P9-DJB-143

NATIVES AND ACADEMICS

Researching and Writing about American Indians

Edited by Devon A. Mihesuah

University of Nebraska Press   Lincoln and London

Acknowledgments for previously published
material appear on page 213, which constitutes
an extension of the copyright page.

⊗ The paper in this book meets the minimum
requirements of American National Standard for
Information Sciences—Permanence of Paper for
Printed Library Materials, ANSI z39.48-1984.

First paperback printing: 1998

Library of Congress Cataloging-in-Publication Data
Natives and academics : researching and writing about
American Indians / edited by Devon A. Mihesuah.
p.   cm.
"The basis for this anthology is the Winter 1996
publication of the American Indian Quarterly's
special issue, Writing about American Indians."—Pref.
Includes bibliographical references and index.
ISBN 0-8032-8243-5 (pbk. : alk. paper)
1. Indians of North America—Historiography.   2. Indians
of North America—Study and teaching.   3. Indians of
North America—Research.
I. Mihesuah, Devon A. (Devon Abbott), 1957–   .
II. American Indian quarterly.
E76.8.N37   1998   970'.00497—dc21   97-30298   CIP

For Henry and Fern Mihesuah

Contents

Preface ix

Introduction 1
Devon A. Mihesuah

American Indian History or Non-Indian
Perceptions of American Indian History? 23
Angela Cavender Wilson

Grandmother to Granddaughter: Generations
of Oral History in a Dakota Family 27
Angela Cavender Wilson

Commonalty of Difference: American Indian
Women and History 37
Devon A. Mihesuah

Special Problems in Teaching Leslie Marmon
Silko's *Ceremony* 55
Paula Gunn Allen

Comfortable Fictions and the Struggle for Turf:
An Essay Review of *The Invented Indian:
Cultural Fictions and Government Policies* 65
Vine Deloria Jr.

Ethics and Responsibilities in Writing
American Indian History 84
Donald L. Fixico

Licensed Trafficking and Ethnogenetic
Engineering   100
Susan A. Miller

American Indian Intellectualism and
the New Indian Story   111
Elizabeth Cook-Lynn

Cultural Imperialism and the Marketing
of Native America 139
Laurie Anne Whitt

On Revision and Revisionism: American Indian
Representations in New Mexico 172
Theodore S. Jojola

American Indian Studies Is for Everyone 181
Duane Champagne

Why Indian People Should Be the
Ones to Write about Indian Education   190
Karen Gayton Swisher

The Contributors 201

Index 205

· Preface
·
·
·
·
·
·
·
·
·
·
·
·
·

The basis for this anthology is the Winter 1996 publication of the *American Indian Quarterly*'s special issue, "Writing about (Writing about) American Indians." As a historian, I have always been intrigued with the contrast between how American Indian cultures and histories are interpreted and portrayed by non-Native scholars and how Indians see themselves and their past. When the *Quarterly* editor, Morris Foster, heard my idea for a special edition, he responded by reserving an issue for a collection of essays authored by Indians. Not surprisingly, Native scholars who contributed papers did so with enthusiasm. The ideas and beliefs they express are not just those of serious academics but also of American Indians who usually do not express their ideas in print. There has been enough interest in the first anthology to warrant this slightly expanded and revised book; many readers desired a text they could use for their class discussions on methodology of researching and writing about Indians. It is our hope that this volume will give them much to talk about.

Prior to the publication of the first anthology, I was anxious about the adverse reactions readers might have to the essays. Apparently some potential contributors were also anxious and felt it would not be in their best interests to make public their opinions. I discussed my concerns with numerous non-Indians, some of whom were cautious and advised me not to pursue publication of the anthology. Others felt that despite the controversy, hurt feelings, and possible retaliation these topics were likely to engender, the collection was essential in helping non-Indians understand what Native academics think about researching and writing about Indians. Not everyone cares about what Indian scholars think, however, and the contributors know it. Nevertheless, nobody was deterred from stirring up debate about methodology and ethics.

All the topics the contributors discuss have the potential to be volatile. We are aware that scholars tend to be territorial about their subject areas and often are not appreciative of suggestions, much less of criticism about their methods and motivations for writing about American Indians.[1] Three topics—the use of oral histories as source material, remuneration to tribes for information received, and the question of who benefits from research on Indians—appear to be the most sensitive areas of discussion. As we predicted, some readers have taken offense to the opinions expressed. Since the publication of the *Quarterly*'s special issue, some contributors have faced the reality that their stances are not accepted by many scholars, and they are accused by some as being "oppositional," "political," "radical," or "emotional." They also are the recipients of general sniping: "You think you know it all," "You're trying to speak for all Indians," and "What great works have *you* written?" Those of us who have been perceived as "not fitting in" with mainstream academia have continued with our work, slightly bruised, perhaps, but undaunted. We still believe that our discussions are necessary. After all, the ideas we present are similar to those Indian scholars have expressed verbally to each other for years. None of us pretend that we have all the answers, but we do believe there are alternative ways of researching and writing about Indians.

One reason for the anthology was to remind scholars that many Indians are not satisfied with the manner in which they have been researched or with how they and their ancestors have been depicted in scholarly writings. Indians do not view themselves as "objects of study," nor do they appreciate scholars who have made lucrative careers from studying their histories and cultures. Because many established scholars and graduate students continue to use the same timeworn methodologies and sources without offering insightful answers to old questions about American Indians, another goal of this book is to offer suggestions scholars might use to produce more critical, creative, and well-rounded interpretations of Indian histories and cultures. We are, incidentally, trying to take our own advice and are the first to admit that it is not easy.

Note

1 An example of territoriality is Gerald D. Nash's response to "revisionist historians" who are attempting to paint a clearer picture of the formation of the American West, in "Point of View: One Hundred Years of Western History," *Journal of the West* (January 1993): 3–4; "New Battleground of American West Academia," *Arizona Republic*, Wednesday, May 19, 1993, A4.

Introduction

DEVON A. MIHESUAH

The most common argument expressed by the contributors to this anthology is that works on American Indian history and culture should not give only one perspective; the analyses must include Indians' versions of events. Many authors of books hailed as the "New Indian History," however, have never consulted tribal people for information. Referring to the problem, Angela Cavender Wilson writes in her first essay, "American Indian History or Non-Indian Perceptions of American Indian History?" that this type of work is not really American Indian history; rather, it is Indian history interpreted by non-Indians and should be labeled as such. She explains that a complete assessment of a tribe's history should take years of research in libraries and archives *and* communication with the tribal people in question.

Many scholars who write the "New Indian History" or "New Western History" are doing nothing new and different. Where are the Indian voices? Where are Indian views of history? We appreciate Patricia Nelson Limerick's attempts at revisionist western history, yet her commentaries on Indians are sketchy, and we are puzzled at her support of Ramón Gutiérrez's book on Pueblos.[1] Despite its insightful introduction, Nancy Shoemaker's uneven anthology, *Negotiators of Change: Historical Perspectives on Native American Women* (Routledge, 1995), features only one essay that utilizes Indians' version of history.[2] Only two authors in Colin G. Calloway's *New Directions in Indian History* (University of Oklahoma Press, 1988) mention the need for including Indian voices.[3] *Ethnohistory*'s two recent special issues, "Women, Power, and Resistance in Colonial Mesoamerica" (vol. 42, Fall 1995) and "Native American Women's Responses to Christianity" (vol. 43, Fall 1996), are both well-written, useful anthologies (especially the former), but they incorporate almost no indigenous viewpoints. Despite Patricia Galloway's impressive display of academic sleuthing in *Choctaw Genesis 1500–1700* (University of Nebraska Press, 1995), the 1996 Erminie Wheeler-Voegelin Prize winner used no Choctaw informants, many of whom could have contributed information about early Choctaw sociocultural life.[4]

Other new books and articles on Crows, Cherokees, Indian literature, multiheritage Indians, and Indian women—deemed by some the "New Indian History"—serve as testaments to writers' lack of desire to even try to talk with Indian informants to better understand Indian cultures. Merely offering mundane descriptions of what happened in the past is nothing more than the "Old Indian History."

Many scholars agree with anthropologist Edwin Ardener's statement that oral histories are unreliable as source material because "the memory of [past] events has been totally restructured."[5] Perhaps that is true in some cases, but according to Cahuilla thinker Rupert Costo, "There is a great and rich store of information still locked in the hearts and minds of Indians all over the nation."[6] So why aren't more Indians consulted about their versions of their peoples' past? Despite the expertise of numerous Indians about their tribe's history and culture, many are not university educated and are not taken seriously by most members of the academic community. Many historians and anthropologists also argue that Indians cannot accurately recount their past using oral traditions. They refuse to use informants, believing modern Indians' versions of their tribes' histories are "fantasies." But are not some written records fantasy? Are not some writings of some army officers, missionaries, explorers, and pioneers who encountered Indians exaggerated and biased? Are not some uses of statistics illusory? Using the Native voice exclusively may not yield a precise picture of past events, but neither will the sole use of skeletal remains, midden heaps, or non-Indians' diaries, government reports, and letters.

Wilson explains in her second essay, "Grandmother to Granddaughter: Generations of Oral History in a Dakota Family," that among Indians with strong cultural connections to their tribes, histories and information about their culture are transmitted orally and are essential for cultural identity and survival. Each generation understands its responsibility to remember stories for its children, and listeners are expected to repeat the stories with accuracy. Both the storyteller and the listener benefit from the recital, unlike many instances where only the researcher reaps the rewards of fieldwork.

Using oral histories, however, is not easy. First, as I discuss in my essay, "Commonalty of Difference: American Indian Women and History," there is no one Indian voice. Different members of one tribe may have different interpretations of the same stories, and not all Indians can accurately recall tribal stories (provided that they have even heard them in the first place). Does the use of Indian voices guarantee an accurate assessment of lives and history? Some informants may not be culturally aware, yet naive researchers may take their word as truth just because they are Indians. A case in point are the *Kiowa Voices* books (Texas Christian University Press, 1981 and 1983) in which Maurice Boyd interviewed multiheritage Kiowa informants, some of whom later joked to me that they "made up" songs and stories because "he wouldn't know the difference." Another example is Diana Meyers Bahr's *From Mission to Metropolis: Cupeño Women in Los Angeles* (University of Oklahoma Press, 1993). The three women Bahr used as informants—three generations of one family—have little knowledge of Cupeño culture and history and, according to other Cupeños, are hardly known among the tribe. Because Bahr chose not to interview Cupeños who were educated about tribal customs, the result is a book that offers nothing much but the ramblings of women who are less than marginally Indian.

Another difficulty researchers face is that the best interpreters of some stories are not just members of the same tribe but members of the same family. Listeners who do not come from an oral tradition may not understand the stories. In addition, as Paula Gunn Allen discusses in her essay, "Special Problems in Teaching Leslie Marmon Silko's *Ceremony*," some writers may discover that tribes do not want their histories and stories textualized. Tribes may not want the listener to hear the complete version for religious or social reasons.[7] Sensitive researchers know that if tribes are not willing to aid them they should abandon the project and not interject their own versions of tribal history, but how often does this happen? Many American Indian scholars feel as Allen does, that certain aspects of tribal culture should be off limits to scrutiny. In regard to Silko's *Ceremony*, Allen states, "I believe I could no more do (or sanction) the kind of ceremonial investigation of *Ceremony* done by some researchers than I could slit my mother's throat. Even seeing some of it published makes my skin crawl." Researchers who are privy to intimate details of tribal life must use discretion when writing so they do not reveal information the tribe deems private or sacred. Serious consequences can befall transgressors, both non-Indians who use sensitive data and Indian informants who are expected by their tribes not to divulge tribal religious and cultural information.

The problem with many books and articles about Indians is not with what is included but with what is omitted. There are many works on tribal histories and cultures that are fine examples of library and archival research, but the search usually ends there. During a recent family visit, my father-in-law, Henry, a full-blood Comanche, read "The Comanche Shield: Symbol of Identity," a chapter in Clifford Trafzer's anthology, *American Indian Identity: Today's Changing Perspectives* (Sierra Oaks, 1989), a superficial book touted as a "fine collection of original works which examine this significant question [Indian identity]." Instead of learning something new about his shield and identity, Henry succinctly summarized Christopher H. Bentley's contribution: "This doesn't tell me anything." Indeed, Bentley's chapter details what a shield might look like, but it tells absolutely nothing about how shields relate to Indian identity. Bentley should have consulted Comanches who could have told him.[8] These difficulties raise the question, Why was this essay included? Because it was about Indians?

What can be done, scholars ask, if we are confronted with an apparent unavailability of Indian voices to consult? Choosing another topic is not an acceptable solution for many scholars. Instead, some argue the merits of using stories of "related" tribes. Others believe "sensitively" interpreting non-Indian sources will suffice. Some prefer the method of "upstreaming," used in Richard White's *The Middle Ground: Indians, Empires, and Republics in the Great Lakes Region, 1650–1815* (Cambridge University Press, 1991), as the technique to use in speculating about past cultures. Scholars, however, can find Indian voices—if they bother to look.

From a conscientious ethnohistorian's standpoint, scholars can only strive for accuracy by scrutinizing all available written data, by incorporating the accounts and interpretations of the participants and descendants of the participants—both Indian and non-Indian—into their analyses, and by holding their pro- or anti-Indian biases in check.

Not every writer does this, however. Anthropologist James Clifton has commented that "over the past several decades Indians have become the central actors in editing and revising, in garnishing, enlarging, and serializing the narrative's substance, busily occupied with inventing their own preferred images."[9] And he is right. Indians have been busy editing and revising incorrect and incomplete histories about their tribes, but it has not been Indians who have written the vast majority of works about Indians. Some non-Indian writers have done precisely what Clifton accuses Indians of having done: "inventing their own preferred images of Indians," or, as Vine Deloria Jr. puts it in "Comfortable Fictions and the Struggle for Turf: An Essay Review of *The Invented Indian: Cultural Fictions and Government Policies*," creating their own comfortable fictions. Drawing from sources produced largely by non-Indians, many scholars write as if they and other members of their profession have the monopoly on the truth. "For most of the five centuries," writes Deloria, "whites have had unrestricted power to describe Indians in any way they chose." Indeed, many authors of comfortable fictions sit in positions of power, setting the standards for how we should write about Indians. In this capacity they often bestow awards on books they perceive as being most accurate representations of people they have learned about through secondary information. Donald Fixico's stance in "Ethics and Responsibilities in Writing American Indian History" is that works exuding the non-Indian perspective and excluding non-written data should be considered unbalanced and even unethical. Fixico's statement is a strong one, but perhaps a warranted one considering that many authors who have not attempted to find Indians' voices have won prestigious awards and fellowships and their books are acclaimed as models for other authors to follow.

Susan Miller's chapter, "Licensed Trafficking and Ethnogenetic Engineering," focuses on two books that are notable because they both won awards, and because they both cause distress to peoples whose ancestors are depicted in inappropriate ways. Richard White's *The Middle Ground: Indians, Empires, and Republics in the Great Lakes Region, 1650–1815*, refers to tribes such as the Winnebagos and Wyandots in terms unsuitable to their descendants while relegating them to the past as if they no longer exist; in effect, according to Miller, White "ignores a people while insulting their ancestors." Furthermore, "tribes keep their own histories," and, as opposed to White's version, their histories "often begin and end with the living." But White is not the only author who has created a version of Indian history that may be at odds with the people he studies.

Ramón Gutiérrez's controversial but much-heralded *When Jesus Came, the Corn Mothers Went Away: Marriage, Sexuality, and Power in New Mexico, 1500–1846*, illustrates the inability of a non-Pueblo to accurately give a clear "vision to the blind" and "voice to the mute and silent"—in this case Pueblo Indians. Numerous Pueblo readers, including Theodore Jojola and others who participated in the Organization of American Historians' April 1993 symposium on the book, argue that the work has "no merit for representing Pueblo thought."[10] Gutiérrez uses no Pueblo accounts, which was unfortunate because Pueblos had much to say about the topic. The book also contains other serious flaws and misconceptions that its editors and award-givers ignored. Stanford University Press did not send this manuscript to any Pueblo tribal council during the editorial process. Is this selective review process indicative of the desire of some publishing houses to profit from any book that happens to be about Indians regardless of quality or of Indians' opinions about the product?

Elizabeth Cook-Lynn expresses her concern about the University of Nebraska Press's series on biography, American Indian Lives, in her essay "American Indian Intellectualism and the New Indian Story." Despite the series' focus on Indian reminiscences, she opines that "ethnographic biography is not an Indian story at all. . . . The writer almost always takes sides with the 'informant,' " with the result being "a manuscript . . . that will satisfy any voyeur's curiosity . . . manuscripts [that] are, by and large, fantasies of Indians as non-conformists to American cultural restrictions." These stories, therefore, are "neither history nor art in terms of Native intellectualism."

Perhaps the tribes should tell us whom they prefer to write about them. For example, among recently published books is one by William T. Hagan on Quanah Parker.[11] While this biography is an excellent summary of Anglo-American accounts of Quanah, it has none of the rich oral stories that Comanches still tell about their famous ancestor. Conversely, Morris Foster's award-winning *Being Comanche: A Social History of an American Indian Community* (University of Arizona Press, 1991) is a thorough ethnographic work that relies heavily on the viewpoints of Comanche informants. Foster, an anthropologist, spent long days with Comanche families (he lived with some, in fact) and is viewed with much respect by the tribe. Fortunately for the field of ethnohistory, Foster was presented the Erminie Wheeler-Voegelin Prize for his work, and the tribe was delighted.

Another issue Miller addresses, as have others, is who bestows these awards and why. Obviously, Gutiérrez's awards committees were not comprised of Pueblo Indians, nor have Indians had the opportunity to voice their opinions on who is worthy of receiving MacArthur Foundation awards. In fact, few committees that reward authors who write about Indians even have Indians as members. Are award committees that include Indian scholars and tribal historians even feasible within our professional organizations? Anything is possible, but as long as senior scholars, publishers, and administrators continue to view Indians as unable to review works about themselves adequately, problems similar to those found in White's and Gutiérrez's studies will be repeated and published. Because the criteria used in evaluating these books are the biased, non-Indian society standards, Miller suggests that it may be fruitful for Indians to form their own awards committees within the tribal college system and use standards common to Indians' communities to assess and reward books about Indians.

Why do historians and anthropologists write about Indians anyway? I regularly receive letters from European students wanting "to study Indians" at Northern Arizona University because the Navajo and Hopi reservations are nearby. One student wrote, "I want to study Indian religions—Navajo or Hopi—I don't care which." Does this desire to study Indians stem from curiosity? Or is it simply to receive a degree, grant, fellowship, or tenure and promotion? Could that have been the motivation behind a recent National Endowment for the Humanities teachers' seminar on Indians held at the University of Oklahoma, a conference that singularly failed to provide insight into how to interpret tribal histories? The Institutional Review Board at Northern Arizona University has recognized this problem and now asks researchers *why* they chose their projects and if the findings will benefit the tribes or the authors.[12]

Indians appreciate accurate historical and anthropological works that focus on their histories and cultures. If a tribe has no tribal historian, it generally will rely partially on studies written by outsiders. Many writings about Indians, however, seem to be useful to the authors only. Consider Ruth Behar's *Translated Woman: Crossing the Border with Esperanza's Story* (Beacon, 1993). Behar, a thoughtful anthropologist, used moneys from her prestigious MacArthur and Guggenheim grants to spend several years in Mexico writing the life story of one Mexican Indian woman. The book earned Behar scholarly notoriety, but what, exactly, did the subject receive in return? The last page tells us that the Spanish-speaking informant heard only a few passages of the completed manuscript. The author even includes excerpts from her teaching evaluations, an entire chapter on herself, and the oft-repeated statement that she is Cuban-American (presumably in an attempt to legitimize her reasons for research and to educate readers about cross-cultural encounters). While some reviewers consider this format "enlightening," others find the book pretentious and question its usefulness beyond helping the author come to grips with her identity.

The subjects of research usually receive few, if any, benefits from the lucrative research grants awarded to scholars each year. Ironically, some of these scholars bask in the glow of scholarly notoriety while the tribes they write about dismiss these same works as fiction. In his 1991 essay "Research, Redskins, and Reality," Vine Deloria Jr. tells how many Indians view researchers: "The researcher has the luxury of studying the community as an object of science, whereas the young Indian, who knows the nuances of tribal life, receives nothing in the way of compensation or recognition for his knowledge, and instead must continue to do jobs, often manual labor, that have considerably less prestige. If knowledge of the Indian community is so valuable, how can non-Indians receive so much compensation for their small knowledge and Indians receive so little for their extensive knowledge?"[13] Deloria also comments about anthropologists specifically: "When we stop and think about it, we live in a society so rich and so structured that we have the luxury of paying six-figure salaries to individuals who know a little bit about the pottery patterns of a small group of ancient people, who know something of the language of an Indian tribe, or who specialize in ledger-book drawings or plant knowledge of remote groups of desert-dwelling tribal peoples."[14]

Deloria also "can see no useful purpose for any additional research or writing on Indians, other than as a form of entertainment." Many scholars who study Indians disagree with this statement, for researching and writing about Indians is not only a form of job security, it also shapes the writer's identity. Years ago a prominent, award-winning historian commented to me, "Writing about Indians is what I do; it's who I am." This scholar, and others like him, are not about to stop publishing just because Indians may not like their work.

Other non-Indians focus their artistic energies on Indians for monetary reward. Laurie Anne Whitt writes in "Cultural Imperialism and the Marketing of Native America" how non-Indians have expropriated spiritual knowledge and rituals and have successfully marketed Native America for themselves through the copywriting of traditional indigenous music, the patenting of indigenous genetic resources, and human cell lines of indigenous people. Theodore S. Jojola, in "On Revision and Revisionism: American Indian Representations in New Mexico," discusses how entrepreneurs—art gallery and tourist shop owners, movie and television producers, and even academics—mold Indian images into marketable items. Businesses profit while Indians often remain poverty stricken.

Scholars who proclaim themselves to be the caretakers of tribes' histories, or those who publish sensitive information not intended for textualization, cause tribes to be suspicious of anyone who wants to write about them. Despite what many writers may believe, Indians do not necessarily like being studied, not even by established scholars whose careers and identities are based on studying Indian histories and cultures. Cook-Lynn throws cold water on the ambitions of many writers by stating what many of us know: many Indians "despise [writers'] curiosity about their lives." Dozens of writers remain strangely oblivious or demonstrably uncaring about what uneducated Natives think. Most Indians reside outside of academia and don't make tenure and promotion decisions.

Tribes do have the power to limit or banish research on their turf. Hopis routinely express displeasure at intrusive researchers who textualize and publish information about their traditional religion, and the tribes have instituted stringent regulations on research. Because of the volumes of incorrect and repetitious history written about Oklahoma Cherokees, the tribe is taking steps to monitor research conducted on its members. The Navajo tribe has recently publicized that it is weary of serving as a "guinea pig" for researchers and will tighten its research guidelines. The San Carlos Apache Tribal Council passed a resolution in 1995, adopting as policy the *Procedures for Research Activity and Recording,* which establishes "protections for their traditional culture."[15] It appears that other tribes may follow suit.

Although some tribes have adopted research guidelines, it does not mean that they want to eradicate research on their histories and cultures. Often they suggest that a solution to the imbalance in the numbers of Indian and non-Indian writers is to encourage more Indians to write their histories. But there are few bona fide American Indian historians, cultural anthropologists, or educators who write.[16] The majority of published Indian writers are novelists and poets. In addition, many Indians, especially "New Indians," are not always knowledgeable about their tribes' histories and cultures.[17]

A potential example is Hertha Dawn Wong, who discovered her Indian blood while completing her book, *Sending My Heart Back across the Years: Tradition and Innovation in Native American Autobiography* (Oxford University Press, 1992). Wong informs us in the prologue that in 1984 she "had little idea" that she was part Native American, yet much of what her mother taught her "reflects traditional values long associated with Native American cultures." One wonders what that means, exactly, since she claims to be a descendant of an unnamed "Plains tribe." In addition, her great grandfather "*may* have been Creek *or* Chickasaw *or* Choctaw *or* perhaps Cherokee" (emphasis mine). While one cannot fault Wong for being interested in her genealogy, she does illustrate another problem that New Indians bring to academia, which is the use of authoritative voice. Wong correctly assesses the "borders" from which she writes as being "a very crowded space these days." To be sure, more than a few "undocumented mixed-blood persons" write from an Indian view-point because they might possess a modicum of Indian blood. But many of these Indians do not even know to which tribe they belong and were not raised with a tribal connection. What sort of Indian voice is this? Does it tell us anything about any tribe?

While non-Indian historians and some Indians have made careers speaking for tribes and interpreting cultures besides the ones to which they belong, many Indians will not write about tribes other than their own, even if they have insights into those cultures. When it comes to speculating on Others' motivations and world-views, many Indians are simply uncomfortable and won't do it. As Pawnee historian James Riding In commented during a conversation on this topic, "it is stressful enough trying to document correctly one's own tribal history."

Choosing to write about groups other than one's own can be interesting but also can cause anxiety to the author. I experience a nagging feeling that I am being nosy when writing about Others. My colleagues have labeled this emotion "hypersensitivity." I chose to write my first book on the Cherokee Female Seminary because its sociopolitical aspects are intriguing and because five of my ancestors attended the Male Seminary. But Cherokee is not the tribe in which I am enrolled, nor are they the people with which I identify. Conducting the requisite archival research did not leave me feeling intrusive, but my presumptive analysis and documentation of the tribe's intratribal factionalism and social values did. Not being a part of the group, I did not want to make even educated guesses about the motives and world-views of traditional Cherokee women who left behind no memoirs and who had few descendants to inform me of their lives. Ironically, this is precisely what reviewers want to read about. If Cherokees want information about their traditions and thoughts published, let them write it themselves or recruit someone to write it for them. Although I do not profess expertise on my tribe's history or culture, as a biracial Choctaw/French female I feel more at ease—and more useful—writing about my own tribe, writing about larger issues that affect all Indians such as repatriation and stereotypes, or writing fiction.

Another concern expressed by Indian scholars is that their writings are likely to be scrutinized more aggressively than non-Indians' works, especially if they incorporate oral histories or if they write from an Indian viewpoint. Some Indians fear they may be taken to task for not incorporating what they deem "tainted" documentation, that is, information derived from burial ground desecration research or from tribal informants who were unaware that their comments would be textualized. Indeed, for many Indians, writing about Indians is a personal, emotional, and political exercise.

The main readership of Indian history and anthropology are academics, usually non-Indians. Many Indians would like to write primarily for an Indian audience but are nervous about utilizing new methodologies that might accurately present their tribal histories. "How would traditionalists recount the past?" they ask. "How can I replicate these unfamiliar storytelling techniques?" At the same time, they are well aware that their new history-telling styles may not find acceptance. After all, non-Indian readers hold authoritative positions at universities and foundations. Cook-Lynn writes that because white America recognizes "no American Indian intellectual," male and female Indian scholars have "no intellectual voice with which to enter into America's important dialogues." (And these dialogues include how to write about Indians.) Despite the increasing number of published works authored by Native writers, Cook-Lynn observes that "the greatest body of acceptable telling of the Indian story is still in the hands of non-natives"[18] . . . and in the hands of Natives who write like non-Indians.

To gain their colleagues' acceptance, some Indian scholars have resigned themselves to compromise. They write histories that include tribal viewpoints in large measure buttressed by theories formulated by non-Indians. While it is important that scholars become theoretically informed, Indians should define their own perspectives on Indian history and culture instead of relying solely on the thoughts and dictates of anthropology and history theorists.

Still, we must not omit from our analyses the works that have been published. Indians are not the only persons with knowledge about Indians. Not all Indians have been taught all aspects of their histories and cultures, let alone been thoroughly trained in historical and anthropological theories and methodologies. In an attempt to establish a voice devoid of non-Indian influence, some Indian graduate students push the concept of essentialism, an idea that may have some merit but is also dangerous.[19] Many Indians would be satisfied if only Indians wrote about Indians. Some prefer not to read anything written by white men and women, not understanding that having a command of the canon of the field is the only way to establish a point of departure. If there are problems with previous works about Indians, how can one correct these histories if one hasn't read them? Conversely, how can the reader recognize incorrect works if she or he doesn't know the correct versions?

To be sure, some Indians have empirical knowledge that non-Indians lack in areas such as tribal religions, kinship, social mores, and oral stories. As Karen Gayton Swisher points out in "Why Indian People Should Be the Ones to Write about Indian Education," most non-Indian scholars do not have the passion that only a writer involved personally in the topic can generate. In addition, unlike most non-Indians who write professionally about Indians, Indians retain an often emotionally charged commitment to Indian issues that extends well beyond academia. Grayson Noley, a Choctaw educator at the University of Oklahoma, has commented that Indians may write better histories because they are "less willing to assign [to] complex social characteristics such vacuous explanatory categories as 'superstition,' or 'habit' or 'custom'. . . . American Indian researchers, because of what we might call a life-connection, likely will pursue not less but more rational explanations. Thus, the reality of this connection . . . also provides an impetus, a genuinely compelling motive, for more exhaustive research."[20]

In "American Indian Studies Is for Everyone" Duane Champagne expresses his belief that "Indian scholars do not have a sole monopoly on Indian studies." Most Indian scholars agree with him. But is an American Indian Studies (AIS) program the best avenue to take in order to learn about Indians? Apparently many people believe so, for universities across the country have developed or are in the process of developing AIS majors or minors programs at the undergraduate and graduate levels. Most non-Indian students take AIS courses because they have "always been interested in Indians" and want to know more about them.

Many Indian students, however, are more than curious. They are concerned with issues pertaining to tribal sovereignty and federal Indian policy and its effect on people. Some Indian students face the reality of high rates of alcoholism, suicide, disease, drop-out, unemployment, and depression among their tribes. Many tribal leaders argue that educated Indians should return to their tribes to work as physicians, attorneys, educators, and counselors to serve as role models. Troubled Indians prefer to be counseled by Indians, preferably by members of their own tribes, but are there enough Indian counselors? Who represents tribes in legal matters? Are there enough Indians in law school, or will tribes continue to depend upon non-Indians for legal advice? What about physicians and nurses? Engineers? Environmental scientists and business managers? Articulate spokespeople to represent tribal interests? If Indian governments cannot make policies because they don't know how, then non-Indian entities, often uneducated about Indians, will. It makes sense that scholars, administrators, tribal leaders, and community members should be thinking in terms of what can be done to solve these problems. Pursuing an AIS degree may not be an adequate way to address the myriad dilemmas Indians deal with on a daily basis.[21]

Further, it has been argued by opponents of AIS degrees that the job outlook for graduates is poor. What does one do with an Indian Studies degree? Some students receive their bachelor's degrees in AIS and then enroll in graduate programs, but not every history, anthropology, or literature department will accept a student without a degree specific to that discipline (much less a new faculty member with a Ph.D. in AIS). Others have jobs guaranteed to them before graduation; they can afford to spend time studying for interdisciplinary degrees.

Some students emphasize a marketable area—such as nursing, accounting, or counseling—with the intent of working with Indians
and utilizing the AIS minor as useful background information. Active
involvement in an AIS minor program is one way to offer students
an opportunity to learn about different aspects of Indian cultures.
It also can offer them the interdisciplinary training they need to
begin investigating the complexities of tribal life. Having access to
a network of scholars well versed in Indian studies from a variety of
fields can help students formulate their theoretical and methodological groundwork.

Many Indians—and non-Indians—argue that more Indian faculty
are needed to give students the perspectives they may not receive
from non-Indian scholars. Unfortunately, many intelligent, well-
trained, and well-published American Indian scholars still have to
contend with comments such as "Qualified faculty of Indian extraction do not exist."[22] After only seven years as a history professor I
can attest to the reality that Indian scholars still endure accusations
that courses on Indians are not important, that our lectures are "too
politically correct," and that we obtained jobs because of our race. Although some Indians may have their positions only because they are
Indian, others are hard-working, superior scholars who have to deal
with backlash jealousy and racism from colleagues (many of whom
are inferior scholars) who assume that all Indians are incompetent.

Conversations with my Indian peers at other schools reveal that
while it is the norm for many non-Indians to speculate on the academic abilities and cultural affiliations of their Indian colleagues,
when Indians attempt to challenge the ways their tribes have been
portrayed in works of history, anthropology, and literature, or to
question the way Indians are perceived as scholars, our concerns
are often overlooked. When Indian academics discuss methodology,
conversations invariably turn to how to deal with the resistance
other academics have over how we choose to focus our energies.
Writing about topics that may have political and cultural meaning
to Indians often bothers our colleagues who do not approve when

academia and activism are bound together. We must also contend with academics who are distressed when sessions at scholarly conferences are composed of Indian people, and with those who believe Indians cannot accurately write about themselves because they are too close to the topic. There is a dearth of Indians, especially Indian women, writing about their tribes and cultures and few role models are available to inspire up-and-coming Indian writers. Indian people have reason to be concerned about who is and will be writing about Indians.

Obviously, Indian academics face many concerns when it comes to writing and teaching about Indians, and many non-Indians wrestle with some of the same problems, such as how to understand the Other and how to teach a well-rounded version of United States history. At universities across the country, sensitive scholars band with Indians to challenge standards and books they find unacceptable and to expose scholars who claim to be Indian but are not. With more Indians completing graduate school, our professions are going to see aggressive attempts at correcting incomplete American Indian ethnohistory, and real attempts at writing "New Indian History."

The following essays discuss some of the most important issues regarding researching and writing about American Indians. I remind readers that no one Indian voice exists; there are many points of view about oral history, ethnic fraud, Indian studies programs, and, in fact, about every other issue associated with writing, teaching, and interpreting Indians. Although the contributors to this book are Indians, they are not the only ones aware of or concerned about these problems, nor are they the only scholars attempting to find answers to them. Anthropologists have pondered their roles as interpreters of Others' cultures for decades.[23] With similar variety of insight and sensitivity, historians continue to debate the definition of the "New Indian History," the viability of ethnohistorical methodologies, and the ability (or inability) of Indians to write their own histories.[24] Indeed, among scholars who write about Indians, these issues remain the main points of contention.

Notes

My sincere thanks to Morris Foster, James Riding In, Robert Williams Jr., and Donald E. Worcester for their comments, suggestions, and encouragement.

1 Patricia Nelson Limerick, "Stop Dancing or I'll Flog Myself," *New York Times Book Review*, July 12, 1993, 21.

2 Paivi H. Hoikkala, "Mothers and Community Builders: Salt River Pima and Maricopa Women in Community Action," 213–234.

3 Willard Rollings, "In Search of Multisided Frontiers: Recent Writing on the History of the Southern Plains," 79–96; and James Riding In, "Scholars and Twentieth Century Indians: Reassessing the Past," 127–150.

4 I am not suggesting that Choctaw informants could have supplied Galloway with all the information she needed about Choctaw genesis, but at least she could have incorporated their views with her other evidence. A case in point is on page 29: "Contrary to legend, the Choctaws did not literally emerge from the earth of the Nanih Waiya mound." Perhaps, but many Choctaws take offense to her statement nonetheless.

5 Edwin Ardener, "The Construction of History: 'Vestiges of Creation,'" in *History and Ethnicity*, ed. Elizabeth Tonkin, Maryon McDonald, and Malcolm Chapman (New York: Routledge, 1989), 22–33.

6 Quoted in Donald A. Grinde Jr., "Teaching American Indian History: A Native American Voice," *Perspectives* 32 (September 1994): 1.

7 See Joseph H. Suina, "Pueblo Secrecy Result of Intrusions," *New Mexico Magazine* (January 1992): 60–63, for a discussion of secrecy among Pueblo tribes.

8 Leonard Riddles (Blackmoon), for example, is a Comanche with little formal education but much empirical knowledge about his tribe's history and culture, including Comanche shields, and would have helped Bentley immensely.

9 James A. Clifton, *The Invented Indian: Cultural Fictions and Government Policies* (New Brunswick NJ: Transaction Publishers, 1990), 19.

10 "Commentaries," *American Indian Culture and Research Journal* 17:3 (1993): 153.

11 William T. Hagan, *Quanah Parker: Comanche Chief* (Norman: University of Oklahoma Press, 1995).

12 See Devon A. Mihesuah, "Suggested Guidelines for Institutions with Scholars Who Conduct Research on American Indians," *American Indian Culture and Research Journal* 17:3 (1993): 131–140.

13 Vine Deloria Jr., "Commentary: Research, Redskins, and Reality," *American Indian Quarterly* 15 (Fall 1991): 466.

14 Vine Deloria Jr., "Conclusion: Anthros, Indians, and Planetary Reality," in *Indians and Anthropologists: Vine Deloria Jr. and the Critique of Anthropology*, ed.

Thomas Biolsi and Larry J. Zimmerman (Tucson: University of Arizona Press, 1997), 210.

15 "San Carlos Apache Elders' Cultural Advisory Council Procedures for Research Activities and Recording, February 7, 1995." San Carlos Apache Tribe, PO Box O, San Carlos, Arizona, 85550.

16 The *American Indian and Alaskan Native Professors Directory, 1995*, published by the Center for Indian Education at Arizona State University, Tempe, is a compilation of Indian academics from a variety of fields. Caution should be exercised in using the directory, for the professors and students listed are *self-identified* as Indian; supplying proof of tribal membership is not a prerequisite to having one's name included in the list.

Ethnic fraud in university settings is not wanting. Fact is, some scholars who once were not Indian now are because they are aware that most universities will not ask them to prove it. Other scholars have sifted through archives in desperate attempts to find an Indian ancestor in order to prove that they really do "belong." Kent Carter discusses this phenomenon in "Deciding Who Can Be Cherokee: Enrollment Records of the Dawes Commission," *Chronicles of Oklahoma* 59 (Summer 1991): 174–205; and "Wanabes and Outalucks: Searching for Indian Ancestors in Federal Records," *Chronicles of Oklahoma* 56 (Spring 1988): 94–104. See also Vine Deloria, *Custer Died for Your Sins: An Indian Manifesto* (New York: Avon Books, 1969), 10–12.

Fraudulent Indians engender several far-reaching problems. One is monetary: students and scholars often claim to be Indians in order to secure tuition, jobs, grants, and research funding, which may deprive deserving Indians. Another is that many fraudulent Indians and New Indians attempt to speak authoritatively about "their" tribes' history and culture. Fraudulent Indian writers are profiled in *Indian Country Today*: "Indian Writers: Real or Imagined," September 8, 1993; "Indian Writers: The Good, the Bad, and the Could Be," September 15 and October 6, 1993; and letters to the editor in subsequent issues. Gerald Vizenor discusses writers who assume "postindian nicknames" in attempts to appear authoritative. "The autoinscriptions of postindian nicknames are texts, commercial instruments that endorse the simulations of identities in the absence of the heard, and the absence of performance, or memories of the tribal real." See "Native American Indian Identities: Autoinscriptions and the Cultures of Names," in *Native American Perspectives on Literature and History*, Alan R. Velie (Norman: University of Oklahoma Press, 1995).

The government-imposed taxonomy has caused difficulties for many Indians. Some Natives find incorrect blood quantums listed on their Certificate of Degree of Indian Blood, and a very few individuals may not be listed on tribal rolls at all. However, if they have cultural ties to the tribe (unquestionably a major portion of the definition of "Indian"), the tribe should be able to confirm their claims. This lack of verification is so commonplace in academia today that people who say they are Indian but cannot produce proof of tribal membership seem to outnumber those Indians who ᴖan. One solution may be to have on- and off-campus Indians join search committees and interview "Indian" applicants to assess their knowledge of and connection to their tribes.

There is a need for more Indian writers, but it is a challenge for many Indians to complete school, for reasons that Indian readers know well. Incorrect perceptions of Indian women lend little support to those wanting to become writers. For example, an undergraduate Navajo woman came to my office two years ago to announce she wanted to quit school because of the result of a survey she had made for her journalism term paper that dealt with peoples' beliefs about Indian women. Two hundred answers revealed that most non-Indians view Indian women as "baby makers" with "pretty hair and eyes." She continues to feel self-conscious in class because she believes this is how all the other students think of her.

17 "New Indians" are especially troublesome because they often have no cultural ties to tribes whatsoever, but they write as if they do. Part of the blame for this surge of Indianness lies with fellowship-granting foundations that fund projects submitted by anyone claiming to be an Indian, and with institutions that create positions for Indian scholars and fellowships for Indian students— some of whom are mediocre—and offer larger salaries to attract them.

18 Hopi anthropologist and writer Wendy Rose also addresses the reality that non-Indians, rather than Indians, are considered the authorities on Indian culture. "The 'Indian biz' has proven quite lucrative for a number of white-shamans," Rose writes. "Not so the careers of all but a scant handful of Native American writers. The result has been a marked stilling of the genuine voice of Native America and its replacement by the utterances of an assortment of hucksters and carnival barkers." See her essay, "The Great Pretenders: Further Reflections on Whiteshamanism," in *The State of Native America: Genocide, Colonization, and Resistance*, ed. M. Annette Jaimes (Boston: South End Press, 1992) 403–422.

While teaching a course on American Indian women in history, I found it a challenge to "deprogram" students who read New Age literature. Non-Indian females such as Lynn Andrews, who have proclaimed themselves religious leaders, have a strong hold upon young women searching for information on Indian culture and religion.

19 In the context of Indian Studies, *essentialism* refers to the idea that all Indians possess inherent knowledge of their cultures and that professors should show

them leniency because they have a different world-view and a lesser academic background than other students. A few professors who are proponents of essentialism allow students to play on their white guilt and have gone as far as asking Indian graduate students fewer questions on M.A. and Ph.D. comprehensive examinations. Some Indian students have grown openly resentful of professors who do not subscribe to this ideology.

20 Grayson Noley, "Historical Research and American Indian Education," *Journal of Indian Education* 20 (1981): 13–18.

21 Northern Arizona University is in the process of developing a Native American Center, and among the comments received by the organizers is that Arizona tribes do not want the university to emphasize an AIS department. They prefer the university to train students in fields that will "make them effective and more likely to come home to work" (business, accounting, education, engineering, and so forth). Institute for Native Americans, "Concept Paper to Establish a Native American Center," 3, n.d.

22 Joseph R. Conlin to Editor, February 28, 1993, *Chico Enterprise Record*, and Commentary in the *Orion*, December 1, 1993. Conlin, a professor of history at CSU, Chico, asserts that minority professors are "incompetent" and claims that "little more is required of Affirmative Action faculty than to show evidence of a majority of the vital life signs." He asserts that Indian historians should pattern themselves after a non-Indian female scholar in his department.

23 For example, James Clifford and George E. Marcus, *Writing Culture: The Poetics and Politics of Ethnography* (Berkeley: University of California Press, 1986); Ruth Behar, "Women Writing Culture: Another Telling of the Story of American Anthropology," *Critique of Anthropology* 13 (1993): 307–325; James Clifford, *The Predicament of Culture: Twentieth Century Ethnography, Literature and Art* (Cambridge: Harvard University Press, 1988); "Gender, Culture and Political Economy: Feminist Anthropology in Historical Perspective," in *Gender at the Crossroads of Knowledge: Feminist Anthropology in the Postmodern Era*, ed. Micaela di Leonardo (Berkeley: University of California Press, 1991); Clifford Geertz, *The Interpretation of Cultures* (Basic Books, 1973); Micaela di Leonardo, *Works and Lives: The Anthropologist as Author* (Stanford: Stanford University Press, 1988); Catherine Lutz, "The Erasure of Women's Writing in Sociocultural Anthropology," *American Anthropologist* 17 (1990): 611–627; Henrietta Moore, *Feminism and Anthropology* (Minneapolis: University of Minnesota Press, 1988); Kirin Narayan, "How Native Is a 'Native' Anthropologist?" *American Anthropologist* 95 (1993): 19–34; Renato Rosaldo, *Culture and Truth: The Remaking of Social Analysis* (Boston: Beacon Press, 1989); Marshall Sahlins, *Islands of History* (Chicago: University of Chicago Press, 1985); Edward Said,

Orientalism (New York: Pantheon Books, 1978); Margery Wolf, *A Thrice-Told Tale: Feminism, Postmodernism, and Ethnographic Responsibility* (Stanford: Stanford University Press, 1992).

24   Examples of historians' and anthropologists' musings on ethnohistory and writing about Indians include James Axtell, "Ethnohistory: An Historian's Viewpoint," in *The European and the Indian* (New York: Oxford University Press, 1981), 3–15 and Axtell, *After Columbus: Essays in the Ethnohistory of Colonial North America* (New York: Oxford University Press, 1988); Colin G. Galloway, "In Defense of Ethnohistory," *Journal of American Studies* 17 (April 1983): 95–99; James A. Clifton, "The Political Rhetoric of Indian History: A Review Essay," *The Annals of Iowa* 49 (Summer-Fall 1987): 101–111; R. David Edmunds, "Coming of Age: Some Thoughts upon American Indian History," *Indiana Magazine of History* 85 (December 1989): 312–321; Francis Jennings, "A Growing Partnership: Historians, Anthropologists, and American Indian History," *History Teacher* 14 (November 1980): 87–96; William H. Lyon, "Anthropology and History: Can the Two Sister Disciplines Communicate?" *American Indian Culture and Research Journal* 18 (1994): 159–176; Calvin Martin, "Ethnohistory: A Better Way to Write Indian History," *Western History Quarterly* 9 (January 1978): 41–57; Calvin Martin, "The Metaphysics of Writing Indian-White History," *Ethnohistory* 26 (Spring): 153–159 (see also *The American Indian and the Problem of History* [New York: Oxford, 1987] for other essays that superficially address his essay); H. C. Porter, "Reflections on the Ethnohistory of Early Colonial North America," *Journal of American Studies* 16 (August 1982): 243–254; and Francis Paul Prucha, "Doing Indian History," in *Indian-White Relations: A Persistent Paradox*, ed. Jane F. Smith and Robert M. Kvasnicka (Washington DC, 1976).

American Indian History or Non-Indian Perceptions of American Indian History?

ANGELA CAVENDER WILSON

When the topic of writing about Indians comes up the first questions that come to mind are Who is doing the writing? Why? And what do the subjects have to say about this? These are questions that rarely have been considered by those in American Indian history, but they are extremely important when addressing the ethical and moral considerations that arise when subjects who can speak for themselves are written abut by those outside the culture.

American Indian history is a field dominated by white, male historians who rarely ask or care what the Indians they study have to say about their work. Under the guise of academic freedom they have maintained their comfortable chairs in archives across the country and published thousands of volumes on whites' interpretations of American Indian history. Very few have attempted to find out how Native people would interpret, analyze, or question the documents they confront, nor have they asked if the Native people they are studying have their own versions or stories of their past. As long as history continues to be studied and written in this manner the field should more appropriately be called non-Indian perceptions of American Indian history.

To truly gain a grasp of American Indian history, the other historians—tribal and family historians—must be consulted about their own interpretations of and perspectives on history. The majority of academic historians have so far ignored these people and attempted to write in the field with only a portion of the information, using only some of the available sources. If an archive somewhere were filled with information relevant to a scholar's study, and she chose to ignore it, accusations of sloppy scholarship would be hurled from all directions. But if a scholar in the field of American Indian history ignores the vast number of oral sources, the scholar's integrity is safe—through the use of such excuses as

> "Indians have no records of this time period."
> "I don't know any Indians who will talk to me."
> "Oral sources cannot be validated and therefore are not trustworthy."
> "Fact cannot be distinguished from fancy."
> "Oral accounts change with each generation."

Would historians attempt to write a history of Germany without consulting any German sources? Would a scholar of Chinese history attempt to write Chinese history without consulting Chinese sources? Why is it that scholars in American Indian history have written so many academically acceptable works without consulting American Indian sources? Is it simply because most of our sources are oral rather than written? As more Native people are trained in history and call attention to these contradictions, the excuses used by historians to exclude oral sources in their research will no longer be acceptable.

Stories in the oral tradition have served some important functions for Native people: The historical and mythological stories provide moral guidelines by which one should live. They teach the young and remind the old what behavior is appropriate and inappropriate in our cultures; they provide a sense of identity and belonging, situating community members within their lineage and establishing their relationship to the rest of the natural world. They are a source of entertainment and of intimacy between the storyteller and the audience.

These stories, much more than written documents by non-Indians, provide detailed descriptions about our historical players. They give us information about our motivations, our decision-making processes, and about how nonmaterial, nonphysical circumstances (those things generally defined as supernatural, metaphysical, and spiritual by Western thinkers) have shaped our past and our understanding of the present. They answer many other "why" and "how" questions typically asked by the academic community in their search for an understanding of "the American Indian past." So while archival materials may offer a glimpse into the world-view of Native people, the degree to which they can provide information on the American Indian half of the equation is quite small relative to what can be gained through an understanding of oral tradition.

Work done in the fields of anthropology and folklore often has served to fill this void for historians in recent years, but even this work is often fraught with its own problems. Native people have, in most instances, had very little to say about the interpretations, analyses, and translations developed from the stories they willingly shared. It has been my experience that many of these works are filled with misinterpretations, mistranslations, lack of context, and lack of understanding (although certainly some exceptions exist in which scholars have been successful in incorporating Native voices into their work). At the very least these oral accounts collected by non-Indian anthropologists, ethnographers, and folklorists should be discussed with knowledgeable elders to determine the accuracy of their assumptions and the appropriateness of their use (preferably with those within the same family from which the original information was collected) before they are used in contemporary histories.

Am I suggesting that all historians working in the field of American Indian history begin swarming to Native communities to record stories from our most precious elders? Absolutely not. I would not wish that fate on any Native group. For the few who have the sensitivity to address the ethical issues in the field and the desire for a more complete understanding of American Indian history, I would suggest slowly developing acquaintances with Indian people and giving Native people from the community they are studying the opportunity to comment on their work while it is being written. Not only would this allow Native people input into how their history will be understood by the rest of America, it also would allow the academician the privilege of having community-endorsed work (credited in part to community members, I hope).

This kind of work is not something that can be accomplished on a six-month research grant. Rather, it means years of involvement, building trusting relationships with Native people. The scholar must understand the internal mechanisms Native people have for determining within their own communities whether they have information relevant to a scholar's study, whether they feel a scholar is respectful enough of their culture to share their valuable insights, who within the community is authorized and informed enough to share the information, and what information is appropriate to share. The rewards of this kind of scholarship may not come from a scholar's academic peers. Rather, the personal rewards reflected in the experiential learning process, the depth of understanding in analysis, and a sense of satisfaction in the realization of moral responsibilities should be enough to inspire many historians in the field of American Indian history to take this route.

For those historians who do not have this sensitivity or desire, the contributions they make to understanding the written word are significant, but the limitations of their work must be acknowledged. The idea that scholars can "sift through" the biases of non-Indian written sources sufficiently to get at the Indian perspective is presumptuous and erroneous. These scholars should not discontinue their research in the field, but they should discontinue the pretense that what they are writing is American Indian history. This kind of scholarship remains, instead, American Indian history largely from the white perspective.

Grandmother to Granddaughter:
Generations of Oral History in a Dakota Family

ANGELA CAVENDER WILSON

The intimate hours I spent with my grandmother listening to her stories are reflections of more than a simple educational process. The stories handed down from grandmother to granddaughter are rooted in a deep sense of kinship responsibility, a responsibility that relays a culture, an identity, and a sense of belonging essential to my life. It is through the stories of my grandmother, my grandmother's grandmother, and my grandmother's grandmother's grandmother and their lives that I learned what it means to be a Dakota woman, and the responsibility, pain, and pride associated with such a role. These stories in our oral tradition, then, must be appreciated by historians not simply for the illumination they bring to the broader historical picture but also as an essential component in the survival of culture.

Maza Okiye Win (Woman Who Talks To Iron) was ten years old at the time of the United States–Dakota Conflict of 1862. She saw her father, Chief Mazomani (Walking Iron), die from wounds suffered in the Battle of Wood Lake. White soldiers wounded him while he was carrying a white flag of truce. She also witnessed the fatal stabbing of her grandmother by a soldier during the forced march to Fort Snelling in the first phase of the Dakota removal to Crow Creek, South Dakota. For three years Maza Okiye Win stayed in Crow Creek before she moved to Sisseton, South Dakota. Finally, after more than twenty-five years of banishment from Minnesota, she returned with her second husband, Inyangmani Hoksida (Running Walker Boy) to the ancient Dakota homeland of Mni-Sota Makoce, or Land Where

The Waters Reflect The Heavens.[1] By this time both she and her husband had become Christians and were known in English as John and Isabel Roberts. There they raised their children and three of their grandchildren.

Elsie Two Bear Cavender was born in Pezihuta zizi village in 1906 to Anna Roberts and Joseph Two Bear. She was raised by her grandparents, John and Isabel Roberts. Her Dakota name was Wiko (Beautiful), given to her by one of her great aunts when she was just a girl. Grandma always seemed embarrassed by that name—as though she didn't believe she was Beautiful enough to possess it and certainly too modest to introduce herself that way. But now that she is gone, I can use what I perceive to be a fitting name without embarrassing her. To me, she was always *Kunsi*, or Grandma. She had eight children, four of whom she buried in her lifetime. She was well known for her generosity, her wonderful pies and rolls, and her stories.

Grandma grew up in a rich oral tradition. Not only was she well acquainted with many of the myths and legends of our people, she also possessed an amazing comprehension of our history, and many of her stories revolved around the events of the United States–Dakota Conflict of 1862. Her grandmother, in particular, had carried vivid, painful memories of those traumatic times. Over time, those painful memories of my great-great-grandmother became the memories of my grandmother and, then, they became my memories.

Early on, when I first began thinking about these stories in an academic context, I realized my understandings of oral tradition and oral history were incompatible with those I was finding in other texts. This incompatibility was largely because of terminology. David Henige, in his book *Oral Historiography*, differentiates between oral history and oral tradition, conveying an understanding that seems to be representative of most scholars in the field, when he says, "As normally used nowadays, 'oral history' refers to the study of the recent past by means of life histories or personal recollections, where informants speak about their own experiences . . . oral tradition should be widely practiced or understood in a society and it must be handed down for at least a few generations."[2] These definitions are applicable to Native American oral history and oral tradition only in a very limited way. Native peoples' life histories, for example, often incorporate the experiences of both human and non-human beings. In addition, this definition would not allow for the incorporation of new materials because it would then be outside the "tradition."

From a Native perspective, I would suggest instead that oral history is contained within oral tradition. For the Dakota, "oral tradition" refers to the way in which information is passed on rather than the length of time something has been told. Personal experiences, pieces of information, events, incidents, etc., can become a part of the oral tradition at the moment it happens or the moment it is told, as long as the person adopting the memory is part of an oral tradition.

Who belongs to an oral tradition? Charles Eastman, a Wahpeton-wan Dakota, reveals in his autobiography *Indian Boyhood* the distinct way in which the oral tradition was developed:

> Very early, the Indian boy assumed the task of preserving and transmitting the legends of his ancestors and his race. Almost every evening a myth, or a true story of some deed done in the past, was narrated by one of the parents or grandparents, while the boy listened with parted lips and glistening eyes. On the following evening, he was usually required to repeat it. If he was not an apt scholar, he struggled long with his task; but as a rule, the Indian boy is a good listener and has a good memory, so that his stories are tolerably well mastered. The household became his audience, by which he was alternately criticized and applauded.[3]

This excerpt highlights the rigorous and extensive training required of young Dakota people. The Dakota oral tradition is based on the assumption that the ability to remember is an acquired skill—one that may be acutely developed or neglected. Eastman also describes the differentiation between myths and true stories, necessitating an understanding of history as being encompassed in oral tradition. However, few scholars working in oral history make any distinction between oral information collected from those belonging to a written culture and those belonging to an oral tradition. This is an area that is yet to be explored.

My grandmother, Elsie Cavender, received this type of training. She had much to tell about some of our more popular characters, stories starring our mythical trickster figure, Unktomi, as well as stories about Dakota men and women—mostly belonging to my lineage—who lived and died long before I was born.

In my own family, the importance of specific stories as interpreted by my grandmother was expressed by the frequency with which those were told. As a girl I was acquainted with an assortment of stories from these categories, and I remember having to request specifically those which were not in the historical realm. But I didn't have to request the stories we classify as "history." Those she offered freely and frequently. Especially in the last years of her life, on every visit she would tell stories about the Conflict of 1862, as if to reassure herself that she had fulfilled her obligations and that these stories would not be forgotten.

One of these stories has become particularly important to me since my grandmother's death because it deals with grandmothers and granddaughters, of which I am the seventh generation. Aspects of this story have helped shape my perception of what my responsibility is, as a mother and eventual grandmother, and as a Dakota. This particular story is an excerpt taken from an oral history project I began with my grandmother in 1990. This is an edited version with much of the repetition cut for the sake of clarity and conciseness in this presentation. However, under usual storytelling circumstances, the repetition is part of the storytelling procedure, often added for emphasis. Grandmother titled this portion of the United States–Dakota Conflict "Death March," consciously drawing on the similarities between the removal of Dakota from the Lower Sioux Agency, first to Fort Snelling and then on to Crow Creek, South Dakota, with the Bataan Death March in World War II. After one of our Dakota relatives who had participated in that march related to her his experiences she saw many parallels with 1862 and thought "Death March" a fitting title. This passage is in my grandmother's voice:

Right after the 1862 Conflict, most of the Sioux people were driven out of Minnesota. A lot of our people left to other states. This must have been heartbreaking for them, as this valley had always been their home.

My grandmother, Isabel Roberts (Maza Okiye Win is her Indian name), and her family were taken as captives down to Fort Snelling. On the way most of them [the people] walked, but some of the older ones and the children rode on a cart. In Indian the cart was called *canpahmihma-kawitkotkoka*. That means crazy cart in Indian. The reason they called the cart that is because it had one big wheel that didn't have any spokes. It was just one big round board. When they went they didn't grease it just right so it squeaked. You could just hear that noise about a mile away. The poor men, women, old people, and children who had to listen to it got sick from it. They would get headaches real bad. It carried the old people and the children so they wouldn't have to walk.

They passed through a lot of towns and they went through some where the people were real hostile to them. They would throw rocks, cans, sticks, and everything they could think of: potatoes, even rotten tomatoes and eggs. New Ulm was one of the worst towns they had to go through.

When they came through there they threw cans, potatoes, and sticks. They went on through the town anyway. The old people were in the cart. They were coming to the end of the town and they thought they were out of trouble. Then there was a big building at the end of the street. The windows were open. Someone threw hot, scalding water on them. The children were all burned and the old people too. As soon as they started to rub their arms the skin just peeled off. Their faces were like that, too. The children were all crying, even the old ladies started to cry, too. It was so hard it really hurt them but they went on.

They would camp someplace at night. They would feed them, giving them meat, potatoes, or bread. But they brought the bread in on big lumber wagons with no wrapping on them. They had to eat food like that. So, they would just brush off the dust and eat it that way. The meat was the same way. They had to wash it and eat it. A lot of them got sick. They would get dysentery and diarrhea and some had cases of whooping cough and small pox. This went on for several days. A lot of them were complaining that they drank the water and got sick. It was just like a nightmare going on this trip.

It was on this trip that my maternal grandmother's grandmother was killed by white soldiers. My grandmother, Maza Okiye Win, was ten years old at the time and she remembers everything that happened on this journey. The killing took place when they came to a bridge that had no guard rails. The horses or stock were getting restless and were very thirsty. So, when they saw water they wanted to get down to the water right away, and they couldn't hold them still. So, the women and children all got out, including my grandmother, her mother, and her grandmother.

When all this commotion started the soldiers came running to the scene and demanded to know what was wrong. But most of them [the Dakota] couldn't speak English and so couldn't talk. This irritated them and right away they wanted to get rough and tried to push my grandmother's mother and her grandmother off the bridge, but they only succeeded in pushing the older one off and she fell in the water. Her daughter ran down and got her out and she was all wet, so she took her shawl off and put it around her. After this they both got back up on the bridge with the help of the others who were waiting there, including the small daughter, Maza Okiye Win.

She was going to put her mother in the wagon, but it was gone. They stood there not knowing what to do. She wanted to put her mother someplace where she could be warm, but before they could get away, the soldier came again and stabbed her mother with a saber. She screamed and hollered in pain, so she [her daughter] stooped down to help her. But, her mother said, "Please daughter, go. Don't mind me. Take your daughter and go before they do the same thing to you. I'm done for anyway. If they kill you the children will have no one." Though she was in pain and dying she was still concerned about her daughter and little granddaughter who was standing there and witnessed all this. The daughter left her mother there at the mercy of the soldiers, as she knew she had a responsibility as a mother to take care of her small daughter.

"Up to today we don't even know where my grandmother's body is. If only they had given the body back to us we could have given her a decent funeral," Grandma said. They didn't though. So, at night, Grandma's mother had gone back to the bridge where her mother had fallen. She went there but there was no body. There was blood all over the bridge but the body was gone. She went down to the bank. She walked up and down the bank. She even waded across to see if she could see anything on the other side, but no body, nothing. So she came back up. She went on from there not knowing what happened to her or what they did with the body. So she really felt bad about it. When we were small Grandma used to talk about it. She used to cry. We used to cry with her.

Things happened like this but they always say the Indians are ruthless killers and that they massacred white people. The white people are just as bad, even worse. You never hear about the things that happened to our people because it was never written in the history books. They say it is always the Indians who are at fault.[4]

An excerpt such as this challenges the emphasis of the *status quo*. This account does not contradict the many written texts on the subject, but contributes details not seen elsewhere, details that shift the focus from the "Indian atrocities," which are provided in rich detail in histories written by non-Indians, to "white atrocities" and Indian courage. It exemplifies the nature of the oral tradition in Dakota culture, as it is the story of one family, one lineage, reflecting the ancient village structure and the community that united those with a collective identity and memory. This account by itself will not change the course of American history, or create a theory for or framework from which the rest of the Plains wars may be interpreted. It is not even representative of the "Dakota perspective." Instead, it is one family's perspective that in combination with other families' stories might help to create an understanding of Dakota views on this event and time period. Certainly these stories shed light on the behavior and actions of members of my family that have led up to the present moment.

As I listened to my grandmother telling the last words spoken by her great-great-great-grandmother, and my grandmother's interpretation, "Though she was in pain and dying, she was still concerned about her daughter and little granddaughter who was standing there and witnessed all this," I understood that our most important role as women is making sure our young ones are taken care of so that our future as Dakota people is assured. I learned that sometimes that means self-sacrifice and putting the interests of others above your own. It also was clear through this story and others that although these were and continue to be hard memories to deal with, always there is pride and dignity in the actions of our women.

In addition, my connection to land and place is solidified with each telling of the story. As a Dakota I understand that not only is Mnisota a homeland worth defending, but through the stories I learn where the blood of my ancestors was split for the sake of the future generations, for me, my children, and grandchildren.

Because these stories are typically not told in the history texts, we also must recognize we are responsible for their repetition. The written archival records will not produce this information. These stories are not told by people who have been "conquered," but by people who have a great desire to survive as a nation, as Dakota people. Consequently, these are not merely interesting stories or even the simple dissemination of historical facts. They are, more important, transmissions of culture upon which our survival as a people depends. When our stories die, so will we.

In my last real visit with my grandmother, several months before she was hospitalized in her final days, she recited this story again. I was moving to New York to begin my graduate education, and it was as if she were reminding me where I come from. In the same way, these stories served to validate my identity in a positive way when, as a girl, I was confronted with contrasting negative images of the "Sioux" in school texts. These stories have stabilized me through graduate school and reminded me why I am involved in this sometimes painful process. One of the last video clips we have of my grandmother is of her telling one of our Unktomi stories to my daughter in Dakota. When I watch that scene it becomes apparent to me that the learning of these stories is a lifelong process and, likewise, the rewards of that process last a lifetime.

The contributions of stories such as this should be recognized as celebrations of culture, as declarations of the amazing resiliency and tenacity of a people who have survived horrible circumstances and destructive forces. Some of the greatest stories are those told by Native people and serve as challenges to the rest of the world to be so strong. Native people have an unbreakable belief in the beauty and the significance of our cultures, and this is reflected in our stories. They are testimony to the richness, variety, detail, and complexity of the interpretations of history. Our role as historians should be to examine as many perspectives of the past as possible—not to become the validators or verifiers of stories, but instead to put forth as many perspectives as possible. But, the greatest lessons of these stories are to the young people, the children, and grandchildren of the elders and storytellers, who will gain an understanding of where they came from, who they are, and what is expected of them as a Dine, as an Apache, as a Laguna, as a Choctaw, and as a Dakota.

Notes

1 Chris C. Cavender, "The Dakota People of Minnesota," *Hennepin County History* 47:3 (Summer 1988), 11.
2 David Henige, *Oral Historiography* (London: Longman, 1982), 2.
3 Charles Eastman, *Indian Boyhood* (New York: Dover, 1971; originally published by McClure, Phillips & Company, 1902), 43.
4 Elsie Cavender, Oral History Project with Angela Cavender Wilson, Fall 1990.

Commonalty of Difference:
American Indian Women and History
DEVON A. MIHESUAH

Literature about American Indian women has increased dramatically during the past twenty years. Recent works reflect the progress ethnohistorians have made in re-creating Indian women's histories, and their publications illustrate sensitivity to their positions as interpreters of the lives, cultures, and histories of Others. While female scholars who study American Indian women have made significant inroads into their histories, many interpretations remain incorrect and undeveloped, providing only partial answers to complicated questions about Native women.[1] The majority of writings are devoid of Indian voices and are thereby only partial histories. In addition, most do not connect the past to the present, which is why we should be writing history in the first place.

Numerous feminist scholars have expressed concern over the propensity of writers to ignore the heterogeneity among women, particularly among women of color.[2] American Indian women are especially multifaceted, and with few exceptions this aspect is overlooked. To analyze American Indian women properly, scholars must look beyond gender and class. This essay briefly discusses some of those ambiguous elements: race (or races), tribal social systems, factionalism, culture change, physiological appearance, and personal motivations.

Commonalty of difference
There was and is no such thing as a monolithic, essential Indian woman.[3] Nor has there ever been a unitary "world-view" among

tribes and, especially after contact and interaction with non-Indians, not even among members of the same group.[4] Cultural ambiguity was and is common among Indians. Traditional Native women were as different from progressive tribeswomen as they were from white women, and often they still are.[5] Even within a single tribe (and sometimes within the same family), females possess a range of degrees of Indian blood, skin and hair colors, and opinions about what it means to be Indian.

Indian women share the common context of gender and the "common core" of struggle against colonialism (genocide, loss of lands, encroachment onto their lands by Euro-Americans and other Indians, intermarriage with tribal outsiders, population loss from disease, warfare, and removal) and the consequent tribal cultural change and identity confusion. What appear to be similarities among women may actually be differences, however, because cultural disparities between tribes over issues such as religion, social systems, and economies, caused Indian women to react to common experiences of externally induced adversity and change in dissimilar ways.

Authors can challenge notions of fixed identity among Indian women by investigating their subjects' allegiances to tribal traditions, their definitions of ethnicity and self, their emotions, and physical appearance.[6] Reconstructions of the intricacies of Indian women's lives must be specific to time and place, for tribal values, gender roles, appearances, and definitions of Indian identity have not been static.

"Class"

Do economics account for Indian women's inferior status (as Marxist feminists might argue)? Or are socialist feminists correct in their assertion that a low economic position combined with gender is a better explanation? While Indian women may be oppressed because of their lesser economic status, capitalism and gender should not be construed as the only forces of oppression operating against them.[7] Native women were gender oppressed (most notably after contact with Euro-Americans) and, like other women, still are.[8] What many feminist theorists ignore is that women of color also are subjugated because of their race. In regard to Indian women, because of their varied economic situations, social values, appearances, and gender roles, they are oppressed by men and women—both non-Indians *and*, interestingly enough, other Indians as well.

We know of the oppression of Indian women at the hands of non-Indians, but what about inter- and intra-tribal racism and sexism? Tribes have long experienced factionalism, between those who cling to tradition and those who see change as the route to survival, whether it be tribal, familial, or personal survival. Intra-tribal factionalism might also be termed "culturalism," a form of oppression that dovetails with racism. Indians in tribal power positions, either political, economic, or social, often use expressions of culturalism against those who do not subscribe to their views.

After Indians adopted new value systems, members of a single tribe often viewed each other from different economic and social classes. Indians with a high "level of acculturation" might have viewed themselves as more enlightened than others whom they deemed as less enlightened, uncivilized, or heathens.[9] Usually, but not always, mixed-bloods had more money and material goods than full-bloods and were able to maneuver themselves into tribal leadership positions. These wealthy families often were educated, progressive, and Christian and did not value tribal traditions. Many saw themselves as morally superior to the uneducated, non-Christian, and less wealthy traditionalists (who were usually, but not always, full-bloods). Their "white blood" also contributed to their feelings of importance. From their point of view, they were in the superior class.[10]

Women situated in the upper level of one "class" did not necessarily belong to the higher echelon of the other. Lack of wealth placed some Indian women in a low economic category, but as far as they were concerned their cultural knowledge put them in a higher social grouping. Those who valued tribal tradition and resisted acculturation believed themselves to be "more Indian" than the "sellouts." Many biracial

Indians may have been more wealthy and educated than full-bloods, but, among traditionalists, wealth and education were not enviable social traits. LaVera Rose, a Lakota, makes the observation in her master's thesis on biracial Lakota women that the full-blood Lakotas looked down on biracial women because of their cultural naiveté, and many still do.[11]

To complicate the issue, full-bloods often adopted attitudes similar to progressives. Ten years ago I conducted an interview with a ninety-eight-year-old Cherokee woman. When I asked if she spoke Cherokee and attended stomp dances—a logical question considering that she was a full-blood and descended from a prominent Cherokee leader—she answered, "Hell no, I'm no heathen." There are other examples too numerous to recount, but the point is that the issue of who held tribal political and social powers, and why, is one of the threads that should wind through almost every aspect of our studies of Indian women.

Indian women as activists

Chandra Talpade Mohanty writes in her anthology, *Third World Women and the Politics of Feminism*, that women of color, or "third world women," all have the "common context of struggle."[12] Indeed, women of color may still struggle against colonialism, racism, and stereotypes, but as multiheritage progressive Indian women illustrate, their struggles have not always been the same nor have their strategies of resistance.

White feminists tend to focus on gender oppression and to overlook racial issues, thus alienating many Indian females. Traditional Indian women have been more concerned about tribal or community survival than either gender oppression or individual advancement in economics, academia, or other facets of society. In *The State of Native America*, Annette Jaimes argues that some Indian women hold white feminists in disdain because they view them as constituents of the white supremacy and colonialism that oppresses Indians.[13] In fact, some Indian women see some biracial Indian women feminists in almost the same light.

Indian women who participated in the takeover at Wounded Knee in 1973 washed clothes, prepared food, and stayed in the background while the flamboyant males spoke to the media. Deb Lamb's research on the takeover reveals that some Indian women could not have cared less about the opinion white feminists held about what appeared to be their subservient roles.[14] Many Indian women concede that male American Indian Movement leaders were and are sexist, having learned misogynist ways of thinking from white society. Nevertheless, the women agree that combating racism against their tribes is more important than personal gain. One woman present during the takeover sums up the differences between white and Indian ways of thinking about feminism: "In your culture you have lots of problems with men. Maybe we do too, but we don't have time to worry about sexism. We worry about survival."[15] To some feminists, domestic duties may seem less important than some men's roles, but these women felt empowered in their domestic sphere. Numerous Indian women assert that they are not "unfulfilled." They refuse to be victims of gender oppression by taking charge of their lives, reveling in their roles and status as women who hold their tribes together.

Two alternative terms that can be used to describe Indian women may be *tribalist* and *womanist*, but most Indian women are either comfortable in their "subservient" positions or are too busy working to preserve their cultures to worry about the labels non-Indians assign to them.[16]

Multiheritage women

Shortly after Native tribes had contact with Euro-Americans, a generation of mixed-race Indians emerged. Some of these individuals still appeared phenotypically Indian and retained their cultural values. Others may have adopted the ways of their non-Indian parent (almost always the father, initially) but physically appeared to be Indian. Continued intermarriage with Euro-Americans and other mixed-bloods resulted in multiheritage women whose appearances and cultural adherences were often indistinct, not only to themselves, but to researchers as well.

Defining the racial backgrounds and cultural adherences of Indian women is crucial to forming an accurate portrait of their lives. To date, research on multiheritage Indians as "cultural brokers" or "cultural mediators" makes a broad generalization without a sociological understanding of the mixed-heritage person.[17] What elements comprise a person's racial identity? These might include physical appearance, acceptance by the racial reference group, commonalties of culture and psychological identification with the group, percentage of biological heritage, and government and tribal restrictions.[18] How do these elements contribute to the psychological and sociological makeup of Indian women with bifurcated racial and cultural backgrounds? What are the expressions of Indian identity? Do multiheritage Indian women mirror Stonequist's model of "marginal" people—those of mixed heritage who live lives of frustration, unable to fit comfortably into any group?[19] Or, do these women absorb cultural traits of all their heritages, making them more like McFee's proposed "150% Man"?[20] Are there categories in between?

For the most part, scholars have ignored the role that appearance once played and still does play in Indian women's lives. Appearance is the most visible aspect of one's race; it determines how Indian women define themselves and how others define and treat them. Their appearance, whether Caucasian, Indian, African, or mixed, either limits or broadens Indian women's choices of ethnic identity and ability to interact with non-Indians and other Indians.

In the past, appearance played a crucial role in status and ease of travel (that is, both physical and sociocultural "traveling") to different cultural groups and societies or "worlds," as defined by Maria Lugones.[21] Consequently, many mixed-heritage white-Indian women had numerous "worlds" open to them, while most full-blood Indian women and those of mixed black and Indian heritage did not.

Progressive, biracial Indian women, especially those who appeared to be predominantly Caucasian (some of whom looked white after one generation of intermarriage), often defined their identity in white society's terms, not those of traditional tribal societies. For example, by the early nineteenth century many Cherokee and Choctaw women who possessed as little as 1/128 Indian blood looked to be white and had adopted the value systems of their white or mixed-blood fathers, including Christianity, acquisitiveness, and the use of African slaves. Many of these women and those of subsequent generations often had little or no knowledge of their tribes' cultures, yet they retained an Indian identity.

While enrolled in boarding schools, some Indian women were influenced by publications such as *Godey's Ladies Book* and strived for the Victorian ideal of the "True Woman." Because many of these Indian women were educated and wealthy and appeared Caucasian, they felt at ease in the white world. Women who looked phenotypically Indian or African-American (many Oklahoma freedwomen enslaved by Indians possessed significant amounts of Indian blood)[22] were not as welcome in white society. The latter were also barred from Indian society.

Many biracial Indian women who looked Caucasian were concerned with issues of gender and economic and social class and not with those of race. Some Indians—especially educated Christianized ones—aspired to be like whites, while at the same time many traditional, dark-skinned women had no desire to fit into white society. Phenotypically looking Indians often felt inferior when they began judging themselves by white standards. After all, they could alter their cultural adherence but not their appearance. How did this desire to be white affect their behavior toward other women and men in the tribe, and how did other Indians react to them?

How have life experiences compared for mixed-race women and men? Have mixed-heritage women had an easier time blending into white society than have mixed-blood men? Turn-of-the-century census records of the Five Civilized Tribes reveal that many white men married full- and mixed-blood women, but few white women married Indian men—even those of mixed-blood.[23] Why did whites see these women as desirable but not the men? (And why are so many white women today attracted to Indian men?) Perhaps one reason is that opportunistic white men targeted wealthy Indian women for marriage to better themselves. Perhaps another reason Indian women were desirable was that women of some tribes were viewed as more "civilized" than others because many of them were Christian and educated (but so were many of the men). What compelled women of some tribes to marry whites and to adopt the lifeways of non-Indians? Some may have believed that by marrying someone from the "superior" race they were improving their lot. Perhaps they married out of affection for one another, but this angle has only been explored in works of fiction.

Women and power

Some anthropologists argue that Indian and white men did not take power away from women because women never had it to begin with. Many of us disagree with literature that portrays males as leaders and women as followers, with no say or control in tribal affairs.[24] In many cases Indian women did indeed have religious, political, and economic power—not more power than the men, but at least equal to what the men had. Women's and men's roles may have been different, but neither was less important than the other. If we look at tribal societies at contact and trace the changes in their social, economic, and political systems over time through interaction with Euro-Americans and inter-tribal relations, we find that women did have power taken from them, and Indian males did as well.

Gender roles changed over time, and Europeans were among the catalysts for that change. For some Indian women intermarriage with white men meant that children no longer belonged to their clans, property no longer belonged to them, and men made the rules. Among some Southeastern tribes women were farmers, but after contact and intermarriage they were forced indoors to use the looms, while Indian men were obliged to work the fields. After the loss of bison and confinement to reservations, men of the Plains tribes could no longer hunt.

The spiritual traditions of many tribes include a female divine spirit. Euro-Americans pressured tribes to convert to Christianity, which included the acceptance of a male God, thus reinforcing the superiority of males. Euro-Americans preferred to deal with men only, perhaps moving women into less pivotal positions. Intra-tribal conflicts developed between those who preferred the old ways and those who adopted Euro-American values. Have frustration and confusion over the loss of traditional gender roles and the adoption of white society's values contributed to spousal abuse among Indians today? Many writers have explored how colonialism changed tribal life, but few have written about how Indian women have made the best of what colonialism has wrought.[25]

Contributions

Because many authors write from a patriarchal or white feminist perspective, the value of Indian women is vastly underrated. Despite overwhelming oppression at the hands of whites, Indians have persevered, but it has not been only the men who were the catalysts for survival, adaptation, and development. Women have been just as crucial to the economic, social, religious, and political survival of tribes.

Indian women are usually evaluated by standards set by white society—and that usually means male bias. Writings on the history of Indian women have focused on the most notable Indian women—Pocahontas, Sacajawea, Susan LaFleche, and a few others—because of their interaction with whites or their success in the white world. But while Sacajawea was helping Lewis and Clark, surely other Shoshone women were doing important things within their tribes.

Scholars should chronicle the accomplishments of Indian women but should use different means of evaluation besides white society's standards. If women's work is evaluated according to a male or feminist bias, then Indian females' duties do appear inferior to men's roles. Indian women from tribes in Indian Territory earned terminal degrees in the mid-1800s, and, while some non-Indians may have respected an Indian woman with a doctorate, not all Indians saw such work as an admirable accomplishment (and many still do not). How do we evaluate the behavior of progressive Indians? If we use white standards, then obviously it is impressive that these women acted so much like whites. If we use traditional standards, their aspirations to imitate whites was tragic, because they were forced to abjure their own cultures. What were the standards of the tribe? When tribes are fractured along social and cultural lines, writers need to look at several sets of standards.

Indian women as real people

Aspects that have gone mostly unaddressed in historical works are the feelings and emotions of Indian women, the relationships among and between them, and their observations of non-Indians. We have extrinsic knowledge of how women interacted with each other during events such as childbirth and healing and puberty ceremonies. We also know what was required of women if they held certain tribal roles. We have photographs showing the clothes women wore and how they styled their hair during various time periods. The intriguing mystery is, What was behind their solemn gazes?

Women worked and socialized together throughout their lives, but we have scant evidence about their relationships with family and friends. What did Northern Plains women discuss as they sat together during the long, cold months making clothes and bead and quill work? Were their conversations much different from what their modern descendants talk about during winter days while performing the same work? What about women of the Southwest who spent hours together grinding corn and preparing food? Did they gossip, joke, and seek advice from each other as they do today?

Colonialism was a powerful force that affected women in countless ways. How did the women feel about intruders onto their lands, the devastation of their ways of life, the cultural changes they underwent to survive? Did Indian women discuss strategies to resist the onslaught of colonization, or did they conspire with the men? Surely they speculated about the intruders as intently as Euro-Americans speculated about them. Thoughts and personal dramas hold our attention and are what endear the women to us, especially if we encounter a semblance of ourselves in them. Historians might argue that depictions of personal conflicts, confusions, and expressions of happiness are best left to novelists, but I believe that without the inclusion of feelings and an understanding of motivations, the histories of Indian women—of all Indians—are boring, impersonal, and, more important, merely speculation and not really Indian history.

Source material

If writers want to find out about what Indian women think, they should ask Indian women. If they want to know about past events and cultures they should do the same thing. More authors—non-Indian *and* Indian—need to follow the examples of Julie Cruikshank, Marla N. Powers, and Ruth McDonald Boyer, women who have spent a good portion of their lives getting to know the people they write about, making certain that the women's voices are heard.[26] Unfortunately, many scholars, historians in particular, have been loath to use Indian oral accounts as source material (an issue that is discussed further in the introduction and in Angela C. Wilson's essay "Grandmother to Granddaughter"). Almost every "resource guide" or "annotated bibliography" lists the requisite secondary source material, government documents, and tribal records, but few inform researchers about oral history collections, recorded interviews, or locations where personal narratives might be stored.[27]

Even fewer writers use literature and poetry as resources. Because many Indian women writers possess empirical data that cannot find acceptance in historical or anthropological works, literature is one effective outlet for their stories.[28] Scott Momaday has commented that "language is the repository of . . . knowledge and experience."[29] Would the textualization of oral stories or of literature composed from influences of oral stories not have messages of import for readers?

Works written by culturally aware Indian women are derived from their consciousness, filled with experience and knowledge of tribal ritual. Chicana feminist Alvina Quintana says that when women writers free their writings of patriarchal discourse, language becomes "a vehicle for the demystification through self-representation of that unity we call woman."[30] Indeed, it is through their writings that we can learn that Indian women were and are powerful; they were and are as complex as their cultures are diverse. Their works are worth a look.

If modern Indians have no knowledge of their tribes' stories, or even if they have plenty of it, writers must also read written accounts for information. The problem is that most observations of Indian women were written by Euro-American men, who judged them by the same standards that they judged women of their own societies. Many non-Indians misunderstood tribal kinship systems, gender roles, and tribal spiritual and social values. Their observations also reflected their biases and, perhaps, their desire to manipulate reality to accommodate their expectations.[31] For example, almost all historical and cultural studies of the Choctaws examine only the male tribal members. Choctaw women, even the wives of prominent tribal leaders, are rarely mentioned. When they are discussed, their roles as Choctaws are described by non-Indian men who evaluate women's roles by their own European, male-oriented standards. Some early commentaries portray Choctaw women as useful tribal members because they prepared food or bore children, but they are also characterized as subservient drudges with no economic, political, or social influence on the tribe. These viewpoints are incorrect. In the pre-contact period, Choctaws were successful agriculturists; the women tilled soil, sowed seed, and harvested crops. Men hunted deer and turkeys and fished the numerous Mississippi and Alabama waterways, while women dressed and prepared the game. In addition, women made clothes, reared children, and held positions of religious importance. Descent was matrilineal, and women retained control over tribal property.

We know that some Europeans' views of Indian women were distorted, but to assess properly what women's lives were really like, information on the Europeans' value systems and women's spheres must coordinate with the tribes' accounts of their past.

There is much to do to give voice to Indian women. Many books and articles about Indian women desperately need new interpretations. Their social, religious, political, and economic roles have been the focus of numerous articles, but few authors use demographic data or Indian women themselves as sources of information. Those who eschew an analytic treatment of women but who utilize only one or two informants believe that approach is sufficient to write the "New Indian History." It is not.[32] Granted, the myriad lifestyles of Indian women render them difficult to write about. Taking the less arduous route of writing descriptive, non-analytical history—the traditional method for the majority of scholars who study Indians—will continue to have serious repercussions on American Indian history, for without understanding the complexity of Indian females, we cannot hope to comprehend the whole of tribal existence.

Notes

Thanks to Joseph Boles, Terry P. Wilson, and Donald E. Worcester for conversations that inspired this essay.

1 Although they depend primarily on non-Indian sources and some on feminist theory, most do not use Indian informants. Many Indians feel non-Indian theoretical conceptions do not apply to Indian studies, period. My opinion is that some simply need altering to fit the needs of ethnohistorians.

There are, unfortunately, few [tribally enrolled] Indian women historians and cultural anthropologists with terminal degrees who write: Brenda J. Child (Red Lake Chippewa), Jennie R. Joe (Navajo), K. Tsianina Lomawaima (Creek), Jean O'Brien-Kehoe (White Earth Chippewa), Bea Medicine (Lakota), and Devon A. Mihesuah (Oklahoma Choctaw). It is hoped that more native scholars will complete their degrees and will write, which will supply ethnohistory with the viewpoints it lacks.

2 For example: Gloria Anzuldua, ed., *Making Face, Making Soul/Hacienda caras: Creative and Critical Perspectives by Women of Color* (San Francisco: Aunt Lute Books, 1990); Evelyn Brooks-Higgenbothan, "The Problem of Race in

Women's History," in *Coming to Terms: Feminism, Theory, Politics*, ed. Elizabeth Weed (New York: Routledge, 1989), 122–133; bell hooks, *Ain't I a Woman?* (Boston: South End Press, 1981) and *Feminist Theory: From Margin to Center* (Boston: South End Press, 1984); and Gerda Lerner, "Reconceptualizing Differences among Women," *Journal of Women's History* (1990): 106–122; Chandra Talpade Mohanty, ed., *Third World Women and the Politics of Feminism* (Bloomington: Indiana University Press, 1991).

3   See Elizabeth Spellman, *Inessential Woman: Problems of Exclusion in Feminist Thought* (Boston: Beacon Press, 1988).

4   Calvin Martin discusses his idea of an Indian world-view in *American Indians and the Problem of History* (New York: Oxford University Press, 1986). While Martin is correct in his assertion that traditional Indian thought is much different from Euro-American thought (whatever that is), one problem with his discussion is that there is no one world-view among tribes.

5   The term *traditional* changes over time. An Indian who speaks her tribal language and participates in tribal religious ceremonies is often considered traditional, but that term is applicable only within the context of this decade, because chances are that she wears jeans, drives a car, and watches television—very "untraditional" Indian things to do. Plains Indians who rode horses in the 1860s are considered traditional today, but they were not the same as their traditional ancestors of the early 1500s who had never seen a horse.

6   For a discussion of identity and difference, see Shane Phelan, *Getting Specific* (Minneapolis: University of Minnesota Press, 1994).

7   Fredrich Engels, *The Origin of the Family, Private Property and the States* (New York: International Publishers, 1972); Karl Marx, *A Contribution to the Critique of Political Economy* (New York: International Publishers, 1972); Ernest Mandel, *An Introduction to Marxist Economic Theory* (New York: Pathfinder Press, 1970); Richard Schmitt, *Introduction to Marx and Engels* (Boulder CO: Westview Press, 1987); and Nancy Holmstrom, "A Marxist Theory of Women's Nature," *Ethics* 94 (April 1984): 186–211.

8   Alison M. Jaggar, *Feminist Politics and Human Nature* (Totowa NJ: Rowman and Allanheld, 1983).

9   In "The 150% Man, A Product of Blackfeet Acculturation," *American Anthropologist* 70 (1969): 1096–1103, Malcolm McFee proposes that the "levels of acculturation" concept may be an inaccurate form of categorization because, in his view, "new ways can be learned without abandoning the old." This statement is indeed true, but because some Indians did abandon their "old ways" in an attempt to become more like the dominant society (for a variety

of reasons), I find the phrase "level of acculturation" appropriate in many instances.

10 I introduce the issue of social classes among Cherokees in " 'Too Dark to be Angels': The Class System among the Cherokees at the Female Seminary," *American Indian Culture and Research Journal* 15 (1991): 29–52. In retrospect, I am sorry that I did not use an alternative form of categorization.

11 Lavera Rose, "*Iyeska Win*: Intermarriage and Ethnicity among the Lakota in the Nineteenth and Twentieth Centuries," Master's thesis, Northern Arizona University (May 1994).

12 Chandra Talpade Mohanty, Ann Russo, and Lourdes Torres, Introduction to *Third World Women and the Politics of Feminism* (Bloomington: Indiana University Press, 1991), 1–47.

13 M. Annette Jaimes, *The State of Native America: Genocide, Colonization, and Resistance* (Boston: South End Press, 1992), 311–344.

14 Deborah Lamb, "The Participation of Women in Wounded Knee II: Indian Activism or Feminist Action?," paper presented at American Indian Family and Tribal Community Conference, Kalamazoo MI, 1993.

15 Madonna Gilbert, quoted in Susan Braudy, "We Will Remember Survival School: The Women and Children of the American Indian Movement," *Ms. Magazine* 5 (July 1976): 94.

16 Melissa Dyea, a Lagua Pueblo, discussed these differing forms of feminism (tribalism and womanism) in "*Kawaik Nako*: Laguna Women and Their Changing Roles," paper presented at Western History Association annual conference, 1994.

17 For current discussions of Indians as "cultural brokers" see Clara Sue Kidwell, "Indian Women as Cultural Mediators," *Ethnohistory* 39 (1992): 97–107; Margaret Connell Szasz, *Between Indian and White Worlds: The Cultural Broker* (Norman: University of Oklahoma Press, 1994); and Frances Karttunen, *Between Worlds: Interpreters, Guides, and Survivors* (New Brunswick: Rutgers University Press, 1994).

18 For discussions of racial and ethnic identity see Harold R. Isaacs, *Idols of the Tribe: Group Identity and Political Change* (New York: Harper & Row, 1975); and A. Bandura and A. Huston, "Identification as a Process of Incidental Learning," *Abnormal and Social Psychology* 63 (1961): 311–318. For theoretical foundations indispensible to the study of mixed-heritage peoples, see L. Brown and Maria P. P. Root, *Complexity and Diversity in Feminist Theory and Therapy* (New York: Haworth, 1990); *Race, Class, and Power in Brazil*, ed. P. M. Fontaine (Los Angeles: University of California Center for Afro-American Studies, 1985); *The Idea of Race in Latin America, 1870–1940*, ed. Richard Graham (Austin: University of Texas Press, 1990); *Acculturation:*

Theory, Models, and Some New Findings, ed. A. M. Padilla (Boulder CO: Westview, 1980); *Racially Mixed People in America*, ed. Maria P. P. Root (Newberry Park CA: Sage Publications, 1992); *The Multiracial Experience: Racial Borders as the New Frontier*, ed. Maria P. P. Root (Newberry Park CA: Sage Publications, 1995); W. J. Scheick, *The Half-Blood: A Cultural Symbol in Nineteenth-Century American Fiction* (Lexington: University Press of Kentucky, 1979); and Paul Spickard, *Mixed Blood: Intermarriage and Ethnic Identity in Twentieth Century America* (Madison: University of Wisconsin Press, 1989).

19 Everett Stonequist, *The Marginal Man: A Study in Personality and Culture Conflict* (New York: Russell and Russell, 1937). Stonequist's view of marginality is negative. He described the "marginal man" as one who lives in "psychological uncertainty" between two worlds, one of which is dominant over the other. Although his theory is flawed in a variety of ways, it nevertheless provokes numerous questions such as, Cannot a person actually "live in two worlds"? Are all marginal persons "pathological personalities," as he implies? Most important, What are the positive aspects of being marginal?

20 McFee, "The 150% Man."

21 Maria Lugones, "Playfulness, 'World'-Traveling and Loving Perception," *Hypatia* 2 (1987): 3–19.

22 Jack Forbes, "Undercounting Native Americans: The 1980 Census and the Manipulation of Racial Identity in the United States," *Storia Nordamericana* 5 (1988): 5–47. Forbes estimates that up to 70 percent of African-Americans have some Indian ancestry.

23 M1186. Roll 1. Index to the Five Civilized Tribes. Final Dawes Roll and M1186. Enrollment Cards for the Five Civilized Tribes, 1898–1914, Rolls 2–93, at Federal Archives, Washington DC and Fort Worth TX.

24 For discussions of Indian women and power, see Michelle Zimbalist Rosaldo and Louis Lamphere, eds., *Women, Culture, and Society* (Stanford: Stanford University Press, 1974); Eleanor B. Leacock's essays "Women in an Egalitarian Society: The Montagnais-Naskapi of Canada" and "Women's Status in Egalitarian Society: Implications for Social Evolution," both in *Myths of Male Dominance: Collected Articles on Women Cross-Culturally* (New York: Monthly Review Press, 1981); *Women and Colonization: Anthropological Perspectives*, ed. Mona Etienne and E. Leacock (New York: Praeger, 1980).

25 Paula Gunn Allen discusses the enduring power and self-confidence of Indian women in her essay "Where I Come From Is like This," in *The Sacred Hoop: Recovering the Feminine in American Indian Traditions* (Boston: Beacon Press, 1986), 43–50.

26 Julie Cruikshank, particularly *Life Lived Like a Story: Life Stories of Three Yukon Elders* (Lincoln: University of Nebraska Press, 1990); Marla M. Powers, *Oglala*

Women: Myth, Ritual and Reality (Chicago: University of Chicago Press, 1986); and Ruth McDonald Boyer and Narcissus Duffy Gayton, *Apache Mothers and Daughters: Four Generations of a Family* (Norman: University of Oklahoma Press, 1992).

27 Rayna Green, Native American Women: A Contextual Bibliography (Bloomington: Indiana University Press, 1983); Francis Paul Prucha, *A Bibliographical Guide to the History of Indian-White Relations in the United States* (Chicago: University of Chicago Press, 1977); *American Indian Women: A Guide to Research*, ed. Gretchen Bataille and Kathleen M. Sands (New York: Garland, 1991); and *American Indian Women: Telling Their Lives*, ed. Bataille and Sands (Lincoln: University of Nebraska Press, 1984).

The *Living Legends Oral History Collection* at the Oklahoma Historical Society in Oklahoma City contains dozens of taped interviews of male and female Oklahoma tribe members that were conducted in the 1970s. These interviews reveal interesting details regarding the informants' lives and their views on Indian identity and tribal politics. *The Indian and Pioneer Histories*, edited by Grant Foreman, contains thousands of interviews of Oklahomans as part of the Works Projects Administration. Although poorly indexed and of uneven quality, the collection is nevertheless useful for researchers with patience. It includes short autobiographies, interviews (usually conducted by individuals with apparently no knowledge about Indians), and geneaologies of Indian women who were born in the mid–nineteenth century. Indians who attended boarding schools left behind diaries, letters, newspaper editorials, and alumni association newsletters. Two recent works bear witness to the plethora of past and present Indian voices available for writers' consideration: K. Tsianina Lomawaima, *They Called It Prairie Light: The Story of Chilocco Indian School* (Lincoln: University of Nebraska Press, 1994), and Devon A. Mihesuah, *Cultivating the Rose Buds: The Education of Women at the Cherokee Female Seminary, 1852–1910* (Urbana: University of Illinois Press, 1993).

28 For example, Paula Gunn Allen, Elizabeth Cook-Lynn, Louise Erdrich, Janet Campbell Hale, Joy Harjo, Linda Hogan, Wendy Rose, Leslie Silko, and Lucy Tapahanso.

29 N. Scott Momaday, "Oral Traditions of the American Indian," speech given at Brigham Young University, 1975.

30 Alvina E. Quintana, "Women: Prisoners of the Word," in *Chicana Voices: Intersections of Race, Class, and Gender* (Colorado Springs: Colorado College National Association for Chicano Studies, 1990), 208–219.

31 A perceptive take on the idea that Euro-Americans used more imagination than facts in chronicling Indian history and culture is historian Curtis M.

Hinsley's description of nineteenth-century digging, excavation, and collection of Indian remains and cultural objects as a deeply psychological and patriotic exercise. Hinsley writes that scholars, young men, and politicians were all contributors in "creating" the new American nation by imposing their versions of Indian history and cultures onto American history. They even created their own identities by "absorbing and domesticating their predecessors . . . into themselves. . . . Digging in the prehistoric dirt and constructing heroic tales on what they found, these men . . . faced the challenge of replacing a heritage of heroism built on classical literature with an identity constructed of shards and bones and preliterate silence. No wonder they kept digging." See his essay, "Digging for Identity: Reflections on the American Cultural Background of Repatriation," *American Indian Quarterly* special issue, "Repatriation: An Interdisciplinary Dialogue," 20:2 (Spring 1996): 180–196.

In *The View from Officer's Row: Army Perceptions of Western Indians* (Tucson: University of Arizona Press, 1990), Sherry Smith utilizes letters, diaries, and government reports to inform us of what non-Indians believed to be true about Indian women. In 1876 Richard Irving Dodge, a career military man, wrote *The Plains of North America and Their Inhabitants* (reprint, Newark: University of Delaware Press, 1989), a book replete with a patriarchal discussion of Indian females that tells us more about the Eurocentric author than it does about his subjects. For a discussion of how Euro-Americans viewed Indians, see Rachel Doggett, ed., *New World of Wonders: European Images of the Americas, 1492–1700* (Washington DC: The Folger Shakespeare Library, 1992); Rayna Green, "The Pocahontas Perplex: The Image of Indian Women in American Culture," *Massachusetts Review* 16 (Autumn 1975): 698–714; and Hugh Honour, *The European Vision of America* (Cleveland: Cleveland Museum of Art, 1975). Today, the reality of Indian women is altered by romance novels, movies, and the multi-million-dollar "Indian Maiden Art" industry.

32 This is not to imply that only non-Indians are writing incomplete histories. Plenty of Indians have not yet demonstrated their abilities to analyze their own peoples properly. Gretchen M. Bataille's *Native American Women: A Biographical Dictionary* (New York: Garland, 1993) is an interesting commentary on non-Indians' opinions about who has "influenced the development of the history of the United States." There is little argument about the historical figures—but some of the modern Indian women included are by no means influential scholars.

Special Problems in Teaching

Leslie Marmon

Silko's *Ceremony*

PAULA GUNN ALLEN

Before I get to the special part, I want to make a few comments about classroom use of sacred materials. Maybe a good place to start is at the point a television commercial calls "book smart," thence to what the same commercial terms "street smart." If we are "book smart" we will define "sacred," and if we are "street smart" we will check out the lay of the land.

For the purposes of this discussion, I'm taking "sacred" to refer to any material that is drawn from ritual and myth. This definition might extend to include "little stories," the kind that are told to children, and it certainly includes most arcane information that can be culled from a variety of scholarly or native sources.

"Street smart" is fairly simple in the commercial, but it's a bit complicated in a university setting. It's easy enough to discern the lay of the land from a white professor's point of view and teach ethically in the best academic tradition, unworried about treading on sacred ground. Ethically, a professor is responsible to provide students with the most complete, coherent information available, and, in teaching Native American literature, providing the best information includes drawing from ritual and mythic sources that have a bearing on the text under consideration. Indeed, I myself have argued elsewhere that teaching a native text without recourse to ethnographic as well as historical glossing is an exercise in obscurity, because texts, either derived from or directly connected to tradition, are firmly embedded within the matrix of their cultural base. But to use the oral tradition directly is to run afoul of native ethics, which is itself a considerable part of the tradition. Using the tradition while contravening it is to do violence to it. The ethical issue is both political and metaphysical, and to violate the traditional ethos is to run risks that no university professor signed up for, in any case.

The protectiveness of native people, particularly Pueblos, toward their traditions is legendary, but the reasons for that protectiveness are perhaps not so well known. Among the Pueblos, a person is expected to know no more than is necessary, sufficient and congruent with their spiritual and social place. One does not tell or inquire about matters that do not directly concern one. I was raised to understand that "street smart" around Laguna meant respecting privacy and modesty, and that to step beyond the bounds of the required propriety was to put myself and others at risk. One did not inquire about or tell about matters that were not hers or his to know or discuss. As my grandmother deftly phrased the requirements, one was to mind her p's and q's as well as her own beeswax.

Recently, I discovered that the sense of propriety I was taught is not confined to Lagunas or even the Pueblo world. As recorded in *Survival This Way,* Ray Young Bear tells Joe Bruchac about an experience he had that taught him the lay of the land in the Midwest. He had contracted with Harper & Row for a book of Indian folktales. He decided he didn't want to draw from published sources for his volume but would go directly to the source. To that end, he wrote a number of people inquiring after storytellers around the Midwest. In a year or so he still had not received a reply. "I took this as a sign that the whole concept of telling a story is still regarded with a lot of veneration among Native American tribes," he says (pp. 347–348). He wrote the publishers saying "there were a whole lot of Native American spiritual leaders throughout the United States who were becoming increasingly aware of people who were making profits out of Indian culture" (p. 348). He still thought he might do a book on only Mesquakie stories, so he checked with his grandmother and other people. Eventually he came to the conclusion that it wasn't possible.

The first and only stories we could have picked from Mesquakie people were published by William Jones, who was a protege of France Boas, in the early 1900s. I tried to tell my relatives that there had been previously published material on Mesquakie people by our forefathers. I thought it would still be possible to, at least, try and share some stories now before they are forgotten. But this idea of trying to keep a culture free of what would be called cultural contamination is still very prevalent among the Mesquakie. It would be easier just to forget the stories and not publish them at all. If one attempts to do that, they are risking their lives. As my grandmother told me, "I used to hear stories about William Jones being here on the Settlement when I was young. He must have gone around with a bag over his shoulder, collecting these stories. But what happened to him? He went overseas and was killed by the Philippines or some other tribe in those islands in the Pacific." She uses that as a reference and I think it is a reference that must be heeded. (p. 348)

Young Bear raises a couple of issues: the distinction that is being made by this erstwhile contact is pretty much across the board. "If it's ours, it's not for sale." He also discovers that what was told to a white ethnographer is not to be re-told by a Mesquakie, *lest tragic consequences ensue.* Preserving tradition in print is not worth the price.

Preserving tradition with the sacrifice of its living bearers seems at best reasonless, at worst blasphemous. If people die as a result of preserving tradition in the White way of preservation, for whom will the tradition be preserved?

But that's an Indian attitude. In his article "Life and Death in the Navajo Coyote Tales" published in *Recovering the Word,* the white folklorist Barre Toelken tells a similar though more elaborate tale about the risk of violating the traditional ethic. He was working with Dine on a cycle of Coyote stories when he came up against the same bottom line Young Bear stumbled on. Essentially, he was told that in continuing to probe the stories—perhaps even in recounting them—he was courting not simply his own death but that of his children or wife, his loved ones. Toelken names two levels of meaning at which one might explore narratives of Dine only at one's peril as Medicine, which he lists as Level III and categorizes as ritual of a restorative nature concerned with order, and Level IV, which he names Witchcraft, also categorized as ritual but destructive in nature. This level is, according to Toelken's scheme, concerned with disorder, "(aimed at individuals, contrary to community values)." He comments that "Level III, while fascinating, involves such heavy implications for Level IV that I think it should also be left alone by outsiders" (p. 400).

"The Navajos believe that language does not merely describe reality, it creates it," Toelken comments (p. 390), and adds "Since words and narratives have power to heal, they may also be used to injure and kill" through the selection of certain parts of the coyote narratives for incorporation into "witch's" rituals, but "instead of integrating the story with a model of order and restoration," they incorporate it into a structure modeled on disorder by using the elements "separately, divisively, and analytically" (p. 396).

Because of the power of language, and because one singer warned Toelken himself that he was flirting with becoming a witch or being seen as one, asking, "Are you ready to lose a member of your family?" (p. 395).

> Since my questions had been selective and analytical, since I was clearly trying to find out exactly what was powerful about Coyote stories, since I stood to gain by this knowledge, the old singer wanted to warn me of two possible dangers: If I became a witch, I would lose someone from my family; if others *thought* I was a witch, someone might try to kill someone in my family. In either case, Navajo informants would assume that my detailed knowledge indicated witchcraft, and no one would be willing to tell me stories any more. (pp. 396–397)

In the white world, information is to be saved and analyzed at all costs. It is not seen as residing in the minds and molecules of human beings, but as—dare I say it?—transcendent. Civilization and its attendant virtues of freedom and primacy depend on the accessibility of millions of megabytes of data; no matter that the data has lost its meaning by virtue of loss of its human context. Yet traditional materials, sacred or social, have meaning within the traditional, day-to-day context of the people who live within it.

But the white world has a different set of values, one which requires learning all and telling all in the interests of knowledge, objectivity, and freedom. This ethos and its obverse—a nearly neurotic distress in the presence of secrets and mystery—underlie much of modern American culture. Witness the John F. Kennedy murder investigations, the bumper stickers that command us to Stop the Secret Government, the conspiracy fever that motivates right- and left-wing organizations, the Irangate hearings, the Watergate hearings, and the cry for full disclosure in political, personal, and scholarly arenas. Indeed, entire disciplines have been developed on exactly the penchant for knowing everything possible that characterizes American ideas of adulthood, though the earlier American belief in privacy is strongly at odds with this trend.

The dilemma in American culture is reflected in American institutions such as universities, where it is doubly dangerous to be short on particulars. It might do harm to oneself and one's dependents. In the field of Native American Studies, the drawing card is largely exactly those matters that we are not to divulge. My students, usually "wanna bes" to at least some degree, are voraciously interested in the exotic aspects of Indian ways—and they usually mean by that traditional spiritual practices, understandings, and beliefs. Drawing their attention from the object of their longing to more mundane literary concerns and practices is troublesome. At every least opportunity, they vigorously wrest the discussion from theme, symbol, structure, and plot to questions of "medicine," sacred language, rituals, and spiritual customs.

Their interest isn't dampened by the arcane lore contained in much of the literature I teach. Numerous poems and novels such as *Cogewea,*

The Half Blood, Fools Crow, House Made of Dawn, and *Ceremony,* as you all know, contain a number of references to arcane matters. My tendency is to feel ambivalent about the whole thing. I believe that to illuminate the works I must say something about the spiritual matters, the beliefs, practices, and ceremonialism the text is alluding to. On the other hand, I shy away from answering many particular questions because I find them offensive. It's not a reaction I plan ahead of time, by the way; in fact, it's not a reaction I have been more than peripherally aware of until working on this paper. But it's one I find myself in conflict with during every lecture and every discussion.

Ceremony is a novel that I find particularly troublesome, and I tend to non-teach it, if you can picture such a thing. I focus on the story, the plot and action. I read the novel quite differently from how it is read by many. I believe I could no more do (or sanction) the kind of ceremonial investigation of *Ceremony* done by some researchers than I could slit my mother's throat. Even seeing some of it published makes my skin crawl. I have yet to read one of those articles all the way through, my physical reaction is so pronounced.

I teach the novel as being about a half-breed, in the context of half-breed literature from *Cogewea* on. Certainly, that is how I read the novel the first time I read it—as a plea for inclusion by a writer who felt excluded and compelled to depict the potential importance of breeds to Laguna survival. The parts of the novel that set other pulses atremble largely escape me. The long poem text that runs through the center has always seemed to me to contribute little to the story or its understanding. Certainly the salvation of Laguna from drought is one of its themes, but the Tayo stories, which, I surmise, form their own body of literature, would have been a better choice if Silko's intention was to clarify or support her text with traditional materials.

Tayo is the name of one of the dramatic characters around Keresland. Perhaps in some story I am unfamiliar with, he is involved with Fly or Reed Woman. But the story she lays alongside the novel is a clan story, and is not to be told outside of the clan.

I have long wondered why she did so. Certainly, being raised in greater proximity to Laguna village than I, she must have been told what I was, that we don't tell these things outside. Perhaps her desire to demonstrate the importance of breeds led her to this, or perhaps no one ever told her why the Lagunas and other Pueblos are so closed about their spiritual activities and the allied oral tradition.

Two instructive events were used as a reference to convey to me what behavior was expected with regard to passing on Laguna materials. I was told that an anthropologist, Elsie Clews Parsons, had come to Laguna to collect material for her study of Pueblo religion and social culture. They had given her information readily enough and everything seemed fine. But when Parsons published the material, Lagunas saw how she treated their practices and beliefs, and they were horrified. In accordance with her academic training, she objectified, explained, detailed, and analyzed their lives as though they were simply curios, artifacts, and fetishes, and discussed the supernaturals as though they were objects of interest and patronization. Her underlying attitude for the supernaturals, the sacred, and the people who honored them didn't evade notice. The Lagunas were "red-haired," as my mother would say. Coincidentally (or not so coincidentally) the terrible drought deepened—the same drought Silko depicts in *Ceremony*—and in its wake many other ills visited the Pueblo. Personal horrors and society-wide horrors ensued; the discovery of uranium on Laguna land, not far from where the giantess's head and her headless body had been flung by the War Twins, the development of nuclear weapons near Jemez, the Second World War, jackpile mine, water and land poisoned by nuclear waste, the village of Paguate all but surrounded by tailing-mesas almost as perfectly formed as the natural mesas all around. It's hardly any wonder that they shut it down. All entry by non-traditionals to dances and stories was cut off. They witnessed firsthand the appalling consequences of telling what was private for reasons that far exceed simple cultural purism.

While Silko details these horrors in *Ceremony,* she does not attribute them to security leaks. She is poignantly aware of the closure of village life to outsiders and depicts the pain such exclusion brings; she is aware of the discovery of the uranium used to bomb Hiroshima and Nagasaki, she is aware of the devastating drought, the loss of self that the entire Pueblo suffered in those years, yet she is unaware of one small but essential bit of information: the information that telling the old stories, revealing the old ways, can only lead to disaster.

Growing up in Cubero, I was not told all these details about the Parsons affair and its repercussions; it is only upon reflection that I can connect the uranium and the bomb as one of the disasters that ensued. But to bring the story even closer to home to me, I was told about my cousin, from another Pueblo, who had written about her life in the pueblo as a school exercise. The exercise was published, and she was somewhat lionized locally, being a child and having notably developed writing skills. She was to do another book, one that told some stories from her Pueblo, but before that project got well underway, she was called before the tribal council and told in no uncertain terms that she must not complete it. I remember being told a person who told those stories might wake up dead in a ditch somewhere. I no longer remember the details clearly, but I think there was another story about exactly that happening to someone who had carried tales.

Now, I've been to college, even to graduate school. I suppose I should be like Rocky in *Ceremony,* able to dismiss these things with a wave of my hand, attributing them to superstition, or seeing them as quaint reminders of a lost past. What's the use in being educated if you still believe in such things? Besides, unlike Rocky, I am a breed. I have even less reason to honor the traditions and heed the references I've been given. And I suppose that, valuing my career and my job—which is a very good one—I have even less reason to honor the Laguna way.

But childhood learning dies hard. In the classroom or before the keyboard, I find myself physically ill when I attempt to override those early lessons. My body, breed as it is, rebels against the very idea that such violations might proceed from me. For years I have had a some-what different attitude toward materials from other tribes, like those in the Midwest. But reading Young Bear's comments, I realize that even that territory—which, for reasons of ignorance coupled with the availability of information from midwestern Native communities, I had seen as open to such use—is not.

Reading Young Bear's comments have required me to see that my difficulties in teaching *Ceremony,* which are considerable, are extended to every writer and work I teach. Being faced with the ethical dilemma caused by my modicum of native awareness, I have specialized in teaching contemporary literature to avoid as many ethical violations as I could, believing that I might teach it and evade or avoid queries about arcane matters. By and large I have succeeded in doing so, giving a few generalized lectures on native spiritual systems and avoiding discussing any in particular detail. I have gone so far as to learn as little ritual or myth as possible in any particular detail to further buttress my defense against ethical violations.

But satisfying my ethical concerns poses a serious ethical problem: pedagogically, I believe I should give specific information to students; discover and teach what the directions of Tayo's movements mean, what constellations figure in the story, and what their significance at Laguna is; what prayers, rituals, and spiritual activities occur at the Pueblo that have bearing on the novel; and how these elements propel the narrative and combine to form its overall significance.

Ethically, as a professor, I see this kind of methodology as necessary; but ethically, as an Indian, I can't do it. Contemplating my dilemma in cold, hard prose here, I begin to despair; no, I begin to understand some of the reasons for my extreme ambivalence in doing what I do, some of the reasons I find teaching in Native American Studies so painful, and some of the reasons why some of the poems and fiction I've been working on for years is stymied.

At this point I don't have any solutions or resolutions in mind. Sadly—and frustratingly—a human life isn't a television commercial OR a novel; it seldom structures itself along classical lines of conflict, crisis, and resolution. Probably I will continue to teach and write, more aware of the source of my conflict, perhaps more able to render that conflict articulate. I think I will feel more secure about my tendency to fail at my professional responsibilities by choosing my Native obligations over my academic ones, and find more precise ways to teach away from forbidden territory while illuminating the texts in more prosaic, less titillating ways. For, make no mistake, many students come to be titillated by Indian lore, seeing—however unconsciously—Native spiritual life as a curious artifact, as they've been conditioned to see all things Indian. They will find themselves disappointed, but then that's not new. Perhaps they will find themselves ever more aware that Native people are people, and their ways are not a spectacle but simply, and significantly, a way of life.

References

Bruchac, Joseph, ed. *Survival This Way: Interviews with American Indian Poets,* Tucson: University of Arizona Press and Sun Tracks, 1987.

Swann, Brian, and Arnold Krupat. *Recovering the Word: Essays on Native American Literature.* Los Angeles: University of California Press, 1987.

Comfortable Fictions and the Struggle for Turf:
An Essay Review of *The Invented Indian:*
Cultural Fictions and Government Policies

VINE DELORIA JR.

In the appendix of *The Invented Indian,* a collection of essays edited by James Clifton purporting to critique the modern configuration of Indian affairs, is a list entitled "Criticisms of Non-Conformers," sixty-four slogans which are frequently hurled at the people who look askance at the antics of modern Indians and their supporters. The inclusion of this list, more than the essays in the collection, tells us a great deal about the scholars who have made contributions to this work. They visualize themselves as the rebels, non-conformists against a rising tide of romanticism and nonsense which they feel is promulgated by Indians and their friends for wholly political purposes. Thus we deal, in this collection, not with Indians but with the self-image of the writers and their view of how the Indian world should properly be constructed.

A jacket quote further illuminates the reader. Penny Jessel, identified as a Shawnee woman, tells us that reading *The Invented Indian* brought to mind an incident when a Golden Eagle landed on her shoulder: "The editor and authors are able to soar among the clouds, look down and view the whole scene with sharp eyes. They evaluate what they see with clear logic. . . . Considering the beating they may take for this book, they are brave. I applaud them for simply telling the truth. They are right." Thus the reviewer is placed at a disadvantage from the very beginning, since any critical analysis of the essays contained herein will be understood by the authors as trying to introduce even more pro-Indian fictions into a scene which they are trying to reform. Nevertheless, their point of view, that they are rebels fighting against insuperable odds to bring truth to Indian affairs, is misleading and needs some extended analysis.

The first point which we must consider in reviewing any set of essays that pretends to offer an objective view of Indian affairs is that there never has been an objective point of view regarding Indians and there never will be. Conflict between red and white has been the predominant characteristic of race relations for half a millennium and will continue to influence all efforts to bring about an interpretation of what the invasion of this continent has meant—to both Indians and non-Indians. For most of the five centuries, whites have had unrestricted power to describe Indians in any way they chose. Indians were simply not connected to the organs of propaganda so that they could respond to the manner in which whites described them. The modern Indian movement, in an effort to strike back and recover ground unnecessarily lost during the preceding five centuries, has made a lot of mistakes, has overly romanticized episodes, beliefs, and moral positions, and has made a lot of people uncomfortable. But it is not yet time that we should swing over to an overt attack on what Indians are saying and doing with the excuse that Indians have over-emphasized their strong points and covered up their weaknesses.

It is singularly instructive that the reviews of *Dances with Wolves* were mostly critical, and strong objections were raised by conservative columnists who took great pride in pointing out the brutality of Indian warfare, the presence of slaves in some Indian societies, and the great strides which industrial America has made in two centuries. This evidence is cited to justify dispossession of the Indians. If you balance *Dances with Wolves* against the hundreds of films which distort the image of Indians, create stereotypes of brutality and incoherence, and justify a fictional western history, it is not difficult to see that the trend of the conservative moment is simply to deny any criticism of the old comfortable fictions. The essays in this book have a similar goal and consequently they are hardly objective and have as their political agenda the rolling back of whatever inroads and changes the authors believe Indians have made in recent decades. That political agenda is permissible—but just say so. Don't cloak the collection in a mist of piety which purports to restore balance and objectivity to the modern scene.

Rarely should a reviewer undertake a personal attack on the authors of essays, and I provide my perspective realizing that I am getting close to that prohibited area. However, the initial claim of objectivity which may fool the casual reader should be placed within a larger background so that the points of view of the people writing these essays can be more easily understood. They are hardly the luminaries of their profession. Clifton, Tooker, Gill, Kehoe, de Mille, and Feraca are known within Indian circles but known as bitter people eager to criticize Indians at the drop of a hat, and if a listing were made up evaluating the professional standing of the authors of these essays perhaps only Tooker and Gill would be ranked anywhere near the top of their fields. Thus we are not dealing with the giants of anthropology, history, and literature, or even the pretty tall people, but with average if not below average scholars who are not taken seriously by their professional colleagues precisely because their point of view is known and is known to exclude objectivity on many occasions.

The collection has an undertone of emotions that struck me as important to the discussion of the motivation of these authors. The authors, for the most part, seem to be very disappointed that modern Indians do not act like the Indians of their undergraduate textbooks or the movies they enjoyed as children, and they seem determined to attack contemporary expressions of Indian-ness as fraudulent and invalid because modern Indians fall short of their expectations. Part of the authors' goal is to excoriate Indians for not being their own ancestors and behaving as such. Indians in store-bought clothes have no romantic value whatsoever and are just pale imitations of "real" Indians, and that is a good bit of the message of these essays.

More profound, however, is the unarticulated assumption that social science scholars, particularly the people represented here, should always control the definitions that people use to describe and communicate. I know Clifton, Gill, Feraca, and Tooker personally, and when I think back to comments and conversations I have had with them I remember their anxious concern over authority and definitions—who will the public identify as the people who "really know"? In this respect these scholars only mirror the struggle that has been occurring for the past generation. Should Indians be allowed to present their side of the story, or will helpful and knowing whites be the Indian spokespeople? This battle has taken up my adult life. Am I as an Indian entitled to write about the Indian view of nature and religion or is this task properly suited to Lynn Andrews and Doug Boyd? These authors are defending their entrenched advantage of being the people who "really know." Thus Tooker expects to be heard in lieu of the traditional Six Nations chiefs because, after all, she has studied the Six Nations and therefore is entitled to represent them before the public and any other interested parties.

If this collection of essays is placed in the proper political context, that is, in the arena in which the struggle for authority and control of definitions is primary, we can then properly evaluate the contents of the book and come to some intelligent conclusions. A review of the respective essays and a demonstration of the errors and hidden agendas may be useful in showing that these are indeed second-rate scholars on a holy mission of stopping the barbarian hordes (Indians) at the gates before they overwhelm the old citadels of comfortable fiction. This analysis may be overly long. It is an effort to come to grips with some of the points that these authors feel are important to make against a generation of Indians determined to give some balance to the manner in which things Indian are presented to the public.

James Clifton: Memories and Exegesis. This essay might be better entitled "The Academic Meets the Real World." The early trauma that Clifton suffered in his academic career was triggered by his role as a witness in the Indian Claims Commission, which he suspected was simply a contrived way that Indians got money from the federal government. Attaching himself to people he felt represented the real Potawatomis, Clifton rejected the other people of Indian ancestry who were attracted to the claims process and its subsequent awarding of monies. Clifton's description of Brantley Blue, Lumbee Indian commissioner on the Indian Claims Commission, belies his objectivity since he characterizes the Lumbees as "born again Indians," people not Indians in his eyes and therefore unworthy and ineligible to participate in Indian activities.

Clifton's next trauma was encountering the poverty programs where, unfortunately, he ran into the resurgent Menominee people seeking restoration of their tribe from its forced and ill-fated termination. He found their militancy distasteful, refusing to understand their side of the story and feeling uncomfortable at the thought of living between two definitions of Indian identity which were being attacked by both liberals and conservatives. Most distasteful, however, seems to have been the fact that the Menominees who were seeking restoration had a B.S., an M.S.W., and an Ll.D. Here, as I have noted before, is the clash of authority. How could the educated Menominees not listen to a man with a Ph.D.? Clifton found that a number of Menominees, perhaps the first generation to really see what the federal government was doing to them, were his peers in educational achievements—in effect they had stepped out of his comfortable fictions and were determined to use modern methods to restore the fortunes of their people.

The point that Clifton misses in his emotional recounting of his Indian experiences is that of tribal identity and purpose. Who is to tell any group of Indians that they must submit meekly to the machinations of Congress or a state or county government and forfeit what they feel in their hearts is their personal and community identity? Definitions of social science, that Indians are only full-bloods, only traditionals, or only people who still speak the tribal language, all fall away before the reality of rural living, experienced in a small Indian community. But somehow, the reasoning is elusive. Clifton believes the Menominee activists were wrong. What does "wrong" mean here, if not the belief that the resurgence goes against prevailing social theories of how Indians are supposed to behave?

Finally, it appears, Clifton was simply overwhelmed by the many changes taking place around him. Witness one of his complaints: "Today, a conference about Indians without Indians prominent on the agenda, or, even better, acting as sponsor-hosts is nearly an impossibility" (p. 16). Well, so what? Are we to restore the old patterns of conferences and have whites such as Clifton telling other whites something about Indians? Indeed, that is Clifton's goal, and what he misses more than anything else is that fine sense of superior status which he received as a new Ph.D. who had actually "studied" Indians and therefore knew more about them than they did themselves.

Fellow scholars knew perfectly well what Clifton had in mind in this collection. He cites examples of two scholars who refused to have their works included in this collection, one for fear of Indian retaliation and the other when Clifton refused to certify that some of the authors did not have racist views on Indians. So his subterfuge and pretended objectivity did not snare the more intelligent scholars. But Clifton's essay ends with a fine diatribe, suggesting that I will eventually write a book entitled *Columbus Was Red* and castigating the *Indian Historian* (now out of print), the *American Indian Culture and Research Journal,* and the *Northeast Indian Quarterly* for presenting special issues giving the Indian point of view. In Clifton's mind there is no valid Indian point of view, for indeed there are no real Indians— except of course the people with whom he has worked and who agree with him—whoever these people are.

I think Clifton and his authors have a right to their point of view, but why do they, in almost every instance, deny the right of Indians to have the same privileges? Clifton's argument, if one follows the essay point by point, is that the modern Indian point of view is wrong because *Indians do not have the right to have a point of view* when scholars know reality to be different. Here, then, we have the crux of the problem. Clifton et al. are simply fighting for the right to continue defining Indians in whatever manner they see fit. This attitude is somewhat akin to spending one's time arguing whether it was an alligator or crocodile that bit off one's arm. It is simply a silly, petulant, adolescent response to the fact that the world has changed.

James Clifton: The Indian Story: a Cultural Fiction. Not content with whining through his introduction, Clifton then constructs his own version of the Indian version of history and criticizes it. Part of this essay critiques recent literature, primarily titles which appear to be favorable to the Indian version of the story. I have no quarrel with Clifton's caricature of our current version of the Indian story because I do the same thing to the anthros' interpretation. All of us do it, and we should simply admit it and not adopt the pious holier-than-thou pretense that we don't. If Clifton really wanted a strange version of history, he should read the opinions of the United States Supreme Court and see how they treat the history of Indians and whites—it is wholly fictional and courts are supposed to be fact-finding bodies.

Christian Feest—The Pocahontas Myth and the Pamunkey. Feest is a European, undoubtedly originally schooled in Indians by Karl May's novels about the Apaches, who later discovered that Indians do not live in tents and hunt buffalo anymore and has been terribly disappointed ever since. His short essay criticizes the Pamunkey because they have adopted the Pocahontas myth as part of their own heritage and proudly displayed pictures of Pocahontas and Captain John Smith. It is unfortunate that Feest was not a Pamunkey Indian, surrounded by insensitive whites who could not have distinguished Geronimo from a Pamunkey, who would have demanded that the Pamunkeys wear war bonnets, make adobe bricks and Santa Clara pottery, and attend Thanksgiving celebrations. Indians can clearly relate to the pressure, experienced throughout one's life, of meeting the fictional expectations of whites. Thus to imply that the Pamunkeys were dishonest in adopting Pocahontas is clearly derived from a disappointment in not finding the original Pocahontas waiting to fulfill one's expectations.

Lynn Ceci: On Planting Corn in the Manner of the Indians and *Carol Mason: Maple Sugaring in the New World.* These two essays are the epitome of white disappointment, since they are devoted to the proposition that Indians did not plant corn with fish fertilizers or make maple sugar until the whites taught them how—or at any rate until after pre-contact times—or at least these are monstrous lies promulgated by Indians. The arguments are hardly suitable for adults. What the authors are protesting are the lies of the previous generation of whites who wanted to believe these things about Indians. Why then should Indians become the butt of accusations of misleading the whites? I have never heard an Indian say that his or her personal or tribal identity stemmed from the truth or falsity of these propositions. So it is not really a debate. It is simply two white scholars venting their frustrations at learning that a childhood teaching—and they certainly weren't taught by Indians—was false. So go argue with your mother.

Elisabeth Tooker: The United States Constitution and the Iroquois League. Some years ago Bruce Johansen published a little book entitled *Forgotten Founders* which suggested that a number of the ideas of constitutional government developed by the Six Nations had found their way into the thinking of the American Constitutional fathers. A wave of nauseous panic spread through the old boys' network of Iroquois studies, since a commoner had dared to write in a field already dominated by self-appointed experts. Donald Grinde, not realizing that he was entering the sanctum sanctorum of anthropology, then published *The Iroquois and the Founding of the American Nation,* further elaborating on this heresy which was becoming an open scandal.

Damage control measures went into effect, and soon Grinde and Johansen found their NEH grant proposals turned down by readers who emphasized the orthodox interpretation of Iroquois studies. Conservative newspaper columnists, learning of the controversy, promptly marched into historical debates of which they had no knowledge whatsoever, and chastised Johansen and Grinde, and proposals by the two scholars to have open debate over the topic were generally turned aside as if mere physical contact with the two would be a sign of incipient heresy.

Into the fray rode Dr. Elisabeth Tooker, and in an article published in *Ethnohistory,* abridged for publication in this book, Tooker articulated her own version of the Six Nations government and demonstrated, to her satisfaction, the impossibility of the Six Nations having any relevance at all for American constitutional thinking. Tooker's argument is so wonderfully naive and anthro-centric that it makes the informed observer of the debate weep for her inability to free herself from the blinders which adherence to anthro doctrine has required she wear. Tooker cites a few quotations that have undoubtedly been derived from popular anthologies on Indians and then argues that no one, really not even the Indians, knew anything about the Six Nations form of government until the anthropologists wrote it down. Witness: "Not until Lewis H. Morgan made it a special subject of study and published his findings did an account of the Iroquois form of government become available" (p. 113).

Tooker then cites specific provisions of the Six Nations' documents, as articulated by Morgan, and notes that there was no direct transfer of provisions from the Indians to the American constitution, in effect mistaking plagiarism for influence and knocking the straw horse she has devised all to pieces again. Throughout her essay Tooker advances John Locke as the philosopher of influence in constitutional thinking, citing him with the same reverence with which Christians cite St. Paul. I chastised Tooker publicly at a panel at the American Anthropological Association meeting, chiding her for an appalling lack of knowledge of political philosophy and suggesting that if she wanted to argue properly she might consult *The Federalist* to see that Montesquieu was the dominant intellectual force in the minds of the pro-constitutional fathers, and suggesting that Locke's brief effort to organize a landed aristocracy in North Carolina had pretty much discredited him with American political thinkers well before the effort to formulate an American constitution. Tooker bolted into the aisle, shrieking, "Tell that to your friends, tell that to your friends."

To find Tooker's original article, in abridged form, reprinted in this collection of essays surprised me, since a little effort on her part could have sharpened her side of the discussion immensely. Perhaps she simply prefers to believe that John Locke was the most influential thinker at that time in American history and does not wish to explore further. That is her privilege, but it doesn't seem a very fruitful contribution to the discussion because it means that the old boys' network of Iroquoian studies simply wants to shout a bit louder and refuses to consider anything except their own belief system.

Johansen and Grinde have collaborated now to produce *Exemplar of Liberty*, published by the *American Indian Culture and Research Journal* (1991), which further extends the scope of materials that must be considered if we are to make sense of this issue. My concern in opposing Tooker and others on the opposite side of the debate is at least two-fold. First, I do not think that ethnographic data, however derived, should have precedence over equally good historical data which has not been used previously simply because anthros look at one kind of material and historians look at another kind. The separation of disciplines must not dominate the search for truth.

More important, as far as I can see, is the fundamental problem which the constitutional fathers faced and which, in my opinion, we have never solved. That question, which Montesquieu attempts to resolve, is the degree to which geography dominates political institutions and whether or not a democracy can extend itself indefinitely over a geographical area, with the subsequent increase in the size of the population to be governed, without seeing its institutions become impotent structures. The genius of the Six Nations political structure, in my opinion, is its ability to spread political sovereignty over three distinct institutions—the Six Nations council itself, the individual tribes, and the nationwide clan system. The constitutional debate really involved allocating political powers and functions between the states and the federal government, and in solving this problem the constitutional fathers had to have given careful consideration to what the Six Nations had already done in solving this vexing question. That the Americans finally split their political sovereignty in at least six pieces—an executive, judicial, and legislative branch for both the national government and the respective states, thus making mush out of political principles—is certainly not the fault of the Indians.

This debate has not really been joined properly because what Johansen and Grinde are saying is simply that considerably more material must be examined before hard and fast conclusions are drawn. Tooker's argument, it seems to me, is simply that the materials, and the arrangement of those materials, that the entrenched scholars of anthropology have amassed, are sufficient to answer all questions regarding the Six Nations—period. The real debate, therefore, is over authority: to whom shall we listen—about anything? Here the credentials of the past, no matter how valiantly won, are just not enough to dominate or close debate on a subject—period.

Sam Gill: Mother Earth: An American Myth. Sam Gill stirred up a great controversy among the uninformed when he wrote this essay suggesting that "Mother Earth" was a white man's invention and not part of Indian traditions at all. Many young Indians were furious because they had uncritically accepted the comfortable slogans of popular culture and felt that Gill had directly attacked their religious sensitivities. After reading Gill's essay I was amazed that people took offense and further astounded that some of his colleagues did not quietly advise him to withdraw it for fear of embarrassing himself and the profession generally.

If Gill's essay is read objectively and dispassionately, it proves to be an unnecessary exercise in demonstrating what inadequate research can lead a person to believe. Gill sets out to show "a lineage of Western writers who have considered the Mother Earth figure as a native American goddess. From their writing a story of Mother Earth emerges, a story attributed to Native Americans but actually created by the writers themselves" (pp. 130–131). Gill then cites Edward B. Tylor (1873), Hubert Bancroft (1882), Albert Gatschet (1890) James Mooney (1896), several lesser known scholars, and more modern authorities such as Mircea Eliade (1958) and Ake Hultkrantz (1979, 1983) as non-Indians who have perpetuated this idea.

Gill cites a speech by Smohalla given in 1885 and argues that "Smohalla's single statement provides almost the only cited evidence on which to base the story" (p. 135) of the Mother Earth goddess. Herein lies a major problem. Gill has expanded his thesis into a book, entitled *Mother Earth* (1990), in which he says:

> Systematically, I reviewed the ethnographic and scholarly literature on native North America. The ethnographic literature produced little, and it surprised me to find that, while scholarly discussions of Mother Earth uniformly considered her to be universal among tribes and to have existed since great antiquity, the majority of evidence used as the basis for these claims was the statement made by Smohalla, with an occasional reference to a statement made by the Shawnee leader Tecumseh.[1]

We can assume, for purposes of discussion, that Gill submitted his essay to Clifton, who then had a devil of a time getting *The Invented Indian* published, leaving a time gap so long that Gill was able to expand his essay into a full book although failing to re-edit his essay and include Tecumseh's speech about Mother Earth. So properly we can look at the essay and Gill's book as articulating the same theme—that Mother Earth as a native goddess was an invention of the white man.

"The story begins," according to Gill, "with a statement attributed to the Shawnee, Tecumseh, who reportedly said in 1810 during a meeting with William H. Harrison, "The earth is my mother and on her bosom I will repose."[2] Gill then suggests that Moses Dawson, who published a historical examination of Harrison and his relationship to Tecumseh, cited the Mother Earth saying of Tecumseh as part of a general process of making the Shawnee chief legendary, implying that perhaps Tecumseh didn't even make the speech. Then citing some similar remarks made by Indians at the treaty council of May 28, 1855, Gill argues:

> We have in 1855 a report of a statement remarkably similar to the statement attributed to Tecumseh at an event forty-five

years before and half a continent away. It is significant that Kip presents this statement as a quotation and that the English word 'reposing' and 'bosom' are central. I see no way to understand this statement as documenting a common belief between the Shawnee, along with other Eastern tribes, and these plateau tribes of the Washington Territory. It indicates to me rather that some of those present in Walla Walla were familiar with the Tecumseh statement so widely quoted in 1855.[3]

Thus Gill sets us straight—whites composed the noblest sentiments previously attributed to Indians.

I would like to point out that Gill's contention that these two quotations are the only references to Mother Earth by Indians only supports the possibility that he is not the best scholar of this generation. He could not have much knowledge of Indians or the source materials dealing with Indians if he could only find these two quotations. As a by-product of researching Indian treaties I have come up with numerous references to Mother Earth. Of course I did not find these references in ethnographic materials—I found them in minutes of councils and treaty negotiations—precisely where the original source materials for both the Smohalla and Tecumseh quotes originated. Indians were not sitting around seminar rooms articulating a nature philosophy for the benefit of non-Indian students after all. They were trying to save their lands from exploitation and expropriation.

Thus on Friday, June 21st, 1776, at a conference in Pittsburgh during the Revolutionary War, Cornstalk, in trying to convince the Mingos of Ohio to side with the Americans in the war, argued: "You have heard the good Talks which our Brother (George Morgan) Weepemachukthe [The White Deer] has delivered to us from the Great Council at Philadelphia representing all our white Brethern who have grown out of this same Ground with ourselves *for this Big [Turtle] Island being our common Mother, we & they are like one Flesh and Blood"* (emphasis added).[4]

And in Sante Fe, in 1892, at a festival celebrating the two hundredth year of the Spanish reconquest of New Mexico, San Juan, an old

Mescalero chief who not many years before had fought the New Mexicans, made a speech. "Many people," he said, "believe that the Apaches do not know God or where He lives. We do. He lives above the clouds, He is our father and the earth is our mother. When we pass to the Great Spirit we go to our homes in the skies, but our bodies remain with our mother who bore us."[5]

I have a number of other quotations of Indians referring to Mother Earth, but I am not going to reveal them for fear that Gill will use them in a revised version of his book and make even worse arguments to prove that white men originated them. Did the same newspaper reporters at Pittsburgh in 1776 attend the negotiations in Washington Territory in 1855 and help Harrison and Tecumseh negotiate in 1810? If Gill was unable to find any other quotes besides Smohalla and Tecumseh, it means that he looked quickly at T. C. McLuhan's *Touch the Earth,* found these two quotes, and began writing his book. Gill merely bears out my original contention that these essays do not represent the highest achievement of the scholarly community but are rather mundane pieces of work.

Leland Donald: Was the Indian Really Egalitarian? Donald takes aim at the question of Indian egalitarianism and finds that a form of slavery existed in some of the Pacific Northwest tribes and on that basis is prepared to deny any sense of parity existing within tribal cultures. Some of these tribes may have had a form of servitude derived from inter-tribal warfare, but their institution of slavery was a far cry from the slavery practiced by whites in the American South. Indian slaves were not a form of property in any way approaching white southern slavery. Did the Pacific Coast Indians have breeding plantations where slave Indians were deliberately bred for market and sold to tribes from other parts of the country? Of course not. Donald's argument simply moves into hyperbole, and he hopes the readers will not notice.

David Henige: Native American Historical Demography as Expiation. Henige attacks demographers who prefer a high count of the aboriginal population and accuses them of moral indignation. I think he has many good points in his argument. Liberals prefer high population counts, conservatives prefer low ones. Neither side of the spectrum has ever given me much confidence in their estimates and I have always resented the manipulation of figures to support such obvious bias—in both directions. One thing is certain, and it can be demonstrated by surveying official government records and estimates beginning with the birth of the republic: the Indian population has always been grossly underestimated in historical times by people believed to be experts. In reading this essay it is good to remember that this is a quarrel between opposing groups of Whites who have political beliefs to protect; it really has no reference to Indians.

Alice Kehoe: Primal Gaia. Kehoe links frauds and charlatans to the idea that Indians were natural peoples with some concern for and knowledge of the environment. The linkage occurs because many Indians are out on the workshop circuit spreading all manner of New Age nonsense, and within the New Age pseudophilosophies is the Gaia concern: the living earth. She attacks the same people who were generally exposed in a series in the *Lakota Times* in the summer of 1991, and so Indians cannot help but applaud her efforts. But who is it that has made such people as Adolph Hungry Wolf, Jamake Highwater, Joseph Epes Brown, Sun Bear, Rolling Thunder, Wallace Black Elk, John Redtail Freesoul, Lynn Andrews, and Dhyani Ywahoo the spokespeople of American Indians? It is the white folks crying for some kind of spiritual reality who have made these people the most visible Indian spokespeople. To my knowledge no Indian tribe has commissioned them to go out and preach the true word. They represent the intense desire of Whites to create in their own minds an Indian they want to believe in, and there is nothing that Indians can do about it. So that makes all Indians frauds? Get off it!!

R. H. Barnes: The Omaha Indians in Anthropology. Barnes simply reviews mistakes in emphasis and interpretation made by several authorities on the Omahas. And again we should ask ourselves why, if scholars are making classical mistakes and writing bad interpretations, does it become a burden to be placed on Indians? It is as if we commit mortal and venial sins simply by becoming the subjects of anthropological research—which is something I have already hinted at in *Custer Died for Your Sins*.

Richard de Mille: Distinguishing Two Components of Truth. I like de Mille's essay, which exposes the Don Juan books as fictional constructions. Everyone should read this essay. But I must issue a word of warning here. When the books first came out I told people they were a fraud and I was met with the accusation, by some rather highly regarded anthropologists, that I was only saying that because I was jealous of Castaneda. If efforts from within the Indian community to expose nonsense are rebuffed and accusations are cast against those willing to speak out against fraud, Indians can hardly be blamed for the perpetuation of this nonsense.

John A. Price: Canada's Indian Support Groups. I do not know enough about the Canadian situation to offer an intelligent critique, so I will not do so.

Stephen E. Feraca: Inside the BIA. Steve Feraca here rants and raves about the initiation of Indian preference in the Bureau of Indian Affairs, first under Robert Bennett and then under Louis Bruce. His basic argument is that no Indian really knows anything about Indians and everyone should be trained before they are allowed to be employed by the BIA—preferably by Feraca. I doubt that this proposition is true. But Feraca's analysis that the BIA has crumbled over the past two decades is undoubtedly true—whether it is due to Indian preference or whether the Bureau, like the Small Business Administration, the National Park Service, or the Department of Agriculture, has simply succumbed to the ravages of time is yet to be determined. To pretend that it would be an efficient organization were it not for Indian preference policies is absurd—it never was anything except a haven for the barely employable.

Alan van Gestel: When Fictions Take Hostages. The author is terribly upset over the fact that eastern Indians have been filing land claims and in many instances have been successful. Indian tribes, he discovers, are legal fictions much the same as the idea that a corporation is a person. So what is the problem? All legal concepts are fictions. Torts are based on the comparative actions of the "reasonably prudent man acting in the same or similar circumstances," contracts are a "meeting of the minds," and so forth. So because these are Indian claims that are being filed we should deny the Indians the benefit of using law and legal procedures to pursue their rights? Is van Gestel an "officer and a gentleman" through act of Congress? I certainly hope so. That would be the ultimate legal fiction.

Christian Feest: Europe's Indians. Feest surveys the various historical images of Indians in Europe. This essay is informative and helpful to those of us who know nothing of European fascination with Indians. But it is ever so depressing—Europeans build up fantasies about Indians the same way American Whites do. And here we thought Europeans were so sophisticated.

Jean-Jacques Simard: White Ghosts, Red Shadows. The author begins his essay: "Indians and Whites do not exist" (p. 333). The remainder of the essay basically argues that these labels are just what keeps the two groups apart. But the argument wanders significantly, making it appear that the author feels deeply about some subject, but never clarifying whether there is any perspective that can be taken to understand Indians and whites. Simard is very disappointed that Indians want federal jobs and funds—as if the rank and file of non-Indians didn't. Simard is very difficult to follow in his reasoning, but I get the impression that he also has a great disappointment that Indians today do not behave as they did in his childhood fantasies. This sentiment seems critical to Simard because he is willing to require higher ethical, moral, and cultural standards for judging Indian behavior than he would apply to a similarly situated group of whites or to white society as a whole. To pretend also that if Indians simply integrated into the majority society, equal justice and opportunity would reign, is simply the old con job of the majority seeking to entice the minority to embrace the fictions by which we hide from our social and political problems.

It was inevitable, given the progress made by Indians in the last three decades, that sooner or later a reactionary attack on us would be made. I am thankful that this group, rather than a group of first-rate minds, saw fit to level the attack. The basic point of view of this group is that we as Indians have severely disappointed them and they do not forgive us. It is as if we have demonstrated that there really is no Santa Claus and they are bitter children at having learned the truth. This feeling is compounded by the fact that these authors have regarded themselves as definitive authorities on Indians and now find their status, indeed their personal identities, threatened by the emergent and militant Indians of the present.

Every Indian should read this book because it does represent the attitude of a significant percentage of American and Canadian citizens who, knowing very little of their own history and having great personal psychological problems, tend to vest their hope for reality in an image of savage nobility which they and their predecessors have created. It is they who have invented and continue to invent Indians. Not willing to admit it, they then blame us for perpetuating whatever images become popular among whites. These people are among the persistent crowd of people exploiting Indians while they pretend in these essays to be advocating the real truth about Indians—another twist in logic, to be sure.

The problems will not go away whether these particular people cease their sniping or not. Understanding the nature and depth of the confrontation between red and white in the Western Hemisphere is difficult and perhaps is really an impossible task for any of us. Certainly we will not benefit from the charges and countercharges that will be made during this year of the Quincentennial. One thing is also certain. The next generation of American Indians must finally find a way to transcend the barriers of communication and provide sufficient information on Indians so that the next generation of whites looks at us realistically and we do not have to face bitter whites who create fantasies about us and then turn against us.

Notes

The Invented Indian was edited by James A. Clifton. New Brunswick NJ: Transaction Publishers, 1990.

1   Sam Gill, *Mother Earth* (Chicago: University of Chicago Press, 1987), 5.
2   Gill, *Mother Earth,* 6.
3   Gill, *Mother Earth,* 44.
4   Cornstalk, Shawnee Chief in speech to the Mingos at the Kickapoo village, June 21, 1776, *Morgan's Journal,* 31–32.
5   Ralph Emerson Twitchell, *Old Santa Fe* (Santa Fe: Mexican Publishing, 1925), 407.

Ethics and Responsibilities in Writing American Indian History

DONALD L. FIXICO

Researching, writing, and teaching American Indian history in a respectful manner calls for a set of professional ethics and scholarly responsibilities. As scholarship evolves, so must the treatment of American Indian history. Such ethics and responsibilities are not currently defined or recorded in any forum, or in any printed material, although historians previously have considered the importance of a fairer treatment of Indians in writing history.[1] The sensitivity of tribal knowledge, especially that of ceremonials, should compel scholars to publicly acknowledge a code of ethics and responsibilities to avoid exploiting American Indians.

Repatriation, the selling of Indian burial remains and imitations of Indian artifacts, and the publication of sensitive Indian knowledge have resulted in a series of controversies forcing Indians to act against whites, and in some cases against Indians where Indians have desecrated tribal properties. The exploitation of American Indians has never stopped. It began with Indian enslavement when a lost Christopher Columbus landed in the Western Hemisphere. Indians have been victimized through centuries of land fraud and disease, the manipulation of warriors as mercenaries, the abuse of Indian women, and the capture of Indian children to meet enrollment quotas in boarding schools.

This essay acknowledges certain moral ethics and professional responsibilities in this field—American Indian history. First this essay will identify those ethics and responsibilities and then provide arguments to convince historians and others of the importance of upholding such ethics and fulfilling responsibilities pertaining to the proper study and writing of American Indian history.

First of all, the field must be carefully defined so the academy, as well as students and writers, understand what is meant by American Indian history. At this date, only parameters can be argued. Is American Indian history also called Native American history and is this acceptable? Is Indian History the history of Indian people and their nations relating only to other Indian nations? To non-Indian nations like France, Spain, Russia, England, or the Netherlands? Or only the United States? Is American Indian history the history of a tribe within itself without reference to outsiders? Or is American Indian history all of these histories *in toto*? Defining the field could be another article as an increasing number of individuals from various fields and backgrounds write about American Indian history.

As a discipline, history is more subjective than some other disciplines in its interpretation and analysis of research. Because of this precarious situation, historians need carefully to consider the moral ethics and professional responsibilities inherent in teaching and writing about Native American history. On the other side of this issue, some American Indians feel that the writing of American Indian history, mostly by non-Indians, is merely another example of the exploitative and unfair treatment of Indian people.

An interesting irony has occurred in the historiography of the American experience. For at least a century, scholars, writers, and historians have neglected Native Americans in writing the history of America. Different schools of thought like the Germ Theory and Turner thesis have encouraged historians to ignore the original inhabitants of the entire Western Hemisphere.[2] Why did this happen, if a scholar's professional responsibility is to be objective in researching historical topics? These approaches described the "white experience," as if Indians did not exist. To write a history of the Anglo-American experience is not wrong, but to claim that it represents the entire history of the American experience is a gross mistake.[3]

Historians, in particular, wrote Indians out of their textbooks for whatever insecure reasons of justifying the past actions of America's heroes, racial bigotry, or white guilt. By ignoring the dark episodes of the destruction of Indians and their cultures, historians in effect denied that these ever happened. Nonetheless, non-Indians have had to face the issue that American Indians, indeed, existed in the Americas well before the accidental arrival of Columbus, and that Native Americans are a vital part of the history of this country. Hence, the writing of American Indian history emerged as a body of literature in the early decades of the twentieth century, although historians continued to vilify Indians as "savages" and "devilish heathens" that a glorified United States had to destroy, exalting a false white supremacy over all minority races in this country.

Whether racially prejudiced or guilt-ridden, patronizing, paternalistic, or romantic, Indian history mainly has been perceived from a white perspective, based on the idea that "the conquerors write the history." More than 30,000 manuscripts have been published about American Indians, and more than 90 percent of that literature has been written by non-Indians.[4] To illustrate this point further, a similar percentage of these non-Indian historians have written about writing or studying American Indian history.[5]

The point here is that non-Indian scholars have sought to define the parameters of the field American Indian history. They have attempted to determine its forms of evidence only as written accounts, professed limited theories, and devised methodologies from a non-Indian tradition.[6] European explorers and military officers recorded accounts of their contacts with American Indians. During the British colonization in the seventeenth and eighteenth centuries, newspapers used negative reports about Indians to sell newspapers. Eager novelists picked up their poisoned pens to embellish on any Indian resistance to intrigue readers with horrific atrocities. In the 1800s, ethnographers recorded notes, wrote articles, and drafted manuscripts describing Indians and their cultures. More ethnographers and anthropologists followed in the late 1800s in desperate efforts to study Native American cultures. These were believed to be disappearing with the buffalo, as the Indian population in the United States declined to 243,000. Careless historians followed ethnographers and anthropologists as a part of the academic community that wrote imbalanced articles and books about American Indians.

Even in the twentieth century, historians have written about the American Indian with very little understanding about "him" (since this was assumed to be a man's history) and the depth of his distinct culture.[7] The ill-trained historian approached Indian history with his or her graduate training for writing mainstream history. Historians borrowed much of their approach from western buffs mostly interested in Indian wars. Next, a small group of scholars emerged to write classical tribal histories. The initial studies were published in the 1930s and 1940s by the University of Oklahoma Press. These works led the way for other presses to produce American Indian books.[8]

The growing scholarly interest in Indians led to a series of conferences in the early 1950s, including the Ohio Valley Historic Indian Conference on November 21, 1953.[9] A number of scholars participated, especially anthropologists involved in Indian claims cases, and this regional conference was expanded into the annual American Indian Ethnohistoric Conference, currently known as the American Society for Ethnohistory. Since then, scholars have struggled to understand the complexity of American Indian history.

In the early 1970s, historians worked to revise the discipline when they recognized that inadequate means were being used to examine Indian history.[10] Historians followed the example of anthropologists using ethnography to study American Indian history.[11] The breakthrough was the distinction of "culture" and the study of it as a part of history.[12] Historians who study Indian history must think in terms of culture, community, environment, and metaphysics.[13]

Ethnohistory has allowed a cross-disciplinary approach using history and anthropology to study American Indian history. Since then, Native American history has been written by geographers, sociologists, and literary writers using a combination of their academic expertise and the tools of historians. The value of the ethnohistorical approach is that it examines society and culture within time periods that also allow it to address historical events. As one ethnohistorian stated, the advantage is that ethnohistory can go beyond the limitations of one discipline by combining two fields.[14] On a cautionary note, another scholar warned that ethnohistory written about American Indians is largely from a Western perspective, while continuing to suppress the American Indian point of view.[15]

A revived interest in Indians was aided by Indians themselves during the rise of the Red Power movement during the late 1960s, when frustrated urban Indians organized protest marches for better treatment of Indian people. Indian activism and Indian militancy such as the occupations of Alcatraz (1969), the Bureau of Indian Affairs (1972), and Wounded Knee (1973) renewed public interest in American Indians. This renaissance resulted in the writing of a deluge of Indian literature and history.[16]

American Indian history is often thought of as a history of Indian-white relations. The fact that the Native peoples of the Western Hemisphere already possessed histories of thousands of years time depth before the arrival of Columbus has had little effect on non-Indians who perceive that only written records comprise history.

Records of relations between the United States and Indian tribes have been numerous and lengthy. The noted Record Group 75 of the National Archives includes more than 11,000 cubic feet of documents collected since 1824, when the Office of Indian Affairs opened. More than 19,000 cubic feet of financial documents from the years 1790–1921 are found under Record Group 217. There are 610 docket cases of the Indian Claims Commission in Record Group 279.[17]

A dependence on documents eliminates other evidence and precludes other methods and disciplines from interpreting Indian history. This singular, focused approach has produced an interpretation that hinges on the white point of view.[18] It is not a balanced history of American Indians, since it yields but one version of a history of two peoples interacting. Rather, it is an Americentric interpretation of Indian history, a point of view that is shared by the majority of American historians writing about the United States, Europe, diplomatic, and general history.

As historians employ the methodologies of other academic disciplines, other forms of evidence and data have emerged. For example, cultural items found underground like pieces of pottery or hunting weapons need to be considered by historians writing about tribal camp life as social history. Ceremonial items would compel historians to consider the religious views and tribal philosophies extrapolated from them.

A discussion of what is meant by American Indian history is important in determining the parameters for this essay. American Indian history is not just one history of all Indian people. Actually it is a field of many tribal histories, complicated by their relations with the United States. At this date, 547 tribes in the United States and Native Alaska communities have been federally recognized. The significance here is the importance of "relations" in Indian history. In many cases, tribes that had foreign relations with European nations before the American Revolution added another level of historical relations with the United States government after. In this light, this series of relations also should include relations between tribes. Considering Indian history from this approach is primarily one of external relations, and studying the history of relations is like studying diplomatic history or foreign policy. It is from this general view of Indian history that studying the relations from a non-Indian, Americentric point of view places American Indians in a marginal history.[19] This kind of myopic history is a violation of professional ethics when scholars are supposed to examine all the evidence and postulate objective analyses. To ignore such narrow interpretations is to further break ethics by choosing not to attempt to balance the historical perspectives.

American Indian history has been viewed as a minority history of less importance by frontier and Turnerian historians who view Indians as a part of the frontier, diplomatic historians who claim that Indians are an internal subject, and domestic historians who hide Indians in footnotes and call them "pawns" in the making of American History.[20] Such Americentric blindness and academic arrogance ignores Indians, and mainstream historians have elected to exile American Indians to "disciplinary banishment."[21] The repercussions are devastating. Each new generation of students learns a misconstrued history of the Americas. Unless critical revisionist textbooks include a more accurate accounting of the role of American Indians in the history of the Americas, Indians could one day be written out of history. In many colleges and universities, Indian history is not taught, but it is even worse when an uninformed, insensitive scholar attempts to teach Indian history. Fortunately, an estimated 250 scholars teach Indian history as a course or as a part of their course on the American West.[22] So, then, the root of bias in mainstream history must rest in the mainstream culture and its conscious and subconscious attitudes toward other peoples' histories. It is ethically wrong to use research to subvert the fair historical representation of other peoples, leaders, and non-mainstream events.

The most important ethical concern is for American Indian history to be included in the scope of the American experience, so that historians would encounter it as a part of their training in graduate school. Indian history should not be regarded as a special or exotic subfield to be pushed aside and ignored. In actuality Indian history has set the foundation of American history. For example, early white settlers adjusted to the environment in ways that Indians had done for centuries. Although the results differed, the environment has had a major influence on all peoples in America. To ignore the historical variable of environment is to view history only from a human perspective, disallowing a broader research focus that includes all factors influencing the facts as they fit together. Unfortunately American mainstream history has placed "man" above "woman" and, indeed, above all other aspects of society, culture, environment, climate, and metaphysical forces.

In brief, ethics in writing Indian history require respect for Native Americans including, preferably, visiting Indian people in their homelands. Interpreting research data and writing to take into account the Indian viewpoint is a most important ethic. After all, Native American history should focus on how and why Indians participated in the American experience. Writing Indian history respectfully also requires avoiding negative terminology such as "savage," "red skin," "Indian plight" and other pejorative names or inappropriate prose that demeans Indian people. Writing proper Indian history would include avoiding suppressing Indians, or writing from an Americentric view. Finally, ethics would include researching and examining all kinds of evidence, including non-written data.

One significant responsibility of all scholarship is to pursue the unknown, especially as it relates to the known. Specifically, mainstream American history presents "one" perspective, which is the known. However, the known history of this particular mainstream perspective fails to challenge itself to experience the unknown or little-known history of American Indians. This narrow vision of history fails to account for the full American experience. Such mainstream myopia fails to understand the other side of historical issues, other historical figures, and Native peoples and their cultures. It is unethical for scholars to claim they are experts on American history; rather, they are specialists.

American Indian communities possess internal histories of relations defined according to their separate cultures. Tribal communities are built on an infrastructure of interrelated societies and roles, such as clans, leaders, warriors, medicine persons, and others. An important part of this network is the community's relationships with the flora, fauna, and metaphysical spirituality. This network is based on sociocultural understanding of a religious nature. Such an understanding of the internal history of what has happened within the community remains foreign to the Americentric historian. This dimension of Indian history cannot be seriously studied until new tools of historical interpretation and new theories can be developed.

The situation requires a basic understanding of the internal and external histories of Native communities. This process is similar to that of using an understanding of United States domestic history and foreign relations to properly study and teach American History. Understanding both the internalness and externalness of tribal communities—even if the assignment is to study or teach the relations of that tribe at war with the United States—is critically important in presenting a balanced history. Unfortunately, this balanced history has been lacking in the practice of American Indian history.

Historians now have an opportunity to study and learn about the internal nature of Indian communities at the tribal or urban levels. This means using ethnohistory or anthropology to comprehend the cultural development of the community. In considering Indian history in this manner, it is necessary to use introspective analysis of how Indians perceive history with regard to tribal language, values, kinship relations, infrastructure, societal norms, tribal beliefs, and worldview. To further this consideration, historians must be willing to acknowledge other means of analyzing history and other sources of facts. For instance, historians will need to turn to other forms of history such as interviews and oral history.

For many years the debate against oral history has gone on despite Studs Terkel winning the Pulitzer Prize for *"The Good War": An Oral History of World War Two* in 1984.[23] Historians must be ready to accept other kinds of history and must approach other disciplines to understand Indian history. Social and cultural history are germane as is the use of historical archaeology to restructure Indian history and understand the internalness of tribal communities. The problem for those who write about American Indians is that written sources have been produced almost exclusively by non-Indians. The alternative is to use oral history and interviews to acquire knowledge about such internal matters as kinship patterns and political organizations.[24]

The need for ethics and responsibilities in teaching and writing American Indian history increases as more individuals pursue the subject. The significance of this dilemma is accelerated as concern about the global environment causes people to turn to tribal philosophies of environmental caretaking. This movement is evidenced in the misguided New Age movement and recent videos, documentaries, and films about American Indians [e.g., *Squanto* (1994), *Last of the Mohicans* (1993), *Lakota Woman* (1994), *Hawkeye* (1994), *The Broken Chain* (1994), and *Dances with Wolves* (1992)]. Non-Indians are increasingly listening to Indian people as a growing number of Indian communities demand input on these projects. Obtaining a tribal viewpoint, a Native feeling, and the other side of history, and then thinking like an Indian and putting yourself in that other position, is mandatory for teaching and writing a balanced history of Indian-white relations.

In summary, the moral ethics of properly working in American Indian history include deliberate removal of ethnocentrism. Improper attitudes have caused scholars to write negative histories about American Indians or to write arrogant histories in which non-Indians see themselves as superior to Indians for whatever insecure reasons. Proper attitude is ethically to subvert racist analysis and subconscious thought about Indians. Respect toward Indian people and their heritage is ethically important. The next ethical step is consideration of Indian viewpoints, while striving to think as an Indian. Disputing the imbalanced scholarship of the past about American Indians becomes a crucial part of the role of the ethical scholar. Moreover, scholars must respect sensitive knowledge about tribal ways and not publish information about certain cultural rituals. The ethic of open-mindedness in considering the value of disciplines other than one's own and being open to other forms of historical data is imperative to piece together a truer picture of the Indian past.

Responsibilities for American Indian history include fair treatment in the portrayal of Indians as well as other minorities within the mainstream society, and balanced treatment in the characterization of Indian males and females. Culture is an important concept in correctly addressing Native American history, as well as analyzing environmental impacts on Indian life. The scholar needs to stretch his or her imagination to ponder the depth of tribal ways and values as these influenced human behavior and history. The scholar must consider the world-view of an Indian group to comprehend its members' sense of logic and ideology. In order to accomplish this task, thinking about the "whole" of Indian life is imperative. After this step, it is essential to define the conception of reality constructed by the Indian community. Mainstream conceptions of reality such as those commonly constructed in the contemporary world cannot be used to study the past. The historian has the responsibility to understand the reality a tribe constructed to constitute its historical experiences of the physical and metaphysical as a whole.

Historians who teach and write American Indian history must examine the whole picture in studying Native American societies and cultures. Such a responsibility also involves examining Indian history from the diverse perspectives of white American views including different bureaucratic positions, missionary beliefs, and humanitarian concerns, as well as from the perspectives of the many tribes. All of these views naturally depend on the subject of study, and it bears repeating that a single Indian voice is impractical. Just as one cannot say that there is one European view, neither can one say that there is only one Indian view of history.

The historian's last responsibility in achieving a true balance is to "think like an Indian." While this may seem impractical, studying tribal cultures enables a scholar to understand individual and group behavior within the tribal community. Thinking of a synthetic physical and metaphysical reality allows the scholar to understand Indians as pro-active instead of reactive in respect to historical events. In gaining such a Native perspective it is necessary to use ethnohistorical methodologies to reconstruct history according to how tribal members remember it.[25]

This extraordinary diversity of perspectives illuminates the sociocultural and political complexity of American Indian history from an external point of view. Combining the external perspective with an understanding of an inner perspective balances the equation, resulting in a proper study of American Indian history. Placing both perspectives within the full context of Indian life in relationship to the natural world is the ultimate goal in analyzing and writing American Indian history.[26]

Notes

1 Almost forty years ago, an insightful Wilcomb Washburn called for a fairer treatment of Native Americans in examining the history of Indian-white relations. In his argument for a moral history of Indian-white relations, he stated, "a moral history of the contact of two cultures calls for wisdom and understanding not normally required of historians and ethnologists." See Wilcomb E. Washburn, "A Moral History of Indian-White Relations: Needs and Opportunities for Study," *Ethnohistory* 4:1 (Winter 1957) 47.

2 The Germ theory suggests that America was settled by Europeans who migrated from east to west, and that the American experience (disregarding American Indians) borrowed its foundation from European ideologies of settling the land and expanded westward. Frederick Jackson Turner introduced his famous thesis at the newly born American Historical Association conference in Chicago in 1893, but in his explanation of the American frontier and development of an American identity, he mentions American Indians only two or three times, and the impact of this view led to two generations of Turnerian historians whose intellectual descendants even today know very little about American Indians and their history. Frederick Jackson Turner's essay "The Significance of the Frontier in American History" is found in his book *The Frontier in American History* (New York: Holt and Company, 1920).

   Colonial Historian Gary Nash wrote almost twenty years ago that in the "consensus school of [mainstream American] historiography . . . [it] was virtually obligatory to ignore Indian history over the last four centuries and to develop historical amnesia about their long history of [Indian-white] relations with the European invaders." In the same article describing a revision of United States history after the 1960s, Nash quotes Indian scholar Vine Deloria Jr., "this 'new' history still plugs a few feathers, wooly heads, and sombreros into the famous events of American history." See Gary Nash, "Review Essay, Whither Indian History?" *Journal of Ethnic Studies* 4:3 (Fall 1976): 69 and 71.

3 Jack Forbes made this point in 1963, and mainstream historians have continued to write in the same "conqueror-consciousness," even beyond 1992 (five hundred years after Columbus's arrival), still purporting an Anglo-American interpretation of this country. Furthermore, Forbes argued that European influence has affected much of the Anglo-American genre of historical writing,

so that colonial American history is perceived as an extension of British history. See Jack Forbes, "The Historian and the Indian: Racial Bias in American History," *The Americas* 19:4 (April 1963): 349 and 350.

4   As of 1991, 127 tribes lack a written history. The ten leading tribes with books written about them are: Eskimo 3,217; Navajo 1,822; Dakota 1,009; Pueblo (including all 19 Pueblo groups) 851; Cherokee (both Oklahoma and North Carolina Cherokees) 808; Chippewa 742; Iroquois 808; Hopi 538; Apache 534; and Seminole 304. See Duane K. Hale, *Researching and Writing Tribal Histories* (Grand Rapids: Michigan Indian Press Grand Rapids Inter-Tribal Council, 1991), 2.

5   The two massive combined reference works of Indian-white literature compiled by Francis Paul Prucha are *A Bibliographical Guide to the History of Indian-White Relations* (Chicago: University of Chicago Press, 1977), 376–379, and *Indian-White Relations in the United States: A Bibliography of Works Published 1975–1980* (Lincoln: University of Nebraska Press, 1982), 140–141.

6   To be fair, an apology is due to a group of sensitive scholars, such as Raymond Fogelson, William T. Hagan, Wilbur Jacobs, Wilcomb Washburn, and certain others, who have clamored for a recognized scholarly Indian view of American Indian history since the 1970s.

7   Sixteen years ago, historian Calvin Martin wrote that historians who wrote about the American Indian had "only the barest understanding" of them. Martin recommended that scholars consider four areas of ethnology—political, ecological, economic, and psychological anthropology—in analyzing Indian history. Furthermore, Martin recommended that, in writing about Indian character and personality, scholars should re-evaluate the "credibility of their sources according to the principle and insights of psychological anthropology." See Calvin Martin, "Ethnohistory: A Better Way to Write Indian History," *Western History Quarterly* 9:1 (January 1978): 41. By the 1980s, the problems in writing and understanding American Indian history were still unresolved, as pointed out in Calvin Martin, ed., *The American Indian and the Problem of History* (New York: Oxford University Press, 1987).

8   The University of Oklahoma Press set a precedent with its Civilization of the American Indian series and by publishing books during this period such as Grant Foreman's works on the Five Civilized Tribes, Angie Debo's *The Rise and Fall of the Choctaw Republic* (1934) and *The Road to Disappearance* (1941), and other tribal histories continuing into the 1950s with works like William T. Hagan's *The Sac and Fox Indians* (1956) and John C. Ewers' *The Blackfeet: Raiders on the Northwestern Plains* (1958). At this date, more than a hundred titles are listed in the Civilization of the American Indian series.

9   A brief history of the development of Indian ethnohistory as a field is explained by Francis Jennings, "A Growing Partnership: Historians, Anthropologists, and American Indian history," *The History Teacher,* 14:1 (November 1980): 88–90.

10 In 1973 historian Wilbur Jacobs wrote that "a wider basis of truth" was needed for "a better understanding of what has happened in the past." He called as well for an understanding of the "Indian point of view," and that a balance was needed to offset the "widely accepted interpretations . . . in our textbooks and in many learned journals." Furthermore, Jacobs refuted the application of the Turnerian school of historical interpretation that excluded American Indians and other minorities. See Wilbur R. Jacobs, "The Indian and the Frontier in American History—a Need for Revision," *Western Historical Quarterly* 4:1 (January 1973): 43. In another article, Jacobs observed that historians such as Ray Billington in *Westward Expansion: A History of the American Frontier* 4th ed., (New York: 1974) and Wilcomb E. Washburn in *The Indian in America* (New York: 1975) argued that revisionary scholarship in the mid-1970s inspired a pivotal turn in examining the role of Indians in American history. Jacobs called this "a fresh analysis of white frontier history by looking at the past from the perspective of native Americans" [and] "a neglected part of the American past." See Wilbur R. Jacobs, "Native American History: How It Illuminates Our Past," *American Historical Review* 80:3 (June 1975): 596.

11 A primary book instrumental in establishing the ethnohistory of American Indians is Francis Jennings, *The Invasion of America: Indians, Colonialism, and the Cant of Conquest* (Chapel Hill: University of North Carolina Press, 1975). Francis Paul Prucha noted that between 1970 and 1975, a deluge of books about the political history of Indian relations and federal Indian policy appeared as more major studies were written than in any previous period in American Indian historiography. See Francis Paul Prucha, "Books on American Indian Policy: A Half-Decade of Important Work, 1970–1975," *Journal of American History* 63:3 (December 1976): 658–669.

12 Francis Jennings has carefully explained that Edward Burnett Tylor was able to separate "culture" from "race" in his scholarly arguments in a *Britannica* article. Jennings goes on to state that "Culture . . . is the product of human intelligence and activity, susceptible to modification by individual invention, group innovation, or imitation, changing within individual lifetimes and from generation to generation." However, Indian history is a complexity of several subjects and human history and human culture are only portions of it. Jennings make a most valid point in arguing that "For historians who think in terms of culture, the contact between two societies with different cultures

becomes something different from a war of conquest or annihilation." See Jennings, "A Growing Partnership," 96–97.

13 One would naturally assume that economics would also need to be studied in understanding Indian history, but the subject of environment and its impact would cover this area while metaphysics would cover religion in understanding the full scope of American Indian reality.

14 Raymond J. DeMaillie, "Sioux Ethnohistory: A Methodological Critique," *Journal of Ethnic Studies* 4:3 (1976): 82–83.

15 Anthropologist Raymond Fogelson termed "ethno-ethnohistory" as making possible an Indian viewpoint written as "a kind of anthropological ethnohistory in which a central role would be given to intensive fieldwork, control of the native language, use of a native time perspective, and work with native documents." See Raymond D. Fogelson, "On the Varieties of Indian History: Sequoyah and Traveller Bird," *Journal of Ethnic Studies* 2:1 (Spring 1974): 106.

16 Russell M. Magnaghi, "Herbert E. Bolton and Sources for American Indian Studies," *Western Historical Quarterly* 6:1 (January 1975): 33. Three helpful historiographic studies of American Indian history are R. David Edmunds, "The Indian in the Mainstream: Indian Historiography for Teachers of American History Surveys," *The History Teacher* 8:2 (February 1975); R. David Edmunds, "Coming of Age: Some Thoughts upon American Indian History," *Indiana Magazine of History* 85:4 (December 1989): 312–321; and Terry P. Wilson, *Teaching American Indian History* (Washington: American Historical Association, 1993).

17 Record Group 75 contains the records of the Office of Indian Trade, 1795–1822, correspondence of the Office of the Secretary of War relating to Indian affairs, 1800–1824, and records of Indian peace and treaty commissions. Record Group 217 contains a wide range of financial records of disbursing officers and claimants regarding tribes, schools, hospitals, and missions. Record Group 279 contains written materials of the Indian Claims Commission consisting of briefs, pleas, hearings, findings, testimonies, and related documents. See Carmelita S. Ryan, "The Written Record and the American Indian: The Archives of the United States," *Western Historical Quarterly* 6:2 (April 1975): 165, 171–172.

18 Donald L. Fixico, "Encounter of Two Different Worlds: The Columbus-Indian Legacy of History," *American Indian Culture and Research Journal* 17:3 (1993): 17–32.

19 Arthur Gilbert, "The American Indian and United States Diplomatic History," *The History Teacher* 8:2 (February 1975): 229.

20 In his famous thesis, Frederick Jackson Turner all but ignored Indians by

casually mentioning them only in a few instances. See Turner's essay, "The Significance of the Frontier in American History."

21 Gilbert, "American Indian and U.S. Diplomatic History," 231.

22 A helpful survey of the progress of American Indian history since its explosion in the early 1970s was conducted by Donald L. Parman and Catherine Price. They concluded that "By any standard—methodology, number of new doctorates, publication of books and articles, and sessions at leading professional conferences—Indian history has established a new legitimacy and respect within the historical profession during the past two decades." See Donald L. Parman and Catherine Price, "A 'Work in Progress': The Emergence of Indian History as a Professional Field," *Western Historical Quarterly* 20:2 (May 1989): 189–193 and 195.

23 Studs Terkel, *"The Good War": An Oral History of World War Two* (New York: Pantheon, 1984).

24 Historian William T. Hagan wrote that in reconstructing American Indian history, the historian has to depend on written sources produced by "white soldiers, traders, missionaries, and government officials," and that oral history is "frequently disappointing, . . . and is more useful as an index of how Indians currently view their past than as a source of hard information." See William T. Hagan, "On Writing the History of the American Indian," *Journal of Interdisciplinary History* 2 (1971–72): 149.

25 In working with memory and the memories of a community, David Thelen observed that collecting history was a cultural act involving constructing history, rather than reproducing it. See David Thelen, ed., *Memory and American History* (Bloomington: Indiana University Press, 1990), ix.

26 Environmental historian Richard White argues that in the initial contact between Europeans and Indians, the former displaced themselves from nature, but failed to distinguish between the "natural man" Indian and the "natural" world of the Americas. The Eurocentric view of placing European society above the natural world due to its developments in technology and scientific study has obstructed mainstream historians from visualizing the full context of Indian history in relation to nature. See Richard White, "Discovering Nature in North America," *Journal of American History* 79:3–4 (December 1992): 882.

Licensed Trafficking and Ethnogenetic Engineering

SUSAN A. MILLER

As a student of history, I follow what historians write about the American tribal peoples, and as a tribal member, I often object. When the topic is the tribes, historians are apt to apply a separate standard, licensing themselves to suspend the rules that govern scholarly procedure.[1] Then they "imagine" the tribes for their own amusement and because they can sell the product. They evaluate each other's images, reward their favorites, and pitch those to readers of history.

In selecting certain books for prizes, committees of historians award the images put forth in those books. Those images then become the likeliest candidates for inclusion in textbooks and transmission into the American historical consciousness. A pair of recent prizewinners illustrate the historians' license to imagine Native America.

The Middle Ground: Indians, Empires, and Republics in the Great Lakes Region, 1650–1815 by Richard White is an excellent work according to historians' standards.[2] In recounting the crisis over control of the Ohio Valley, for example, White takes an innovative down-river vantage and evades the readers' assumption that the events were inevitable. One hardly expects the decisive battle at Fallen Timbers until it is over.[3] The book is full of such gems.

The problem with *The Middle Ground* stems from the author's distance from the people whose histories he examines. White is writing about the histories of Winnebagos, Wyandots, Seneca-Cayugas, Shawnees, Delawares, and other tribes whose members are present today on our social landscape. To someone acquainted with those tribes, his brilliant paragraphs are disappointing. He is not recovering a segment of their past but toying with a story severed safely from their present. He simply ignores the people whose history he is examining.[4] That approach to the writing of history resembles the familiar pattern of extraction of Native resources such as timber and minerals by outside interests that give back nothing to the Native community and move on when the easy profits play out. Committees of the Society of American Historians and the Organization of American Historians awarded prizes to *The Middle Ground,* tacitly endorsing its method.[5]

Ignoring a people's living generations accords with the historians' superstition that the distant past can be seen more objectively than recent times. This superstition rationalizes an important taboo against examining the recent past. Thus, historians ignore the persistence among white Americans of cultural traits advantageous to them at the expense of the tribes. The dishonoring of treaties reflects such traits, and the Lakotas and the Newes can attest that Americans still do that. Still, a writer in *The New Yorker* can refer to the heyday of the Wild West shows as "the decades following the sack of Indian culture" as though, for example, the Lakotas' Black Hills and the Newes' (or Western Shoshones') lands known as Newe Segobia (or much of present Nevada) were not contested today, and as though vigorous examples of "Indian culture" did not depend on the integrity of those lands.[6] The taboo enjoins historians from pointing out that the sacking continues.[7]

So Richard White's "new Indian history" beheads the tribes in his story by disregarding their living generations.[8] Such mutilation can hardly be termed Indian history. The tribes keep their own histories, which often begin and end with the living. White's is a retelling of his own people's account of their long-ago dealings with the tribal nations. That story needed updating for this generation, and White has retooled it in accord with the American hegemonic myth, which leans heavily on the fiction that the consequences of American aggressions are safely in the past.

White trivializes the tribes with his decision to misclassify a disparate assortment of tribal groups under the single and inaccurate label "the Algonquians."[9] If one can accept the grouping of the tribal peoples by nontribal scholars into large categories according to esoterically perceived relations among their languages—and some tribal thinkers cannot—one may reasonably prefer that the writer keep to his own categories. Scholars classify as Algonquians the tribes whose languages are related to that of a people once labeled "the Algonkins."[10] Shawnees, Delawares, Kickapoos, and Anishinabes (Chippewas) speak languages like that. Wyandots (Huron-Petuns), Seneca-Cayugas (Mingos), and Winnebagos do not, but White calls them Algonquians anyway. Wyandot and Seneca-Cayuga languages are related to the "Iroquoian" languages of the six Haudenosaunee nations, the Cherokees, and others. The Winnebago language is "Siouan," related to languages of the Iowas, the Otoe-Missourias, and others.

Throughout Native America, related languages contribute to the complex network of families and tribes that has integrated this hemisphere since long before Europeans arrived. Each tribal person has a place in that network. Native scholars should be wary of relinquishing the network in its full complexity as a model for history.[11] Although White acknowledges the network and gives it some attention, he abandons it when he applies the label *the Algonquians*. He opts instead for the "definition of Native Americans . . . as a separate and single other" that Robert F. Berkhofer Jr. describes in *The White Man's Indian,* a book about white people and images that they have conceived.[12]

This is no quibble. White's reductionism occurs under a license that has real-world repercussions. Where a Winnebago may be taken for an Algonquian, a red pickup may be taken for a red-and-white van as in the case against Leonard Peltier.[13] License to trivialize significant distinctions is a consequential matter. Who decides what is significant, and who benefits?

"The Winnebagos were Siouan," White admits, ignoring an opportunity to acknowledge that they still are.[14] What must Winnebago historian David Smith and his tribespeople think about being conjugated out of the Siouan language family? Although historians resist the temptation to speak of a living colleague as though he or she were dead, casting an entire nation into past tense meets the profession's standard. Thus historiography nurtures Americans' default impulse to vanish the Indian.

Another unwelcome survivor in the historiographic medium is the long list of epithets that Americans apply to Native groups. When White writes about Hurons and Mingos, he is preserving ethnic slurs against ancestors of living peoples. *Huron* appears to have originated among French persons as an aspersion on the hair style of Wendat or Wyandot[te] ancestors.[15] The Mingos of White's narrative survive today as the Seneca-Cayuga Tribe. *Mingo* is identified as an Algonquian word meaning "stealthy, treacherous."[16] Wyandot and Seneca-Cayuga are perfectly good names, and to ignore them in favor of outsiders' labels is a violation of simple etiquette that historians would not allow in other contexts. Imagine introducing two colleagues at a reception: "Lydia, have you met Charles?" If Lydia should respond, "How do you do, Chickenlips?" there would be consequences. Who licensed historians to insult entire nations in the same manner?

It may be argued that the epithets *Huron* and *Mingo* are venerable old insults that have entered standard English, that the groups so labeled were not identical to their descendants of today, and that redressing the epithets would clutter the writer's prose. Nevertheless, the historian who ignores a people while insulting their ancestors expropriates their history. This is one of those messy value conflicts.

White's disregard for the tribes whose histories he extracts is well within historiographic tradition. His image of long-gone, alien, and ultimately trivial peoples rationalizes his own people's present relations with them. By ignoring the living communities that derive from those histories, White appears to regard their members as irrelevant to the discussion of their own pasts as the standard that the historians' profession upholds. How high is that standard?

In *When Jesus Came, the Corn Mothers Went Away: Marriage, Sexuality and Power in New Mexico, 1500–1846,* Ramón A. Gutiérrez violates a list of fundamental procedures of the historians' methods.[17] He neglects to cite the sources of some of his provocative statements of "fact," for example, and he misrepresents material from sources that he cites.[18] In writing about Native peoples of New Mexico, Gutiérrez exercises the historians' license to trivialize significant distinctions: He generalizes the varied ethnographies of the disparate Pueblos into a single composite description, and he cites irrelevant descriptions of non-Puebloan peoples in support of a point about "Puebloan" behavior.[19] Again, one recalls Berkhofer's dictum. Although Gutiérrez fails various scholarly standards, he does uphold the historians' cherished superstition that the act of writing launders inaccuracy from an account. His reliance on Spanish colonial sources—mostly Franciscans—to inform his description of sixteenth-century "Puebloan" culture yields a grotesque, unsubstantiable, and highly marketable image of the Pueblos as a set of aboriginal Gomorrahs peopled by naked, screwing women and men who thought of themselves as "two-legged deer."[20] When challenged by historians—both traditional and scholarly—from the Pueblos, Gutiérrez insists that he arrived at that description by following the historical method. He dismisses the opportunity to balance Franciscans' distortions with traditional histories from the Pueblos on the ground that unwritten accounts are outside the historian's purview.[21] Ted Jojola of Isleta Pueblo replies that because the traditional histories kept at the Pueblos are sacred, their accuracy is guarded diligently enough to make them suitable source matter for scholars.[22] Satirizing Gutiérrez's method, Roxanne Dunbar Ortiz bases an examination of the Catholic past on such observers of Catholicism as Moors, Sephardic Jews, Luther, Calvin, Planned Parenthood, and the Ku Klux Klan, while ignoring Catholic sources on a flimsy pretext.[23]

Despite his mauling of Native history, Gutiérrez's colleagues leapt to reward his book. In the *New York Times Book Review,* Patricia Nelson Limerick declared it "as thoroughly researched as academic history gets."[24] It received at least ten prizes, including one from the Pacific Coast Branch of the American Historical Association and two from the Organization of American Historians. Only later did careful reviews begin to appear, notably by historians Roxanne Dunbar Ortiz, Ralph Vigil, and John Kessell, each of whom had examined Gutiérrez's sources and found the inadequacies in his use of them.[25] But the book was already a success. By citing (however inaccurately) written sources (however ignorant), Gutiérrez had performed an essential rite of the historical method, and his colleagues were satisfied.

Most historians seem to condone Gutiérrez's bizarre imagining of Pueblo peoples, and more than one has remarked privately that those who object to his distortions should stop complaining and write their own versions. Historians do not deserve that luxury, however, of dismissing such historiographic distortion as a harmless postmodern exercise. Distorted images have served repeatedly to justify invasions of communities and murders of families, as, infamously, the misconception of the Ghost Dance provided the rationale for the atrocity against families at Wounded Knee Creek in 1890. Similarly, this generation has seen atrocities at Pine Ridge, presumably at Duck Valley, and elsewhere rationalized by distorted images of Oglala people and the American Indian Movement. Rather than reward distortions, the community of scholars is supposed to provide a corrective context for an individual scholar's excesses. In the case of *When Jesus Came,* the historians bailed out.

If the prizewinning works by Richard White and Ramón Gutiérrez are exemplars of American historiography, then the American historian's Indian conforms to Berkhofer's observation: "the essence of the White image of the Indian has been the definition of Native Americans in fact and fancy as a separate and single other."[26] Historians see the tribal peoples as separate enough to fall outside the profession's usual standards and trivial enough to be lumped into broad nonsensical categories. Under the historians' license, moreover, esteemed scholars fashion images of the tribal peoples from inferior matter, because historians' sources are from outside the tribes (that is, secondary) by definition, and matter deriving from tribal (that is, primary) sources is considered categorically dismissable. Historians reverse the precedence of sources in the discussion of Indians, reviewers look the other way, prize committees reward the most lurid images, the increasingly commercialized scholarly publishing industry calls for more of that toy-Indian product, and by some process of ethno-genetic engineering, monsters like Gutiérrez's Puebloan Woman Doll come onto the market. White's Algonquian is better documented but no less disturbing: That product line leads off with a brown child with a stake through its head.[27]

White's staked child is a documentary image whose use falls well within the standard of historiography. Its murderers are bloodthirsty Native cannibals: Senecas brutalizing Miami children. The prominence of that imagery in the opening pages of a prizewinning work of American historiography challenges the reader to seek other images among the prizewinners to balance the lurid appeal of that one.

Tribal people have never been able to stop the traffic in distorted and sensationalized imagery, but the institutional framework of scholarship might be used to discourage that traffic on the supply side while promoting the development of healthier products. One promising approach frames an article by historian James H. Merrell, who surveyed the literature in colonial United States history published from 1968 through 1988 to determine whether recent findings in ethnohistory were having any influence.[28] He found that his colleagues, with few exceptions, were still repeating debunked myths about colonial America. He epitomized his finding with a biting composite statement in the words of recent writers, who saw the tribes as "part of the landscape" or "savage foes" and were still insisting that Europeans in America had settled a "trackless wilderness."[29] An editor of a Native studies journal would be in a good position to coordinate a periodic review along the lines of Merrell's.

The Cherokee Nation took an effective approach in September 1993 by sponsoring a conference on their own history at Park Hill, Cherokee Nation, Oklahoma. Participants included many of the major scholars who write about Cherokee history. The success of that conference suggests it as a model for Native groups seeking to participate in the discussion of their past.

Finally, historians from the tribes might meet the prize committees head-on by honoring responsible works selected according to responsible standards. A suitable institutional home for such an honor might be found within the tribal college system. The honored writers might be rewarded with something of value other than money, bestowed on an occasion other than a banquet. An annual prize for Indian history, a periodic review, and participation by the nations in the scholarly discourse might provide gates that historians' images of the tribes must pass on the road to the textbooks and into the mind of America.

Notes

1   It is no surprize that American historians differentiate between tribal peoples' history and their own. Americans apply separate standards to tribal and non-tribal people in laws regarding land tenure (unless the common standard is whether one's ancestors were Christians at the turn of the sixteenth century). Americans are governed by a constitution that guarantees freedom of religion to them, while their economic growth dines routinely on the tribes' sacred sites. Even English grammar sets the tribes apart: The "ethnic plural" prescribes a separate rule for pluralizing the names of tribes, separating us grammatically with phrases such as "The Kiowa are. . . ." Yes it do.

2   Richard White, *The Middle Ground: Indians, Empires, and Republics in the Great Lakes Region, 1650–1815,* Cambridge Studies in North American Indian History (New York: Cambridge University Press, 1991).

3   White, *Middle Ground,* 420–68.

4   White dismisses the living tribes by dismissing the method known as upstreaming (p. xiv). Upstreaming is a method of speculating about the histories of communities of people. The stream is a metaphor for time; upstream is towards the past. The scholar identifies an element of a people's culture and speculates that it might have been part of the culture of their ancestors. Obviously, upstreaming can identify only traits that have persisted. It also provides a valuable check: If a trait is present today, historians who declare it absent previously have some obligation to account for its appearance. In

any case, upstreaming is a separate issue from whether one should ignore a people while extracting their history.

5 The Francis Parkman Prize, named for a man who wrote, "Indian traditions of historical events are usually almost worthless" (quoted in Francis Jennings, *The Ambiguous Iroquois Empire* [New York: Norton, 1984], 22, n.39). Here is a case where American historians might respond to Patricia Nelson Limerick's hope, "[d]efending the integrity of the [history] profession . . . that one's ethnocentric predecessors can be credibly and rapidly disowned" (*The Legacy of Conquest: The Unbroken Past of the American West* [New York: Norton, 1987], 219).

6 Mark Stevens, "Chief Joseph's Revenge," *The New Yorker,* August 8, 1994, 30. The newspaper *Indian Country Today* (formerly *Lakota Times*), the electronic newsgroups *soc.cuture.native* and *alt.native,* and the electronic mailing list Native-L are good sources for the recent history of the Black Hills claim and the dispute over Newe Segobia.

7 Taboos are persistent too. Patricia Nelson Limerick produced an entire book, *The Legacy of Conquest: The Unbroken Past of the American West,* debunking for Western History the taboo against recognizing the continuity of past into present. Her chapter "The Persistence of Natives" (180–221) examines the "unbroken past" of the tribes. Her book is a huge success, but her colleagues remain unmindful of the connection between Native past and present.

8 White, *Middle Ground,* xi.

9 White, *Middle Ground,* xi.

10 Frederick Webb Hodge, ed., *Handbook of American Indians North of Mexico,* 2 vols. (New York: Rowman and Littlefield, 1965 [1907–11]), vol. 1, 38.

11 James A. Clifton would prefer that we cease noting our tribal identities (which he understands in terms of genetics) in parentheses after our names. (James A. Clifton, "The Political Rhetoric of Indian History," *The Annals of Iowa,* 3d ser., 49:1,2 [1987], 105.) The lamentable detribalization of white people does not obligate us, however, to detribalize ourselves. If we humored him, we could not recognize each other and respond from our respective positions within the network of tribal relations.

12 Robert F. Berkhofer Jr., *The White Man's Indian: Images of the American Indian from Columbus to the Present* (New York: Vintage Books, 1978), xv.

13 Peter Matthiessen, *In the Spirit of Crazy Horse* (New York: Viking, 1991), 323, 358–59.

14 White, *Middle Ground,* xi.

15 Hodge, *Handbook* 584. "Collectively the Huron . . . called themselves Ouendat (Wendat)," according to Conrad E. Heidenreich in the *Handbook of North*

American Indians (ed. William C. Sturtevant [Washington DC: Smithsonian Institution, 1978-], v. 15; *Northeast,* ed. Bruce G. Trigger, 368). Historian Juanita McQuistion of the Wyandotte tribal organization in Oklahoma says that her people do not use *Huron,* but the name is alive in a Huron Place Cemetery that Wyandots maintain in the Kansas City area. For more information about that group of Wyandots, she refers a caller to a man who lives in that area and to an Indian center in Kansas City. She also suggests consulting the Lorette Hurons of Canada. A comment posted recently to an Internet newsgroup implies that *Wendat* is in use at Lorette. The next step in writing about "Hurons" would be to inquire of members of those Kansas City and Canadian communities.

16 Hodge, *Handbook,* 867. According to Roberta Smith at the offices of the Seneca-Cayuga Business Committee in Miami, Oklahoma, the name *Mingo* is not in use there and is unfamiliar.

17 Ramón A. Gutiérrez, *When Jesus Came, the Corn Mothers Went Away: Marriage, Sexuality, and Power in New Mexico, 1500–1846* (Stanford CA: Stanford University Press, 1990).

18 Roxanne Dunbar Ortiz, commentary in "Commentaries on *When Jesus Came, the Corn Mothers Went Away: Marriage, Sexuality, and Power in New Mexico 1500–1846,* by Ramón A. Gutiérrez," comp. Native American Studies Center, University of New Mexico, *American Indian Culture and Research Journal* 17:3 (1993): 154–158; John L. Kessell, review of *When Jesus Came. . . . Pacific Historical Quarterly* 62:3 (1993): 364–365; Ralph H. Vigil, "Inequality and Ideology in Borderlands Historiography," *Latin American Research Review* 29:1 (1994): 163–164.

19 Kessell, review of *When Jesus Came,* 364; Vigil, "Inequality and Ideology," 163–164.

20 Gutiérrez, *When Jesus Came,* 30.

21 "Gutiérrez Meets His Critics, November 8, 1993," videotape, Native American Studies Center, University of New Mexico, Albuquerque, 1993. Upstreaming might further this discussion: Gutiérrez ascribes certain sexual behaviors to Puebloan ancestors. Puebloan people object that his claims make no sense in terms of present Puebloan conceptions of gender. Rather than invoking the superstitious historians' tenet that excludes unwritten evidence, Gutiérrez might attempt to understand Puebloan gender-based behaviors of the past in light of gender-based behaviors of today. He might try to explain, for example, just when and why those libidinous Puebloan women of his conception lost their zest for Catholic clerics.

22 "Gutiérrez Meets His Critics, November 8, 1993," videotape, Native American Studies Center, University of New Mexico, Albuquerque, 1993.

23 Roxanne Dunbar Ortiz, "When Jan Huss, Martin Luther, and John Calvin Came, the Holy Mother Went Away: Marriage, Sex, and Power in Catholic Culture, 1 A.D. to 1541," unpublished essay.

24 Patricia Nelson Limerick, "Stop Dancing or I'll Flog Myself," *New York Times Book Review*, July 12, 1992, 21.

25 Ortiz, commentary, 154–162; Vigil, "Inequality and Ideology," 155–171; Kessell, review of *When Jesus Came,* 363–365. For a historian's summary of the reception of *When Jesus Came,* see John R. Wunder, "What's Old about the New Western History, Part 1: Race and Gender," *Pacific Northwest Quarterly* 85:2 (1994): 56–57.

26 Berkhofer, xv.

27 White, 4–5.

28 James H. Merrell, "Some Thoughts on Colonial Historians and American Indians," *William and Mary Quarterly* 46 (1989): 94–119.

29 Merrell, "Some Thoughts," 98–99.

American Indian Intellectualism
and the New Indian Story

ELIZABETH COOK-LYNN

The role of Indians, themselves, in the storytelling of Indian America is as much a matter of "jurisdiction" as is anything else in Indian Country: economics, the law, control of resources, property rights. It goes without saying that it reflects our struggle with the colonial experience of our concomitant histories. If that sounds benign, it is anything but that. On the contrary, how the Indian narrative is told, how it is nourished, who tells it, who nourishes it, and the consequences of its telling are among the most fascinating—and, at the same time, chilling—stories of our time.

It is true that "the American Indian intellectual" is to many people a bizarre phrase, falling quaintly on the unaccustomed ears of those in the American mainstream. While there are images of Jewish intellectuals, European intellectuals, British scholars, African novelists, there is no image of an American Indian intellectual. There is only that primitive figure who crouches near the fire smoking a sacred pipe or, arms outstretched, calls for the gods to look down upon his pitiful being. Worse, the drunk, demoralized Chingachgook sitting alongside the road, a medallion with George Washington's face imprinted on it hanging about his neck. Or the Red Power militant of the 1960s.

It is as though the American Indian has no intellectual voice with which to enter into America's important dialogues. The American Indian is not asked what he thinks we should do about Bosnia or Iraq. He is not asked to participate in Charlie Rose's interview program about books or politics or history. It is as though the American Indian does not exist except in *faux* history or corrupt myth.

Yet, the American Indian population is one of the fastest growing minority populations in America and American Indians own and occupy hundreds of thousands of acres of land throughout the country, have earned doctorates and other scholarly credentials and they run their own homelands-based universities and corporations.

In spite of mistaken ideas about American Indian life and public intellectualism, today's Native poets and novelists—many of them professors at American universities, teachers at Native-based colleges, and directors of native-based programs—have been attempting to participate in this country's intellectual dialogues ever since the Kiowa writer N. Scott Momaday won the Pulitzer in 1968. Their writing and research seems on the one hand important, provocative. On the other, its influence on mainstream scholarship, art and dialogue seems minimal. Who, for example, believes that Ted Koppel's "Nightline" is going to drop the news of the O.J. Simpson trial to talk about the impact of a 1994 racist Supreme Court decision *Hagen v. Utah*?

Hagen v. Utah, a case that determinedly deconstructs historical, treaty-established Indian nationhood by further diminishing sovereignty, is a story that needs to be told. Because of the entrenched stereotypes American people hold of Indians, we don't expect it will hit the mainstream news programs under the topic of racism in America. Still, it seems to anyone who has been in bookstores lately, at the movies, or privy to the agonized discussions going on in academia about the "American Canon" that the question of telling Indian stories is still at the heart of what America believes to be its narrative of self.

It is unfortunate that, in spite of the burgeoning body of work by Native writers, the greatest body of acceptable telling of the Indian story is still in the hands of non-Natives. The recent Disney release of *Pocahontas* is evidence of that, if there has been any doubt, and we can expect even more of the same. Much as the title to Indian land is still held by the white American government, the major Indian story is held in non-Indian enclaves though not, like the land, by overt congressional mandate. Rather, we are told, freedom of the press and the First Amendment allow any storyteller to be taken seriously. This means that the works of non-Indians invade every genre, and they can't be written fast enough, it seems.

The so-called popular Indian story is everywhere, in every paperback section of every supermarket, on every book stand. This kind of dime novel approach to the story is well established in American culture though, like anything else, it can no longer be bought for a dime. These novels, though, are the precursors to the narratives of Larry McMurtry (e.g., *Lonesome Dove*) and to the stories of the white-boy exemplar, Kevin Costner, who as a child "wanted to be Indian" and grew up to become successful as star, writer, and director of *Dances with Wolves,* telling the most famous modern Indian story of them all. His movie recharged the flagging paperback industry but, more significantly, geared up the television fare for such characters as Medicine Woman and Buffalo Girls. This brought hundreds of Indians to Hollywood; they hired agents and became actors and actresses, but that's a subject for another time.

Euro-American literary genre influence

In spite of the reality that Indian stories have had their own generic literary development within a tribal language, custom, and experience, the European influence in the newest versions or in translation is almost overwhelming. American writers have never hesitated to plunge into literary fields of exotic origin and call them their own. Thus, the borrowing and trading of literary kinds has flourished.

Anything is useable. The chant. Religious ritual. Coyote. Mother Earth. There is some feeble effort on the part of many thoughtful artists to connect indigenous literary traditions to contemporary forms such as has happened with the remarkable "trickster" figure but, for the most part, these often seem superficial or exploitative.

This means that the Indian story as it is told outside of the tribal genres and the Indian character, has its own modern imprimatur.

In the Costner-style story told in television, movies and paperback, the white protagonist is central. An important generic quality of the white male hero requires that he be helper to the underdog, sensitive to women, and a winner. The white heroine is strong-willed, she will not shirk her duty, and she often knows the history of Indians better than they do themselves, spouting lines about Wounded Knee, federal policy, and why a son-in-law cannot speak to his wife's mother lest he offend some tribal code. Indian characters in this genre often break into a chant at every massacre site, light the sacred pipe during the unexpected quiet moments, and sit cross-legged at gorgeously lighted campfires.

For reasons that are still obscure, Native supervisors and consultants often are employed nowadays by movie and television producers per-haps in an effort to assert authenticity, a relatively new phenomenon perhaps brought about during the militant 1960s and 1970s when "identity politics" reached its nexus, when only blacks could speak for blacks, only women could speak on women's issues. This political agenda may have moved publishing houses and New York editors around to the notion that Indians could now write their own stories, but, in truth, that idea doesn't seem to have improved very much on the Indian story itself. The stereotypes still abound, and the same stories are being told only in a more sympathetic tenor.

An example of how wrong things can go was obvious in a 1995 Disney project. Russell Means, a Lakota activist turned movie actor and leader of the American Indian Movement in the 1960s and 1970s, was quoted in the *Lakota Times,* a Native-owned newspaper based in Rapid City, South Dakota, as saying about the new Walt Disney picture *Pocahontas*: "It's the finest movie to ever come out of Hol-lywood about Indian people." Means, the voice of Chief Powhatan in the Disney blockbuster, is apparently thought by the media to be a historian, a literary scholar, and an art critic all rolled into one. Or perhaps they are simply using his notoriety to make money. In either case, the Pocahontas story is an old story, one that is hotly debated by Native American scholars—none of whom believe the story to be truthful or that all was well in colonial America as the film implied. Because there is thought to be no Native intellectualism, no one thinks to turn to the Native American scholarship that has been done on this period. Historian Angie Debo wrote in *A History of the Indians of the United States* that the Pocahontas story was filled with errors and fantasy, and if the incidents happened at all they were an anomaly in an otherwise barbaric history toward Native peoples. She said it need not be retold except to assuage the United States' national conscience.

Even as we speak, though, there is the idea that to talk about something, you have to have had special *experience*. Everyone knows of the experience of the American Indian Movement media stars of the 1970s such as Russell Means so why not ask him to speak for Indians in any and all matters? It's sad but true that to run an alcoholism treatment center on any Indian Reservation in the country (as an example of furthering this "been there done that" notion of authenticity) your own years of alcohol abuse are your major credential. This idea is called "essentialism" in lit-crit jargon, and it is thought by critics—who paint everyone who speaks out with the same brush—to make its defenders "intellectually disreputable." A redneck comic who is making the rounds puts it: "I don't think you ought to talk about being a redneck unless you are one . . . and I are one." Very funny guy.

Whatever else may be said about experience-based intellectualism, there seems to be no real understanding of the idea as it concerns the *content* of art and scholarship, and some have dismissed it as a "damned if you do, damned if you don't" issue.

Fabulous fictions and the Indian romance novel
Popular fiction about Indians includes the romance novel which—developing out of the nineteenth century novel that disallowed the mating of Indians and whites—has explicit interracial love at its core. Kathleen Pierson, one of the new writers in this genre, was born in Fredricksburg, Virginia, to an Air Force family, raised in

Massachusetts, and educated at Mount Holyoke, South Hadley, Massachusetts. She went to a North Dakota Indian Reservation a couple of decades ago to teach and, while she was there, married a Lakota Sioux man, Cyde Eagle. She is now a successful romance novelist using Sioux themes and settings, and seems to be attempting to lead the way toward harmony and assimilation between the races, with interracial love her major theme.

This is not a new idea for modern white New Englandresses. In fact, one named Elaine Goodale (1863–1953), an early Christian woman among the Sioux, educated at Sky Farm in Western Massachusetts, married a Sisseton Dakota male named Charles Eastman just one year after the Wounded Knee Massacre in 1890, and they both talked openly about their collaboration as a commitment to assimilation. If you look very closely at what has been written and who is doing the writing, this model can seem almost embedded in the history of those times. Nonetheless, it hangs on as a hopeful consequence of that history.

Kathleen Pierson Eagle's *Reason to Believe,* published in 1995 by Avon, is a fictional account of the "power and magic of love." She spends her time crafting "very special stories," her publicity blurbs say. Her genre, if you look at the tips in *Writer's Market,* requires that attraction, passion, idealism, and love be the main themes, that the heroine (white woman, in this case) be self-assured, perceptive, and the hero (Indian male, in this case) be goal-oriented, upwardly mobile, and dynamic. This is known in the trade as classical romance.

I would suspect that Ms. Eagle probably wants her work considered as history because she begins with a reference to the five-year Big Foot Memorial Ride from Cherry Creek, South Dakota, to the Wounded Knee Site (1989–1992) in this way: "For the runners and the riders, and for all those who offered support. May the sacrifices be known, the injustices be rectified, and may the healing touch battered hearts everywhere." In the afterward she and her husband, Clyde, thank such Lakota notables as Arvol Looking Horse, Carol Ann Heart, Ron McNeil, Isaac Dog Eagle, and Howard Eagle Shield. Ms. Eagle also wrote *This Time Forever, Fire and Rain* and has just finished a novel called *Sunrise Song*. The last title is a fictional story about what was called the Hiawatha Indian Insane Asylum for American Indians that opened in Canton, South Dakota, in 1902 and closed in 1934. She claims to have done considerable research into the history of the place, the only remnant of which is a cemetery now in the middle of a golf course. Her "do-gooder" approach to history and fiction seems to find enthusiastic audiences.

Another sub-genre in the romance novel is "intrigue," which includes mystery, suspense, espionage, adventure, and puzzles. Perhaps Tony Hillerman's novels may be described in this way since not even the Navajos and Hopis from whose cultures the plots and characters are fashioned, know what is real and what is not. A third sub-genre is called "period romance" and this category requires the setting to be from 1700 to 1900, and the story should be realistic and its details authentic. The last sub-genre is called "sensuous romance," and this type of story fulfills fantasies and is described as "sizzling but subtle." Committed premarital sex is a requirement; the heroine must be a strong contemporary woman, a match for the hero as together they confront dilemmas ranging from woman-in-jeopardy to horror. These paperbacks are found in every supermarket with titles like *White Squaw, Red Man's Passion,* and *Savage Love.* Much study of this genre is needed in order to understand the historiography that underlies it.

Book lovers love the children's story about Indians

The children's Indian story has long been a staple in the American narrative, and many of these stories are so entwined with European folk tales as to be severely corrupted. A transplanted Englishman, Paul Gobel, who lived in the Black Hills of South Dakota for a time and married a woman from Sturgis, South Dakota, with whom he has a child, has been the most intrepid explorer of this genre in recent times. He has taken Iktomi (or Unktomi) stories, the star stories, and the creation myths of the Sioux, a vast body of philosophical and spiritual knowledge about the universe, to fashion twenty or more storybooks for children ages 3 to 14 which he, himself, has illustrated in a European aesthetic and style. Now living in Minnesota, he has successfully used several people as "informants," including a popular hoop dancer, Kevin Locke, who lives on one of the South Dakota Indian reservations. It is no wonder, when Native cultural philosophy and religion are used to entertain and inform white American children, that the idea of "Indian Intellectualism" in America is dismissed.

The informant-based Indian story has a long tenure in the American literary canon. Gobel—a man who says he showed artistic talent at an early age, was always fascinated by Indians, and long wanted to be considered an *artiste*—has taken it a step further into the popular imagination. Most of all, he simply invades the available written texts, among them Ella Deloria's *Dakota Texts* published after ethnographic work with the famed ethnographer Franz Boas in the early decades of this century.

Gobel takes his place not alongside, but a step ahead of those other white writers of children's stories who, knowingly or not, have long trivialized the rather sophisticated notions the Lakotas have held about the universe for thousands of years. Children's stories about the Bible are one thing but, considering the vast ignorance the average person has concerning native intellectualism, the non-Lakota speaking Englishman's reinterpretation of the native Lakota/Dakota world-view and spirituality through the lens of his own language and art is, at the very least, arrogant.

It has not occurred to anyone, least of all Gobel himself, to ask why it is that tribal writers, except in carefully managed instances, have chosen not to use these stories commercially. If one were to inquire about that, one would have to explore the moral and ethical dimensions of who owns bodies of knowledge and literature. That is a difficult exploration in a capitalistic democracy that suggests anything can be bought and sold. Many white American critics refuse to enter into this debate, believing Native American literature and knowledge cannot "belong" to any single group. A discussion of who "transmits" and who "produces" usually follows. As Americans and

other world citizens enter cyberspace, increased technology will undoubtedly bring more Anglo-American interpretation and definition
to these matters.

In 1995, a children's book, *The Indian in the Cupboard,* turned into a
do-gooder fantasy movie about a toy Indian who becomes real in
much the same way a piece of wood carved by Gippetto became
Pinocchio (a *real* boy). This metamorphosis proves, one supposes, that
there is nothing new in plot making. The media touted this movie
as a marvelous step forward in movie-making about Indians since it
was tribally specific both in language and history, and its purpose was
to teach little white moviegoers to be kind to animals, Indians, and
other feathered friends. Native consultants and actors were part of
the preparation of the story, and this was supposed to give it further
importance.

Biography

If you want to understand the pathology of whites and Indians in
America, it is biography, the "life story," that is required reading.
It is certain that the "Indian informant" model of "transmitting"
and "producing" stories has had acceptance not only in the popular
literary world but in the academic world as well. It probably has its
origins in the rather quick rise of the discipline of anthropology in
the last seven or eight decades, or in the model claimed by ethnographers who have been participants and originators of the American
Indian story since the beginning and have long claimed a "scientific"
methodology. It's a little like the "authorized" or "unauthorized"
biography so prevalent now in American culture that has spawned
not only vicious debate but, in some cases, vicious litigation.

Because of its claim to scholarship, this genre is dominated by the
university presses. The University of Nebraska Press, as an example
of one of the more prolific presses in this genre, has published about
forty titles in the years since its Bison Books classic *Black Elk Speaks* (a
tale of traditionalism) by John G. Neihardt invaded the imagination
of the American public. *Catch Colt* by Sidner J. Larson (a tale of

mixed-bloodedness) is one of the latest in the subsequent series, American Indian Lives, which gives you an idea of how diverse the genre has become. There is an editorial board for this American Indian Lives series (which now has fourteen titles and offers a North American Indian Prose Award annually) and among its members are such scholarly figures as A. LaVonne Brown Ruoff, University of Illinois at Chicago; Michael Dorris, formerly of Dartmouth; R. David Edmunds, Indiana University; Daniel F. Littlefield Jr., University of Arkansas at Little Rock; Alfonso A. Ortiz, University of New Mexico; Kathleen M. Sands, Arizona State University; and Gerald R. Vizenor, University of California, Berkeley. When I talked to an editor at the press she said of the Bison Books: "They have general appeal, and we hope they won't become a disgrace," a remark which unaccountably indicates circumspection on the part of those responsible for the publishing. I am not sure how to interpret this ambiguity.

Many books produced by these academic publishers are used in courses ranging from literary studies to the social sciences and history, under the rubric of Native American literature. This interest shown by university presses is not to suggest that commercial presses have been silent on this subject matter. Indeed, Harpercollins has just taken up the Crow Dog life stories (Mary Moore's and Leonard Crow Dog's stories of the Wounded Knee Uprising of 1973) written by another transplanted European who now lives in New York, an Indian expert and Hungarian/Austrian photographer named Richard Erdoes. Movie moguls Jane Fonda and Ted Turner have recently turned this popular informant/biographer piece done by Erdoes into a television bio now available on video.

I've become particularly interested in the "life story" as it has emerged as a genre in the literature on Indians. I've been asked by editors and agents to write my own "life story," as they send me their regretful rejections to my essays, non-fiction works, and poetry. While I may have a reasonable understanding of why a state-run university press would not want to publish my research that has little good to say about America's relationship to the tribes or art, I am at a loss to explain why anyone would be more interested in my life story (which for one thing is quite unremarkable) than they would in my poetry, for instance, or my essays, which may generate thoughtful discussion where none had before existed.

Though I've referred to the "informant-based" Indian stories as "life story" works, I would like to suggest that they are offshoots of biography, a traditional art form in European literature. Ethnographic biography is not an Indian story at all and does not have significant ties to the interesting bodies of Native literary canons produced culturally and historically. In light of this, the question of the origins of life stories about Indians and the development of that genre seem essential to the exploration of what is called the Indian story in the American literary canon.

Biography, as I understand its literary history, has been a type of writing that was thought to merge with history but was not itself history. Distinguished personages like the Duchess of Newcastle (Margaret Cavandish) wrote biographies in the 1600s, and it was a matter of self-record. Later, anthologies of biographies were written, as in the lives of the saints, and they were among the first kinds of history that I ever read when I was a student who lived near a pitifully biased library at the Catholic Indian boarding school near Fort Thompson, South Dakota. I did not consider them history even then, though I was probably aware that biography was said to have evolved into a form which required considerable research.

Over the years, as is the case in any genre development, methods and principles evolved, although biographical methods were rather strictly adhered to in the early stages. Collecting anecdotes, for example, was thought, in early biography, to be a form of degraded "evidence," but today the anecdotal method seems primary. Delight and entertainment, gossip and scandal have become the style of the day. All of this may account for the interest today's American readers have in the Indian story because its anecdotal nature is difficult to resist.

Indian life stories are an attempt, perhaps, to own the facts of our own lives, to keep private the most intimate facts, or to share them in the way that seems most appropriate. In the face of massive historical distortion of Indian lives over the past two hundred years, this attempt is understandable. But, the truth is people do not "own" their lives at all. As Janet Malcolm suggests in her *New Yorker* essay (August, 1993) on publishing stories about the unfortunate life and death of the white poetess, Sylvia Plath: "This ownership passes out of our hands at birth, at the moment we are first observed." Malcolm goes on to say: "Biography is the medium through which the remaining secrets of the famous dead are taken from them and dumped out in full view of the world," and "The dead cannot be libeled or slandered. They are without legal recourse." This is probably more true of Indians than of any other people on earth.

But what of the living? What of those who "inform," those who give themselves over to a white writer for collaboration and explanation?

"The biographer at work," Malcom says, and this is what applies to the "informant-based" work,

> is like the professional burglar, breaking into a house, rifling through certain drawers that he has good reason to think contain the jewelry and money, and triumphantly bearing his loot away. The voyeurism and busybodyism that impels writers and readers of biography alike are obscured by an apparatus of scholarship designed to give the enterprise an appearance of banklike blandness and solidity. The biographer is portrayed almost as a kind of benefactor, seen as sacrificing years of his life to his task. There is no length he will not go to, and the more his book reflects his industry the more the reader believes that he is having an elevating literary experience, rather than simply listening to backstairs gossip and reading other people's mail. The transgressive nature of biography is rarely acknowledged, but it is the only explanation for biography's status as a popular genre.

In the case of the "informant-based" Indian story, there is no length the biographer will not go to in his search for the "real story." He/she spends every summer for twenty years in an Indian reservation community, attends hundreds of powwows, endures the dust and the tedium of these weekend-long or four-day communal marathons, puts up with the insults from those who despise his/her curiosity about their lives. He/she makes his/her home in some faraway city available as a crash pad for traveling Indians, loans money which he/she never expects to have returned, lends a car, baby-sits, takes on the responsibilities of an "adopted" relative, is thrilled to be given an Indian name which is said to be invested with a mysterious spirituality. Many times this biographer takes an Indian as wife, husband, lover, or "live-in."

After twenty years he/she is thought to be master of this territory on Indian lives and can present a manuscript to a publisher that will satisfy any voyeur's curiosity. These manuscripts are, by and large, fantasies of Indians as non-conformists to American cultural restrictions, Indians as redeemed drunks, Indian grandmothers and grandfathers as legendary figures, quite unremarkable and decent Indians presented on pedestals, Indians as victims of racist America, Indians as mixed-blood outcasts. All in all, these manuscripts describe the significance of individual Indian lives in the tribal parable mode, those stories that exhibit "truth."

In the telling of these stories, the writer almost always takes sides with the "informant" who gives him/her specific answers to specific questions. The writer/biographer is a believer. That is the nature of the relationship between the Indian informant and writer, and that's what gives the story its authority for the reader. Unfortunately, that's also what makes these stories neither history nor art in terms of Native intellectualism. That characteristic is what will ultimately define them as anti-intellectual, and the reasons are many.

For one thing, ambiguity, the essential ingredient of art, literature, *and humanity,* has been sacrificed for "truth" by both the informant and the biographer. Another, more important reason is that in the process of this so-called scholarship, the essential focus is America's dilemma, not questions about who the Indian thinks he/she is in tribal America. I don't mean to say this focus is not an interesting one, nor do I mean to suggest such an inquiry should never be made. But indigenous intellectualism in art, at least, has never had as its major interest the defining of one's self *as an American.* That is a relatively new phenomenon, political in nature, colonialistic in perspective, and one-sided. What distinguishes Native American intellectualism from other scholarship is its interest in tribal indigenousness, and this makes the "life story," the 'self"-oriented and non-tribal story seem unrecognizable or even unimportant, non-communal, and un-connected.

What popular art and literature have to say about what it means to be an American Indian in non-tribal America is not the essential function of art and literature in Native societies. If stories are to have any meaning, Indian intellectuals must ask what it means to be an Indian in tribal America. If we don't attempt to answer that question, nothing else will matter, and we won't have to ask ourselves whether there is such a thing as Native American intellectualism because there will no longer be evidence of it.

The urban mixed-blood Indian and American writing
In American Indian scholarship and art, the works of writers who call themselves mixed-bloods abound. Their main topic is the discussion of the connection between the present "I" and the past "They," and the present pastness of "We." Gerald Vizenor, Louis Owens, Wendy Rose, Maurice Kenny, Michael Dorris, Diane Glancy, Betty Bell, Thomas King, Joe Bruchac, and Paula Gunn Allen are the major self-described mixed-blood voices of the decade.

While there is in the writings of these intellectuals much lip ser-vice given to the condemnation of America's treatment of the First Nations, there are few useful expressions of resistance and opposition to the colonial history at the core of Indian/White relations. Instead, there is explicit and implicit accommodation to the colonialism of the "West" that has resulted in what may be observed as three intellectual characteristics in fiction, non-fiction, and poetry: an aesthetic that

is pathetic or cynical, a tacit notion of the failure of tribal governments as Native institutions and of sovereignty as a concept, and
an Indian identity which focuses on individualism rather than First
Nation ideology. Gerald Vizenor, a major voice in this mixed-blood
discourse explains it this way in "The Ruins of Representation": "The
postmodern turn in literature and cultural studies is an invitation to
the ruins of representation; the invitation uncovers traces of tribal
survivance, trickster discourse, and the remanence of intransitive
shadows."[1] The postmodern conditions, he says, are found in aural
performance, translation, trickster liberation, humor, tragic incoherence, and cross-causes in language games. Almost all of the current
fiction being written by Indians is created within these aesthetics in
contradistinction to the hopeful, life-affirming aesthetic of traditional
stories, songs, and rituals.

The diversity of American scholarship is being developed in substantially different ways from that of the historical educational
pattern of colonial coercion for captive Indians. There are new movements afoot. This means that the Indian story is included in every
genre and most disciplines during this era of the rise of cultural
studies, diversity, and multiculturalism. In this period, the so-called
"mixed-blood" story, often called the "post-colonial" story, has taken
center stage. The bicultural nature of Indian lives has always been a
puzzle to the monoculturalists of America; thus, mixed-bloodedness
becomes the paradigm of preference.

Several publishing influences are perhaps at the heart of this movement. In brief, the loneliness of *Bury My Heart at Wounded Knee,*
written by a white Arkansas writer whose name is Dee Brown, was
published by Holt, Rinehart, and Winston in 1970 and set the tone
for much poignant and sad and angry poetry by Indian and non-
Indian writers during the beginning period of modernity.

In the 1980s, the Louise Erdich saga of an inadequate Chippewa
political establishment and a vanishing Anishinabe culture suggests
the failure of tribal sovereignty and the survival of myth in the

modern world. Edrich's conclusion is an odd one, in light of the reality of Indian life in the substantial Native enclaves of places like South Dakota or Montana or Arizona or New Mexico.

In the subsequent decade, a plethora of stories of the individual Indian life, biographies, and autobiographies of emancipated Indians who have little or no connection to tribal national life, has become the publishing fare of university presses in the name of Native scholarship. This body of work (a recent University of Nebraska Press title is *Standing in the Light: A Lakota Way of Seeing* by Severt Young Bear and R. D. Theisz) is generated by reasons of interest in the social sciences, perhaps, rather than art and literature, since its "storytelling" approach is more pedantic than dynamic. (I discuss this category separately in an essay called "Life and Death in the Mainstream of Indian Biography," which was written for a Canadian Indian journal called *Talking Stick*.)

Several new works in fiction that catalogue the deficit model of Indian reservation life, such as *Skins* by Adrian Louis (Crown) and *Reservation Blues* by Sherman Alexie (Atlantic Monthly Press) have been published in this decade. These are significant because they reflect little or no defense of treaty-protected reservation land bases as homelands to the indigenes, nor do they suggest a responsibility of art as an ethical endeavor or the artist as responsible social critic, a marked departure from the early renaissance works of such luminaries as N. Scott Momaday and Leslie Marmon Silko. Reviews of these works have been published generally on the entertainment pages of newspapers rather than in scholarly journals. Atlantan Ed Hall, a book reviewer editor for *Hogan's Alley,* a magazine of the cartoon arts, says of Louis's first novel, "*Skins* starts in the outhouse and keeps returning there," a comment that is, perhaps, both literally and figuratively true. Gloria Bird, a Spokane Indian professor of the arts at the Institute for American Indian Arts in Santa Fe, New Mexico, in calling Alexie the Indian Spike Lee makes the point that Native cultures are used like props in this fiction, "Spinkled like bait are sage-smudging, stickgame, sweet grass enough to titillate the curiosity of non-Indian readers."[2]

The failure of the contemporary Indian novel and literary studies in Native American studies to contribute substantially to intellectual debates in defense of First Nationhood is discouraging. The American universities which have been at the forefront of the modern study of American Indian experience in literature for the past three decades and the professors, writers, and researchers who have directed the discourse through teaching and writing have been influenced by what may be called the inevitable imperial growth of the United States. Most seem to agree that the Indian story and what is labeled "cultural studies" are the future, but their refusal or inability to use a nation-to-nation approach to Native intellectualism has prevailed.

A "tolerant" national climate with resourceful diversity curricula have forged the apparatuses through which the study of aesthetics, ideology, and identity in native thought have flourished to the detriment of autonomous models in Native studies. In this process there has been little defense of tribal nationhood and the consequences of that flaw are deeply troubling. Indian Nations are dispossessed of sovereignty in much of the intellectual discourse in literary studies, and there as elsewhere their natural and legal autonomy is described as simply another American cultural or ethnic minority. Scholarship shapes the political, intellectual, and historical nation-to-nation past as an Americanism that can be compared to any other minority past. Many successful Native writers whose major focus is "mixed-blood" liberation and individualism seem to argue their shared victimhood through America's favorite subjects about Indians, i.e., despair, rootlessness, and assimilation.

Perhaps no one should be surprised at this turn of events since, officially, American citizenship for Indians made it clear from the beginning in 1924 that Indians were *not* to continue toward successful and progressive roles in their own tribal nation citizenship.

As it is now heard, the American Indian literary voice seems dependent on a university setting. The university is a place where few Indians reside and where the few who are present are notable for their willingness to change tribal traditions to mainstream traditions of modernity, transcribing in English and imagining in art some principles of personal (not tribal) politics and expressing the Indian experience in assimilative and mainstream terms.

The mixed-blood literature is characterized by excesses of individualism. The "I," the "me" story, and publishing projects by university and commercial presses in the "life story" genre are the result more of the dominance and patriarchy most noted in American society than of tribalness. Mixed-blood literary instruction may be viewed as a kind of liberation phenomenon or, more specifically, a deconstruction of a tribal-nation past, hardly an intellectual movement that can claim a continuation of the tribal communal story or an ongoing tribal literary tradition.

The omnipresent and evasive role of the urban mixed-blood Indian intellectual writer has not been examined in its relationship to tribal nation hopes and dreams. Yet its influence cannot be dismissed, since it may be a movement of considerable consequence whose aim seems to be to give instruction to the academic world about what the imperialistic dispossession imposed on American Indians through the development of capitalistic democracy has meant to the individual, emancipated Indian. Unfortunately, the mixed-blood literary movement is signaling that a return to tribal sovereignty on Indian homelands seems to be a lost cause, and American individualism will out. The legacy of this, realistically speaking, is sure to translate into a wider terrain of assimilation and confusion as economic questions and cultural questions and Federal Indian policy questions become more a matter of power than doctrine.

Though there is little documentation in literary studies of how Indians themselves have assessed these matters, there has been the suggestion in informal discussion that the mixed-blood movement is led by those whose tribal past has never been secure. Others believe the rise of such a literary movement is simply the result of the economy and culture imposed by conquest and colonization and politics.

Non-Indian critics of the systems of American colonization and imperialism such as the Italian intellectual Antonio Gramsci, who became the founder of the Italian Communist party, might have suggested that such a movement could be the result of not transmitting ideas and knowledge from and to those who do not belong to the so-called intellectual class. Gramsci might have theorized that American Indians who have become a part of the elite intellectualism of American universities are unable to meet the standards of the true intellectual, that they are failed intellectuals because they have not lived up to the responsibility of transmitting knowledge between certain diverse blocs of society. This would suggest that the mixed-blood literary movement arose as a result of the assimilation inherent in cultural studies driven by American politics and imperialism.

Gramsci has said that it is the function of intellectuals to be at the forefront of theory but, at the same time, to transmit ideas to those who are not of the so-called professional, academic, intellectual class. Indian scholars, on the other hand, suggest that Native intellectuals are more likely to come from non-academic enclaves. A major history/political science/theology scholar, Vine Deloria Jr. (Standing Rock Sioux) has suggested in his serious contemporary work that a turn away from academe toward tribal-knowledge bases that exist at a grassroots level is the answer to the complex dilemmas of modern scholarship in Indian affairs. This presents a distinct dilemma, one that has been brought up in discussions of authenticity but seldom mentioned in terms of theory. Ideas, in general, according to Native American studies disciplinary definitions, are to be generated from the inside of culture, not from the outside looking in. This fact, scholars like Russell Thornton have suggested, has been the feature of Native studies that distinguishes it from anthropology and other social science disciplines which have claimed an "objective," i.e., "scientific" approach. It is evident that the mixed-blood literary phenomenon is not generated from the inside of tribal culture since many of the practitioners admit they have been removed from cultural influence through urbanization and academic professionalization or even, they suggest, through biology and intermarriage. Separation of these writers from indigenous communities (reservation or urban) indicates that this is a literary movement of disengagement.

When writers and researchers and professors who claim mixed blood focus on individualism and liberation, they often do not develop ideas as part of an inner-unfolding theory of Native culture; thus, they do not contribute ideas as a political practice connected to First Nation ideology. No one will argue that Native studies has had as its central agenda the critical questions of race and politics. For Indians in America today, real empowerment lies in First Nation ideology not in individual liberation of Americanization.

The explosion of the mixed-blood literary phenomenon is puzzling to those who believe that the essential nature of intellectual work and critical reflection for American Indians is to challenge the politics of dispossession inherent in public policy toward Indian nationhood. It is not only puzzling, it may be dangerous because there can be no doubt, despite recent disclaimers in the media, about the power of intellectuals at universities to direct the course of American life and thought. More worrisome is the fact that the literary people who are contributing to the Indian affairs debate in academia are in ever more increasing numbers the people who have no stake in First Nation ideology. Their desire to absolve themselves of their responsibility to speak to that ideology, their self-interest in job seeking, promotion, publishing, tenure, and economic security dismisses the seriousness of Native intellectual work and its connection to politics.

A great deal of the work done in the mixed-blood literary movement is personal, invented, appropriated, and irrelevant to First Nation status in the United States. If that work becomes too far removed from what is really going on in Indian enclaves, there will be no way to engage in responsible intellectual strategies in an era when structures of external cultural power are more oppressive than ever.

Moreover, no important pedagogical movement will be made toward those defensive strategies which are among the vital functions of intellectualism: to change the world, to know it, and to make it better by knowing how to seek appropriate solutions to human problems. Teaching is the mode intellectuals use to reproduce, and their reproduction should be something more than mere self-service. How long, then, can mixed-blood literary figures teach a Native American curriculum in literary studies of self-interest and personal narrative before they realize (and their students catch on to it) that the nature of the structural political problems facing the First Nation in America is being marginalized and silenced by the very work they are doing?

Art for art's sake

Today, American Indian artists, novelists, poets, and scholars who are publishing their own works seem to take an *art for art's sake* approach. There are astonishingly few exceptions, like Ray Young Bear and Percy Bull Child. Publishers want to take on only what will have a reasonably wide readership, and it is thought that the purists will not be read. Few discussions about the moral issues in producing art are taken seriously.

Since Momaday published his classic novel, much bad poetry (which should be called "doggerel") and bad fiction (which should be called "pop art") has been published in the name of Native American art. I have not heard much discussion from the Modern Language Association scholars or from literary critics (mostly white) or from inner circles of Native writers who must know (if they have read John Gardener's *On Moral Fiction*) that bad art has a harmful effect on society. Native scholars often suggest that to be critical of the work of fellow Indian writers is a function of jealousy or meanness. It is my opinion that literary fiction can be distinguished from popular fiction. I think a responsible critic will challenge the generic development of what is called Native American fiction by using the idea that there are such concepts as (1) moral fiction and (2) indigenous/tribally specific literary traditions from which the imagination emerges. American Indian writers could discuss what is literary art and what is trash or fraudulent or pop in Native American literatures; there could be a dialogue about what is good or bad and why, but only a few have the stomach for it.

The truth is, Momaday's *House Made of Dawn* is considered a classic in the study of Native American literatures not simply because it adheres to the principles of the oral traditions of the tribes, though that is vital to classic indigenous literatures, nor is it a classic because it seeks out the sources of ritual and ceremony, language, and storytelling although that, too, is essential. It is considered a classic because it is a work that explores traditional values, revealing truth and falsity about those values from a framework of *tribal realism*. It is diametrically opposed to fantasy, which often evades or suppresses moral issues. Momaday's work allows profound ideas to be conceptualized, allows its Indian readers to work through those ideas and move on to affirm their lives as Indian people. It adheres to the Gardner principle and the principles of the oral traditions that good stories incline the reader to an optimistic sense. In too much of what passes for Native American Literature today you couldn't find a significant *idea* with a ten-foot pole let alone find one that is life-affirming to the indigenes.

The art for art's sake phenomenon, more than any other in modern times, seems to thrive on the notion that art (fiction, painting, music, poetry) as a mode of thought is important as a human activity because it is a way of discovering. I can't argue with that. But it also is an idea which, if untrammeled and unexamined, lets Indian artists off the hook and leads us away from what some of us may consider a responsibility to our own tribal traditions. Though modernity suggests the inevitability of that moving away for the sake of a living art, I am not sure that art can be considered art if it ignores its own historical sense.

A major characteristic of many novels written in the 1980s and 1990s in the art for art's sake mode is the interest in the "marvelous," the expression of a magic spirit which leads to an unexpected alteration of reality. *Ceremony* by Leslie Marmon Silko (Pueblo) and *Tracks* by Louise Erdrich (Turtle Mountain Chippewa) are the major contemporary examples of this so-called magical narrative, and they have achieved enormous popularity with their American readers. South American writers like García Márquez and Alejo Carpentier have led this movement and are the major theorists of this North American phenomenon in storytelling, but both Silko and Erdrich have had an enormous influence on the new American Indian story.

Long before either Silko or Erdrich were out of infancy, however, this idea for a continental approach to art rose out of another colonial literature, Spanish American fiction, when Angel Florez wrote as early as 1955 in "Magic Realism in Spanish American Fiction" that "magic realism" attempts to "transform the common and everyday into the awesome and the unreal."[3] Many of the writers of the work Florez spoke of were not Indians, but were from Spain, one of the colonizing nations of the hemisphere, and were not Native language speakers, but speakers of Spanish, as colonizing a language as any. Their interest in magical realism could be thought of, then, as another generic imposition upon the indigenous story. And the question of distortion in American Indian intellectualism or its outright dismissal again looms.

All of this may give evidence to the idea that the Native magical realism writers of our time have moved away from their own traditions and have grounded their work in a reality that is inherently fantastical. A prevailing theory about magical realism expressed by the South American writer García Márquez gives these writers support. He says that the narrative dramatization of magical realism is "usually expressed through a collective voice, inverting, in a jesting manner, the values of the official culture," and by "official" culture he means Euro-American culture. He does not ask the obvious question about how what he terms Third World (and I would term Native) cultures are distorted in the process of these fictional fantasies but that question is as vital as his message of revolution. No one can deny the vitality of his vision when he accepted the 1982 Nobel Prize for Literature and talked about a continent stolen, bathed in blood, its Natives buried in poverty. This is, of course, also the vision of Silko in her newest novel, *Almanac of the Dead*.

One supposes that every age is characterized by a phrase that distinguishes it from any other. "The Age of Reason" and Thomas Paine. "The Age of Anxiety" with Freud and Margaret Mead. Do we accept the idea that the current Indian Story rises out of "The Age of mixed-blood and magical fantasies"? If not, artists and critics must come to understand that popular Native American fiction is as extricably tied to specific tribal literary legacies as contemporary Jewish literature is tied to the literary legacies of the nations of Eastern Europe or contemporary black literature is tied to the nations of tribal Africa.

The dilemma

If it is true that writers are the intellectuals of any nation, the question of how it is that what might be called experimental work in contemporary Native American literature or "pulp fiction" narratives or fantasies will assist us with our real lives is a vital one. Does this art give thoughtful consideration to the defense of our lands, resources, languages, children? Is anyone doing the intellectual work in and about Indian communities that will help us understand our future? While it is true that any indigenous story tells of death and blood, it also tells of indigenous rebirth and hope, not as Americans nor as some new ersatz race but as the indigenes of this continent.

Perhaps much of the work produced in the last decade can be looked upon as a legitimate criticism of existing society, a realistic criticism of a system of untidy ethics written by a new generation of thinkers who are separated from a real Indian past, people who have no Native language to describe the future, young people who are tired of the whining of old people about the loss of their lives, and Indians who think they can rise to the challenge of life on the entertainment pages. But where does it all end?

Does the Indian story as it is told now end in rebirth of Native nations as it did in the past? Does it help in the development of worthy ideas, prophecies for a future in which we continue as tribal people who maintain the legacies of the past and a sense of optimism?

I can think of a few questions more essential for an Indian writer today than these which mean, perhaps, that biographies, individual

Indian life stories, romance novels, Ted Turner television, Costner movies, magic, children's stories, and mixed-blood visions have little or nothing to do with what may be defined as Native intellectualism.

What is Native intellectualism, then? Who are the intellectuals? Are our poets and novelists articulating the real and the marvelous in celebration of the past or are they the doomsayers of the future? Are they presenting ideas, moving through those ideas and beyond? Are they the ones who recapture the past and preserve it? Are they thinkers who are capable of supplying principles which may be used to develop further ideas? Are they capable of the critical analysis of cause and effect? Or, are our poets and novelists just people who glibly use the English language to entertain us, to keep us amused and preoccupied so that we are no longer capable of making the distinction between the poet and the stand-up comedian? Does that distinction matter anymore? Does it mater how one uses language and for what purpose?

Who knows the answers to these questions? Who believes it is important that they be posed? In my generation, Alfonzo Ortiz, a Pueblo (Tewa) Indian who is now a professor at the University of New Mexico, published *The Tewa World* (University of Chicago Press) in 1969 and it became a classic. N. Scott Momaday, a Kiowa, in 1966 wrote the novel *House Made of Dawn,* and it won the Pulitzer Prize for literature and became the quintessential fictional work of modern literary studies. The Lakota scholar Vine Deloria Jr. in 1967 published *Custer Died for Your Sins,* and it became the first of several essential texts he produced for use in the development of Native American studies as an academic discipline. These books were based in history and culture and politics that looked out on the white world from a communal, tribally specific indigenous past. A whole list of writers who do not situate themselves within the mixed-blood or mainstream spectrum such as Momaday, Silko, Ortiz, Young Bear, Warrior, Medicine, Willard, Deloria, Bird, Crum, Woody, Bull Child, and dozens more for whom books matter and intellectualism has meaning, come to mind as people who will become something more than icons for American pop culture.

Since the time thirty years ago when Native American studies began to define itself as a discipline, more Indian writing has been done than ever, more Indians have had their work published, there are more public storytellers than we ever hoped for, but it seems that little of this subsequent writing has the perspective that propelled Ortiz, Momaday, and Deloria toward a scholarship that concerned itself with indigenousness, and almost none of it can be called profound. It does not pose the unanswerable questions for our future as Indians in America.

The question of how Indians claim the story, then, is still a primary and unanswered question. If the works of non-Native storytellers haven't got it right, who says that the modern works written by American Indians, introspective and self-centered, have? Who says the focus of our modern works on the pragmatic problems of the non-communal world of multicultural America are worthy to be the lasting works in our legacy of artistry?

In a 1995 literary review of contemporary fiction by the preeminent Lagunan artist Leslie Marmon Silko which appeared in *The Nation,* we are told that this "United States is this big Indian Reservation."[4] We are told that Indian Country's poverty and violence are the *defining themes* in the new Indian stories and that any Indian Reservation town described in the new works, because of the nature of its poverty, could be any neighborhood in East Los Angeles or the Bronx. Except, we are told, Indian people "use car wrecks and cheap wine, not drive-by shootings and crack, *to make their escape.*" While Silko is talking about the real lives of Indian people on Indian reservations and in America, it is possible that her reference can be taken as a major dimension of literary theory concerning the function of modern Native fiction. This literature is written and it is read for the purpose of "making an escape." The people who are writing these modern stories, Silko says, are "the best we have."

This assessment, supposedly based on a reading of the important works published in the last several decades, is probably shared by many readers and scholars of our time. This assessment makes "escape" the operative word in discussing the function of storytelling; yet any Indian artist, and surely Silko herself, has told us over and over that escapism has never been the thrust of Native storytelling. What are we to think, then? Are we to take this as a warning?

In light of the genre development of modern works illustrated here and in the context of the new novels and short stories being written, the modern Indian story (whether told by an Indian or a non-Indian) seems to have taken a very different course from its traditional path in Native societies. In doing so, it has defined the literary place where the imaginative final encounter may be staged and only time holds the answer to its continuity or rejection or obligation or interdiction. Native intellectuals, dabbling as we are in a rather shallow pool of imagination and culture, must pull ourselves together to examine not only the irrelevant stories of "other" storytellers, but to critically examine the self-centered stories we presume to tell about our own people.

Indian stories, traditions, and languages must be written, and they must be written in a vocabulary that people can understand rather than the esoteric language of French and Russian literary scholars that has overrun the lit/crit scene. Scholars in Native intellectual circles must resist the flattery that comes from many corners, defend freedom, refute rejection from various power enclaves, resist the superficiality that is so much a part of the modern/urban voice. We must work toward a new set of principles that recognizes the tribally specific literary traditions by which we have always judged the imagination. This distinguished legacy—largely untapped by critics, mainstream readers, and Native participants—is too essential to be ignored as we struggle toward the inevitable modernity of Native American intellectualism.

Notes

1 Gerald Vizenor, "The Ruins of Representation," *American Indian Quarterly* 17 (Winter 1993): 7.

2 Gloria Bird, "Telling: The Changing Climate in American Indian Literature," *Indian Artist* (Fall 1995): 65.

3 Angel Florez, "Magic Realism in Spanish American Fiction," *Hispania* 38 (May 2, 1955): 190.
4 Leslie Marmon Silko, "Bingo Big," *The Nation* (June 12, 1995), 857.

References

Brown, Dee. *Bury My Heart at Wounded Knee*. New York: Holt, Rinehart, and Winston, 1970.

Debo, Angie. *A History of the Indians of the United States*. Norman: University of Oklahoma Press, 1970.

Gardner, John. *On Moral Fiction*. New York: Basic Books, 1978.

Gramsci, Antonio. *Further Selections from the Prison Notebooks*. Edited by Derek Boothman. Minneapolis: University of Minnesota Press, 1995.

Vizenor, Gerald. "The Ruins of Representation." *American Indian Quarterly* 17 (1993): 1–17.

Cultural Imperialism and
the Marketing of Native America
LAURIE ANNE WHITT

In 1992, mainstream Euro-America demonstrated the short, selective, and sanitized character of both the national memory and the official history that sustains it by celebrating an anniversary: the Columbus Quincentenary, the "discovery" of the "New World." The vast majority of activities generated by this event were festive and culturally self-congratulatory. Yet there were powerful sub-currents of protest, indigenous and otherwise, in wide evidence, contesting the sharply edited, profoundly revisionist nature of the commemoration. They drove home the moral and methodological implications of the fact that history is not only written from a particular standpoint, but that that standpoint has been of the colonizers, not the colonized.[1] The response of Native America was also a determined assertion of presence and continuity, pointedly captured by the defiant counter spilling over with T-shirts, posters, and bumper stickers: "Still Here! Celebrating 49,500 years . . . before Columbus."

Partly as a result of these cultural dynamics, the writing of history has become more problematic within the general public's awareness. Some began openly to question longstanding practices, notably the racist dimensions of the continued stereotyping of Indian people by Hollywood, the media, and the sporting world.[2] Yet many deeply disturbing aspects of contemporary Western/indigenous cultural relations were left largely unexamined and unquestioned. One of these is a particularly virulent form of cultural imperialism—the marketing of Native America and, most tellingly, of Native spirituality.

Consider, for example, that a leading figure of the New Age recently announced he intended to patent the sweat lodge ceremony since Native people were no longer performing it correctly.[3] Could he receive intellectual property protection from the U.S. government for the sweat lodge ceremony, acquiring the right to prohibit Native people from performing it? To sue them if they do so? Astoundingly, it is at least legally arguable that he could, thereby placing himself in a position to limit the access of Native peoples to their own cultural expressions.[4] Yet, were such to occur, it would be only an escalation (albeit a particularly egregious one) of a phenomenon already deeply entrenched in Western culture, the commodification of indigenous spirituality. The transformation of indigenous spiritual knowledge, objects, and rituals into commodities, and their commercial exploitation, constitute a concrete manifestation of the more general, and chronic, marketing of Native America.[5]

Cultural imperialism is one of a number of oppressive relations that may hold between dominant and subordinated cultures.[6] Whether or not it is conscious and intentional, it serves to extend the political power, secure the social control, and further the economic profit of the dominant culture. The commodification of indigenous spirituality is a paradigmatic instance of cultural imperialism. As such, it plays a politically vital diversionary role, serving to colonize and assimilate the knowledge and belief systems of indigenous cultures. Ultimately, it facilitates a type of cultural acquisition via conceptual assimilation: Euro-American culture seeks to establish itself in indigenous cultures by appropriating, mining and redefining what is distinctive, constitutive of them. The mechanism for this is an oft-repeated pattern of cultural subordination that turns vitally on legal and popular views of ownership and property, as formulated within the dominant culture.

Marketing native America

Whether peddled by white shamans, plastic medicine men and women, opportunistic academics, entrepreneurs, or enterprising New Agers, Indian spirituality—like Indian lands before it—is rapidly being reduced to the status of a commodity, seized and sold. Sacred ceremonies and ceremonial objects can be purchased at weekend medicine conferences or via mail order catalogs.[7] How-to books with veritable recipes for conducting traditional rituals are written and dispensed by trade publishers.[8] A succession of born-again medicine people have—with greater or lesser subtlety—set themselves and their services up for hire, ready to sell their spiritual knowledge and power to anyone willing and able to meet their price.[9] And a literary cult of Indian identity appropriation known as white shamanism continues to be practiced.[10] Instead of contributing to the many Native-run organizations devoted to enhancing the lives and prospects of Indian people, New Agers are regularly enticed into contributing to the continued expropriation and exploitation of Native culture by purchasing an array of items marketed as means for enhancing their knowledge of Indian spirituality.

Recently, the National Congress of American Indians (an organization not exactly known for radicalism) issued a "declaration of war" against "non-Indian wannabes, hucksters, cultists, commercial profiteers and self-styled New Age shamans" who have been exploiting sacred knowledge and rituals.[11] Throughout Indian Country, eloquent, forceful critiques of these cultural developments have been mounted. Writers, intellectuals, activists, and spiritual leaders have joined in identifying and resisting what has been described as "a new growth industry . . . known as 'American Indian Spiritualism'" (henceforth AIS).[12] The phenomena being protested are diverse and include literary, artistic, scholarly, and commercial products intended for consumption in the markets of popular culture as well as in those of the cultural elite.[13]

When the spiritual knowledge, rituals, and objects of historically subordinated cultures are transformed into commodities, economic and political power merge to produce cultural imperialism. A form of oppression exerted by a dominant society upon other cultures, and typically a source of economic profit, cultural imperialism secures and deepens the subordinated status of those cultures. In the case of indigenous cultures, it undermines their integrity and distinctiveness, assimilating them to the dominant culture by seizing and processing vital cultural resources, then remaking them in the image and marketplaces of the dominant culture. Such "taking of the essentials of cultural lifeways," Geary Hobson observes, "is as imperialistic as those simpler forms of theft, such as the theft of homeland by treaty."[14]

It is phenomenon that spans native North America, sparking the fierce resistance of indigenous people in Canada as well as the United States. Lenore Keeshig-Tobias, a Toronto-based Ojibwa poet and storyteller, is a founding member of the Committee to Re-establish the Trickster, an organization devoted to reclaiming the Native voice in literature. The Canadian cultural industry, she protests, "is stealing—unconsciously, perhaps, but with the same devastating results—native stories as surely as the missionaries stole our religion and the politicians stole our land and the residential schools stole our language. . . . (It) amount(s) to cultural theft, theft of voice,."[15] Wendy Rose makes it plain that the issue here is not that "only Indians can make valid observations on themselves" and their cultures; rather, it is "one of integrity and intent": "We accept as given that whites have as much prerogative to write and speak about us and our cultures as we have to write and speak about them and theirs. The question is how this is done and . . . why it is done."[16] Some forms of cultural imperialism are the product of academic privilege and opportunism. The "name of Truth or Scholarship" may be invoked, the cause of scholarly progress, of advancing knowledge.[17] Ojibwa author Gerald Vizenor reproaches the "culture cultists (who) have hatched and possessed distorted images of tribal cultures."[18] Their obsession with the tribal past, he contends, "is not an innocent collection of arrowheads, not a crude map of public camp sites in sacred places, but rather a statement of academic power and control over tribal images."[19] Sometimes the cause is one of ethical progress, of moral duty: "Given the state of the world today, we all have not only the right but the obligation to pursue all forms of spiritual insight. . . . [I]t seems to me that I have as much right to pursue and articulate the belief systems of

Native Americans as they do."[20] On this reading, the colonization of indigenous knowledge and belief systems (and the attendant economic profit that their repackaging brings in the marketplaces of the dominant culture) is not only morally permissible, it is morally mandated.

Whatever its form, cultural imperialism often plays a diversionary role that is politically advantageous, for it serves to extend—while effectively diverting attention from—the continued oppression of indigenous peoples. Acoma Pueblo writer Simon Ortiz underscores this aspect of the phenomenon. Condemning white shamanism as a "process of colonialism" and a "usurping (of) the indigenous power of the people," he charges that

> symbols are taken and are popularized, diverting attention from real issues about land and resources and Indian peoples' working hours. The real struggle is really what should be prominent, but no, it's much easier to talk about drums and feathers and ceremonies and those sorts of things. "Real Indians," but "real Indians" only in quotes, stereotypes, and "interesting exotica." . . . So it's a rip-off.[21]

Keeshig-Tobias refers to it as "escapist" and a "form of exorcism," enabling Canadians "to look to an ideal native living in never-never land" rather than confront "the horrible reality of native-Canadian relations."[22] The extent to which cultural imperialism turns on conceptual colonization, and what is ultimately at stake in this, has been succinctly captured by Oneida scholar Pam Colorado. She contends that the commodification of indigenous spirituality enables the dominant culture to supplant Indian people even in the area of their own spirituality. This moves beyond ensuring their physical subordination to securing absolute ideological/conceptual subordination. If this continues, "non-Indians will have complete power to define what is and is not Indian, even for Indians. . . . When this happens, the last vestiges of real Indian society and Indian rights will disappear. Non-Indians will then own our heritage and ideas as thoroughly as they now claim to own our land and resources.[23] Some practitioners of AIS are genuinely surprised when they are charged with arrogance, theft, hucksterism. They see themselves as respect-fully "sharing" indigenous spirituality, even as they make a living on its commercialization, charging hefty fees to "share" their version of the pipe ceremony and the sweat lodge, and to sponsor New Agers through vision quests. Moreover, they see nothing problematic in this behavior, castigating their critics as "advocates of censorship . . . trying to shackle artistic imagination" or as "Indian fundamentalists" guilty of "reverse racism" and of a selfish refusal to share traditional knowledge.[24] This last is to massively distort what is at issue and the source of indigenous concern. The Traditional Elders Circle, meeting at the Northern Cheyenne Nation, is very clear on the point:

> [T]he authority to carry . . . sacred objects is given by the people, and the purpose and procedure is specific to time and the needs of the people. . . . [P]rofit is not the motivation. . . . We concern ourselves only with those who use spiritual ceremonies with non-Indian people for profit. There are many things to be shared with the Four Colors of humanity in our common destiny as one with the Mother Earth. It is this sharing that must be consid-ered with great care by the Elders and the medicine people who carry the Sacred Trusts.[25]

That those engaged in the buying and selling of products generated by the AIS industry fail to recognize their behavior as reprehensible suggests that the diversionary function of cultural imperialism is operative at the individual level as well, where it deflects critical self-reflection.[26] Hobson speaks of this as an "assumption . . . that one's 'interest' in an Indian culture makes it okay . . . to collect 'data' from Indian people."[27] Ward Churchill describes a comparable devel-opment. New Age practitioners of AIS, he maintains, "have proven themselves willing to disregard the rights of American Indians to any modicum of cultural sanctity or psychological sanctuary. They . . . willingly and consistently disregard the protests and objections of

their victims, speaking only of their own 'right to know' "[28] He characterizes the process as one of self-deception. Their task is to simultane-
ously hang on to what has been stolen while "separating themselves
from the *way* in which it was stolen. It is a somewhat tricky psychological project of being able to 'feel good about themselves' . . . through
legitimizing the maintenance of their own colonial privilege."[29] Such
posturing effectively hides or diverts individuals' attention from the
nature and consequences of their behavior. It is, in Renato Rosaldo's
terms, grounded on a courting of nostalgia, wherein the agents of
colonialism yearn for what they themselves have altered or transformed. "Imperialist nostalgia" has a paradoxical element to it:

> [S]omeone deliberately alters a form of life, and then regrets that
> things have not remained as they were prior to the intervention.
> At one remove, people destroy their environment, and then they
> worship nature. In any of its versions, imperialist nostalgia uses
> a pose of "innocent yearning" both to capture people's imagi-
> nations and to conceal its complicity with often brutal domi-
> nation.[30]

This nostalgia is integral to the cultivation of self-deception. It is a
"particularly appropriate emotion to invoke in attempting to establish one's innocence and at the same time talk about what one has
destroyed."[31]

The cultural politics of ownership
When confronted by their critics, those engaged in the marketing
of Native America frequently do attempt to justify their behavior.
From their reasoning and rhetoric we can elicit some distinctive
features of this variant of cultural imperialism. What we will find
is a rationale that has reverberated throughout the history of domi-
nant/indigenous relations, one that starkly reveals how the cultural
politics of ownership are played out in the context of oppression.

Consider Gary Snyder's response to indigenous protests. "Spirituality is not something that can be 'owned' like a car or a house," he

asserts. It "belongs to all humanity equally."[32] To Alberto Manguel's response to Keeshig-Tobias: "No one," he contends, "can 'steal' a story because stories don't belong to anyone. Stories belong to everyone. . . . No one . . . has the right to instruct a writer as to what stories to tell."[33] Yet those who write and copyright "Native" stories, those white shamans who sell poetry that "romanticize(s) their 'power' as writers to inhabit (Indian) souls and consciousness," and those culture capitalists who traffic in "Indian" rituals and sacred objects are all clearly making individual profit on what "no one" (allegedly) owns.[34] Such responses are both diversionary and delusionary. They attempt to dictate the terms of the debate by focusing attention on issues of freedom of speech and thought and deflecting it from the active commercial exploitation and the historical realities of power that condition current dominant/indigenous relations. In the words of Margo Thunderbird, "They came for our land, for what grew or could be grown on it, for the resources in it, and for our clean air and pure water. They stole these things from us . . . and now . . . they've come for the very last of our possessions; now they want our pride, our history, our spiritual traditions. They want to rewrite and remake these things, to claim them for themselves."[35] The colonists indeed displayed an array of motivations regarding their presence and conduct in America, and it is similar to that of the AIS practitioners currently vending Native Americana. The prospect of profits from speculation lured some to seize Native lands; others, wanting to escape poverty and enhance their lives, regarded themselves as merely "sharing" underused lands; most found it convenient to believe that the indigenous inhabitants of this continent could have no legitimate claims to land.[36]

Analogous reasoning and rhetoric accompany numerous parallel tales of acquisition in contemporary Western/indigenous relations. By examining some of these, we can better elicit the specious justificatory appeals on which cultural imperialism relies to extend and legitimize such practice. Their cumulative weight suggests that cultural imperialism, in its late capitalist mode, requires a legitimating rationale, one that enables the dominant culture to mask the fundamentally oppressive nature of its treatment of subordinated cultures. This rationale is fashioned by invoking legal and popular views of ownership and property prevalent in Euro-American culture and conceptually imposing these on indigenous cultures. It may take one, and usually both, of two forms—an appeal to common property and an appeal to private property. In the first, the dominant culture enhances its political power, social control, and economic profit by declaring the (material, cultural, genetic) resources of indigenous cultures to be common property, freely available to everyone. Thus, whatever the dominant culture finds desirable in indigenous cultures is declared to be part of the "public domain." The second appeal accomplishes the same ends through opposing means, facilitating privatization and the transformation of valued indigenous resources into commodity form. These appeals lie at the heart of cultural imperialism. As we will see, they commonly function in tandem, with the former preparing and paving the way for the latter. Three examples will be examined: (1) the copyrighting of traditional indigenous music; (2) the patenting of indigenous genetic resources; and (3) the patenting of human cell lines of indigenous people themselves. We will see how, through the development of the notion of intellectual property and the articulation of intellectual property laws, the established legal system extends and enforces the practice of cultural imperialism. First, however, to facilitate appreciation of where these examples fall on the continuum of expropriative strategies invoked by Euro-American culture, I offer a few remarks about some of their historical antecedents.

In an earlier day, imperial powers could appeal to three competing legal theories of territorial acquisition to justify their claims to sovereignty over new lands: occupation, conquest, and cession. The first of these, unlike the other two, required that the land be *terra nullius,* devoid of people. According to Blackstone, "if an uninhabited country be discovered and planted by English subjects, all the English laws then in being . . . are immediately there in force."[37] Declaring that the land belonged to no one set the stage for its conversion into private or individual property—a legally protected possession. But other legitimating rationales for the privatizing of property were needed, particularly to accommodate other types of property in addition to land. By declaring the intellectual and cultural properties of indigenous peoples to be in the public domain—that is, to belong to everyone—the stage is equally well set for their conversion into private property. These two rationales (*terra nullius* and public domain) clearly resemble each other. The notion of property belonging to no one is the functional equivalent of the notion of property belonging to everyone; they both serve as the terms of a conversion process that results in the privatization of property. However, while the concept of *terra nullius* enabled the privatizing only of lands, the notion that property in the public domain could come to be owned by individuals applies to other types of property as well, such as intellectual and cultural property. The latter conversion process is addressed below; it might thus be regarded as a legal theory of cultural acquisition, whereby Western intellectual property rights are invoked in the interests of cultural imperialism in order to appropriate valued intangible indigenous resources.

The politics of property is the central historical dynamic mediating Euro-American/indigenous relations. Certainly one of the more obvious examples of this is the General Allotment Act of 1887, which served to privatize communally owned tribal lands. A more recent case is that of the struggle to protect Newe Segobia (Western Shoshone homelands) from further encroachment by the U.S. government. It is a struggle at least as old as the 1863 Treaty of Ruby Valley, in which the U.S. first acknowledged Native title to the land. The Western Shoshone have steadfastly refused payment for the subsequent theft of a large portion of their land, rejecting the government's offer of $26 million in damages for land taken by "gradual encroachment." The eight-hundred-acre cattle ranch of Mary and Carrie Dann has been a focal point in this controversy.

In the early 1970s, the Dann sisters were told that their cattle were trespassing on "public range land" and that they must purchase federal grazing permits to run livestock on "public land." (The terms *public lands* and *public domain lands* designate lands that are subject to sale or other disposal under the general laws of the U.S. or the states.)[38] They have been locked in lawsuits ever since. Their home has been raided by federal agents, their livestock impounded, and their brother imprisoned. They were also recently awarded the "alternative Nobel Peace Prize" by the Stockholm-based Right Livelihood Foundation.[39] Says Carrie Dann, "The real issue is that the United States is attempting to claim control over sovereign Western Shoshone land and people. Our land has never been ceded or deeded to the U.S., so it's not possible for them just to take it and determine that our title to the land has been extinguished."[40]

But the politics of property has never been confined to land. Consider the struggle between Euro-American and indigenous cultures over the ownership of human remains. Since the U.S. claims title to all "cultural property" found on federal public lands, material items of indigenous cultures discovered on these lands belong to the U.S. government, provided that they are at least one hundred years of age.[41] This includes human skeletal materials, which find themselves—together with these other items—thereby transformed into the "archaeological resources" of the dominant culture.[42] Ultimate authority to regulate the disposition of such "resources" rests with the secretary of the interior, according to the Archaeological Resources Protection Act of 1979.[43] Moreover, since the majority of states do not strictly regulate the excavation of Native graves and sacred sites on state or private lands, private landowners have historically been at liberty to sell, destroy, or otherwise dispose of any material remains of indigenous cultures as they saw fit or profitable.[44]

Thus, whether it is legally permissible to dig up a grave, or to display or sell the contents of it, will turn in part on whether that grave is in an Indian or non-Indian cemetery. This discriminatory treatment of skeletal remains has been noted by various critics. C. Dean Higginbotham has observed that "only the burial and religious sites of Native Americans are regularly subjected to archaeological excavation and study in the United States."[45] Walter Echo-Hawk concurs: "If human remains and burial offerings of Native people are so easily desecrated and removed, wherever located, while the sanctity of the final resting place of other races is strictly protected, it is obvious that Native burial practices and associated beliefs were never considered during the development of American property law."[46] Cultural imperialism, then, embraces a spectrum of expropriative strategies. At one end of this spectrum we find legal theories of acquisition that facilitate the dominant culture's ownership of indigenous land and of the material remains of indigenous peoples within the land. At the other end, we find theories of acquisition that rely on laws of intellectual property to legitimate the privatization of less tangible indigenous resources. We can turn now to three examples in which the legitimating rationale of public domain is invoked to provide moral and legal cover for the theft of indigenous cultural and genetic resources.

Musical piracy and letters of marque

Like the rest of U.S. property law, music copyright is based on an individualized conception of ownership. Existing copyright law fails to acknowledge any rights of indigenous communities to their traditional music. Indeed, the United States is among the most reluctant of nations to "consider changes in the copyright law which would give broad rights to intellectual property for 'traditional' rather than individually created culture."[47] Traditional indigenous music is considered to be in the "public domain" and so not subject to copyright.[48] Anyone may borrow extensively from materials in the public domain. Moreover, entire works may be "borrowed" from the public domain and receive copyright protection provided the author or composer has contributed some "modicum of creative work" and is able to meet the "originality" requirement.[49] Originality has been interpreted minimally: A work has originality if it is "one man's alone."[50] Any "distinguishable variation" of a prior work "will constitute sufficient originality to support a copyright if such variation is the product of the author's independent efforts, and is more than merely trivial."[51]

The threshold for originality is particularly low in music: "[A] musical composition is original if it is 'the spontaneous, unsuggested result of the author's imagination.' "[52] It may be achieved by slight variations in the use of rhythm, harmony, accent, or tempo.

Thus, as Anthony Seeger protests, "the real issue is . . . the economic and cultural exploitation of one group by another group or individual." Under existing copyright law,

> there is nothing illegal about taking a piece of "traditional" music, modifying it slightly, performing it, and copyrighting it. When music is owned by indigenous people it is seen as "public domain." If it becomes popular in its "mainstream" form, though, it suddenly becomes "individual property." The song brings a steady income to the person who individualized it, not to the people from whose culture it is derived.[53]

While others are free to copy the original indigenous song with impunity, were someone to attempt to copy the "original" copy (now transformed into the legally protected individual property of a composer who has "borrowed" it from the indigenous "public domain"), he or she would be subject to prosecution for copyright infringement.[54] This includes any members of the indigenous community of the song's origin who cannot meet the requirements of "fair use."[55]

According to the Universal Declaration of Human Rights, "Everyone has the right to the protection of the moral and material interests resulting from any scientific, literary or artistic production of which he is the author."[56] Copyright, then, is recognized as a human right but only as an individual human right. Since copyright laws turn on identifying specific individuals who have produced the work to be copyrighted, they afford no protection to the traditional music of indigenous communities. In response to this, a United Nations agency—the World Intellectual Property Rights Organization (WIPO)—proposed in 1984 a set of "Model Provisions for National Laws on the Protection of Expressions of Folklore against Illicit Exploitation and Other Prejudicial Actions." (In this context, the term *folklore* refers to traditions that transcend the lifespan of individuals. To receive protection, moreover, they need not be "reduced to material form.")[57] Recognizing that "no share of the returns from . . . exploitation is conceded to the communities who have developed and maintained" their traditions, the model provisions would treat as a punishable offense any unauthorized use or willful distortion of folkloric traditions that is "prejudicial to the cultural interests of the community concerned."[58] A review of the model provisions by a U.N. group of experts concluded that, despite a desperate need for protections of this nature, an international treaty would be premature, since there were no (1) workable mechanisms for resolving disputes or (2) appropriate sources for identifying the folkloric expressions to be protected. Accordingly, to date, no country has adopted these provisions; they remain proposals for member states. As Darrell Posey notes, acquiescence to such arguments is "akin to allowing people to steal property whenever the owner has failed to announce his or her possession."[59]

Current copyright laws not only fail to protect the intellectual property of indigenous communities but directly facilitate cultural imperialism by consigning traditional music to the public domain, then providing for its facile "conversion" to private property. In such circumstances, copyrights offer legal and intellectual cover for cultural theft. They give an aura of legitimacy to the privateering activities of individuals who, like Blackbeard and Henry Morgan, have been granted letters of marque and reprisal by the government "so that they could do whatever they wanted."[60] Two critics of the music copyright system have recently demonstrated an emerging pattern in this regard: "[S]ongs from small countries are often picked up and exploited internationally, with the original collector or publisher claiming the copyright on the 'first there, first claim' principle, and with the original *local* composers or 'collectors' getting left out."[61] Their evidence includes various examples of the appropriation by American artists and record companies of the traditional music of the Caribbean, where profits on a single calypso song can easily run in the millions without any of this flowing back to the peoples or countries of its origin. They document in detail the confusion and exploitation that results when "international copyright systems . . . come into conflict with traditional thinking."

> [T]he identity of the actual composer becomes irrelevant in the traditional [calypsonian] system. This "positive" public domain attitude can of course be totally exploited by the legally wise when exposed to a system where the first registered copyright claimant is accepted as the legal owner. . . . It's not easy to merge the cultural norms of a society where music is regarded as a gift to the public with the legal norms of a society where individual ownership is the holiest pinnacle![62]

Genetic imperialism and the "common heritage"

In what has been described as "the last great resource rush," commercial seed and drug industries are extracting, transforming, and commodifying the valuable genetic resources of indigenous peoples.[63] This time around, it is not land or natural resources that imperialism has targeted but indigenous genetic wealth and pharmaceutical knowledge. Indigenous peoples inhabit the most genetically diverse areas of the world, and, once again, "their areas, and their knowledge, are . . . being mined—for information. Unless indigenous rights to this material and knowledge are respected, this gene rush will leave indigenous people in the same hole as the other resource rushes."[64] Corporate and academic scientists engaged in "gene-hunting" and "chemical prospecting" first mine indigenous medicinal and agricultural knowledge. They then identify and extract selected plant materials, process these in laboratories and finally through the legal system—ultimately transforming them into commodities and legally protected private property, for whose use indigenous people must pay. The key first step is to declare that these indigenous genetic resources belong to everyone. As the "common heritage of humankind . . . to be traded as a 'free good' among the community of nations," they are "not owned" by any one people and are quite literally a part of our human heritage from the past."[65] Thus, they are "looked upon as a public good for which no payment is necessary or appropriate."[66] One may then convert these free "public" goods into private property and a source of enormous economic profit.

A current example is the use by the Uru-eu-wau-wau Indians of Brazil of the bark of the Tike-Uba tree in a preparation that acts as an anticoagulant.[67] Reportedly, a large U.S.-based chemical company is attempting to patent these properties of the plant, following a study by corporate scientists of sap and bark specimens provided to them by members of the Goiana Institute for Prehistory and Anthropology.[68] The Uru-eu-wau-wau, protesting this commercialization of their knowledge, are challenging that company's right to patent their traditional medicines.[69] However, as Janet McGowan notes, "much like Columbus' voyage, when it comes to U.S. patent law, it isn't always a question of getting there first, but having the resources to control and protect your discovery. . . . U.S. patent law really protect(s) (and financially reward[s]) the discovery of the known."[70] Despite the fact that some 80 percent of the world's population relies on traditional health care based on medicinal plants and that 74 percent of contemporary drugs have the same or related uses in Western medicine as they do in traditional medical systems, the pharmaceutical knowledge and medicinal skills of indigenous peoples are neither acknowledged nor rewarded. As one commentator observes, "Traditional remedies . . . are products of human knowledge. To transform a plant into medicine, one has to know the correct species, its location, the proper time of collection . . . , the part to be used, how to prepare it . . . , the solvent to be used . . . , the way to prepare it . . . , and, finally, posology . . . curers have to diagnose and select the right medicine for the right patients."[71] Yet, while indigenous pharmaceutical knowledge, like industrial knowledge, has been accumulated by trial and error, "it has been made public with no patent rights attached. . . . What are the ethics behind recording customary knowledge and making it publicly available without adequate compensation?"[72] Such questions are all the more pressing because, often, this knowledge is obtained from specialists in the indigenous community only after the scientist "has established credibility within that society and a position of trust with the specialist."[73] Research in ethnopharmacology cannot ignore the omnipresence of pharmaceutical corporations eager "to analyze, develop, and market plant products," to secure "exclusive rights to pertinent information" collected.[74] While some ethnopharmacologists have worked to develop products managed by indigenous communities, others have been accused of "stealing valuable plant materials and appropriating esoteric plant knowledge for financial profit and professional advancement."[75] Witting or not, this collusion of Western science, business, and legal systems is a potent extractive device:

> [C]ontemporary patent systems tend to disregard the creative intelligence of peoples and communities around the world. Thus the Western scientific and industrial establishment freely benefits from a steady flow of people nurtured genetic material and associated knowledge, and, at times, after only a superficial tinkering, reaps enormous economic profits through patents, without even token recognition, and much less economic reward to the rightful owners of such resources.[76]

Rural sociologist Jack Kloppenburg describes this phenomenon as "the commodification of the seed."[77] He notes that scientists from the advanced industrial nations have, for more than two centuries, appropriated plant genetic resources, yet, "[d]espite their tremendous utility, such materials have been obtained free of charge as the 'common heritage,' and therefore common good, of humanity. On the other hand, the elite cultivars developed by the commercial seed industries . . . are accorded the status of private property. They are commodities obtainable by purchase."[78] The process wholly discounts the tremendous investment of generations of indigenous labor that is involved in the cultivation of specific plant varieties for their medicinal and nutrient value.[79] It credits solely the "chop shop" laboratory labor of corporate and academic scientists who "modify" what they have taken. Victoria Tauli-Corpus, representing indigenous peoples at a meeting of the U.N. Commission on Sustainable Development (CSD), underscores the exploitation and skewed reasoning that is at work:

> Without our knowing these seeds and medicinal plants were altered in laboratories and now we have to buy these because companies had them patented. . . . We are told that the companies have intellectual property rights over these genetic plant materials because they improved on them. This logic is beyond us. Why is it that we, indigenous peoples who have developed and preserved these plants over thousands of years, do not have the rights to them anymore because the laboratories altered them?[80]

The "vampire project": patenting indigenous people

There seems to be little that is indigenous that is not potentially intellectual property.[81] This includes indigenous people themselves or, more exactly, indigenous cell lines. The Human Genome Organization (HUGO) is currently engaged in an NIH-sponsored effort to map and sequence the human genome. This $3 billion project is supposed to be completed in fifteen years. Since the project does not consider population-level variation, a collateral study has been proposed—a "genetic survey of vanishing peoples" known as the Human Genome Diversity Project (HGDP).[82] It proposes to create thousands of cell lines from DNA collected from "rapidly disappearing indigenous populations."[83] Some 722 indigenous communities have been targeted for "collection."[84]

A recent article in *Science* presents the following rationale for such a study:

> Indigenous peoples are disappearing across the globe. . . . As they vanish, they are taking with them a wealth of information buried in their genes about human origins, evolution, and diversity. . . . [E]ach (population) offers "a window into the past" . . . a unique glimpse into the gene pool of our ancestors. . . . Already, there are indications of the wealth of information harbored in the DNA of aboriginal peoples.[85]

Sir Walter Bodmer, HUGO's president, refers to the proposed survey (dubbed the "vampire project" by indigenous delegates to the United Nations) as "a cultural obligation of the genome project."[86] At an HGDP workshop on "Ethical and Human Rights Implications," it was suggested that sampling begin "with the least politically risky groups. . . . If the Project does not proceed carefully and properly, it could spoil the last good opportunity to obtain some of this data."[87] What are "proper procedures?" Dr. Paul Weiss, an anthropologist, proposed the following strategy, according to the summary report: " 'Immortalization' can be a very sensitive term and should be avoided when talking about the intended creation of cell lines. (Someone suggested using "transformation," the standard European practice.) Whether to tell people what you intend to do, as a technical matter, is a difficult question."[88] Not surprisingly, Native rights activists such as Jeanette Armstrong of Canada's En'owkin Center describe the ethics committee as "a P.R. operation for the project."[89]

Indigenous opposition has been extensive and emphatic. After heated debate with Stanford law professor Henry Greely, chair of the HGDP ethics subcommittee, the 1993 Annual Assembly of the World Council of Indigenous Peoples unanimously resolved to "categorically reject and condemn the HGDP as it applies to our rights, lives, and dignity."[90] In January 1994, John Liddle, director of the Central Australian Aboriginal Congress, protested, "If the Vampire Project goes ahead and patents are put on genetic material from Aboriginal people, this would be legalized theft. Over the last 200 years, non-Aboriginal people have taken our land, language, culture and health—even our children. Now they want to take the genetic material which makes us Aboriginal people as well."[91] And at the June 1993 session of the CSD, indigenous representatives described the HGDP as "very alarming": "[W]e are calling for a stop to the Human Genome Diversity Project which is basically an appropriation of our lives and being as indigenous peoples."[92] Project opponents

> believe we are endangered. . . . After being subjected to ethnocide and genocide for 500 years (which is why we are endangered), the

alternative is for our DNA to be collected and stored. This is just a more sophisticated version of how the remains of our ancestors are collected and stored in museums and scientific institutions.

Why don't they address the causes of our being endangered instead of spending $20 million for five years to collect and store us in cold laboratories. If this money will be used instead to provide us with basic social services and promote our rights as indigenous peoples, then our biodiversity will be protected.[93]

They also raised concerns about patenting and commercial exploitation: "How soon will it be before they apply for IPRS to these genes and sell them for a profit?"[94]

The legitimacy of these concerns is without question. Indeed, the U.S. Centers for Disease Control and Prevention (CDC) had *already*, in November 1991, applied for a patent to a cell line created from a Guaymi woman. They did so because of its commercial promise and since "the government encourages scientists to patent anything of interest."[95] However, lack of commercial interest, together with pressure from indigenous organizations and their supporters, prompted the CDC to abandon its application in 1993.[96] The Canadian-based Rural Advancement Foundation International (RAFI) was responsible for discovering the patent application and sounding the alarm regarding it, noting that it "represented the sort of profiteering from the biological inheritance of indigenous people that could become commonplace as a result of the proposed Human Genome Diversity Project."[97]

The justifactory rhetoric embedded in these examples is essentially the same as that invoked by those we encountered at the outset of this essay who are actively engaged in the marketing of indigenous spirituality. In all of these cases, appeals to common property, private property, and usually both in succession constitute the legitimating rationale of cultural imperialism. It enables the dominant culture to secure political and social control as well as to profit economically from the cultural and genetic resources of indigenous cultures. Just as the concept of *terra nullius* once provided legal and moral cover for the imperial powers' treatment of indigenous peoples, the concept of public domain plays a comparable role in late capitalism.

As we have seen, far from being mutually exclusive, these appeals function together to facilitate a conversion, or privatization, process. When intellectual property laws of the dominant culture are imposed on indigenous peoples, the first appeal to common property or the public domain lays the legal groundwork for the private ownership secured by the second. What "flows out . . . as the 'common heritage of mankind' . . . returns as a commodity."[98] This is a particularly effective strategy for acquiring desired but intangible indigenous resources—medicinal and spiritual knowledge, ceremonies, artistic expressions. Ownership of such intangibles may in turn (as in the case of genetic information) lead to control of, and denial of indigenous access to, tangible resources. This is not only "legal theft" of indigenous resources; it is legally sanctioned and facilitated theft. As Vandana Shiva comments, "[C]ommunities have invested . . . centuries of care, respect, and knowledge" in developing these resources, yet "today, this material and knowledge heritage is being stolen under the garb of IPRS (intellectual property rights). IPRS are a sophisticated name for modern piracy."[99] The payoff of imperialistic cultural practice is substantial. There is considerable economic profit to be reaped from the commodification and marketing of indigenous cultural resources. It is also politically invaluable. As the established legal system extends and enforces the practice of cultural imperialism, it brings with it its own legitimating rationale. This, simply put, is a way of speaking about and thinking about what is going on—a rhetoric and a reasoning that plays a politically diversionary role as, at the individual level, it nurtures self-deception.[100] Ultimately, the two appeals explored here constitute a logic of domination—a structure of fallacious reasoning that seeks to justify subordination. The dominant conceptual framework is held to have certain features that indigenous frameworks lack and that render it superior. Such alleged superiority, it is assumed, justifies the assimilation of those frameworks and cultures to it.[101]

This logic of domination figures vitally in the marketing of Native America. If strategies of resistance to it are to be effective, they must be situated within the broader social context that informs it. The extension of the commodity form to new areas is one of the principal historical processes associated with the political economy of capitalism. It provides a way of reproducing the social relations needed if capital is to survive and grow in a particular sector.[102] The development of the notion of intellectual property and the articulation of intellectual property laws is a significant moment in the self-expansion of capital, another instance of "the relentless extension of market assumptions into areas where the market has not ruled."[103] We are, as Christopher Lind protests, "forced to genuflect before the great god market in yet one more area of . . . life."[104] It is also a significant move in the dynamics of power that structure dominant/indigenous relations, in the growth of cultural imperialism. It wrests away from indigenous peoples the power to control their cultural, spiritual, and genetic resources. As Kloppenburg notes, "business interests in the developed nations have worked very hard over the past ten years to put in place a legal framework that ensures that genetically engineered materials . . . can be owned."[105]

Let us be clear about what is being critiqued. It is not the concepts of public domain or common heritage, nor even that of private property per se. It is a particular set of social and power relations—specifically, the dynamic of oppression and domination mediating Western and indigenous cultures—that sustains the practice of cultural imperialism. As outlined here, that practice is one wherein elements of the dominant culture's conceptual framework—notably, its concepts of ownership and property—are thrust upon indigenous cultures and enforced by the power of the state. These concepts tend to dictate the terms of the struggle, to reinforce current relations of power, and to sustain existing inequalities between dominant and indigenous cultures. Resistance to this is pronounced, adamant, and growing.

While indigenous representatives to the Commission on Sustainable Development acknowledged that many of the cultural and genetic resources of indigenous cultures can be shared with the rest of the world, they were resolute that

> we will be the ones who will determine how these will be shared based on our own conditions and our own terms. We cannot buy the arguments that we have to play within the field of existing patent and copyright laws to be able to protect our resources and knowledge. . . . Is there a way of preserving and promoting biodiversity and indigenous peoples' knowledge and technology without necessarily being pushed into the field of intellectual property rights? We are still seeking for the answers to this.[106]

The task is as daunting as it is vital. Morton Horwitz has documented how, during the post-Revolutionary War period, merchant and entrepreneurial groups rose to political and economic power, forging an alliance with the legal profession to advance their own interests through a transformation of the legal system. By the mid-nineteenth century, they had succeeded in reshaping the legal system to their own advantage and at the expense of other less powerful groups in society.[107] A comparable phenomenon appears to be currently in process at the international level. Through coercive instruments such as the GATT, the U.S. and other leading industrial nations have succeeded in furthering their interests at the expense of indigenous peoples and developing nations by strengthening Western intellectual property systems worldwide. All of this demonstrates the degree to which law, as various critical legal theorists have insisted, is a form of politics.[108] The politics of property and ownership that we have seen played out in the various examples above is ample testimony to the fact that, when it comes to dominant/indigenous relations, law has never been separate from politics. Whether as appeals to *terra nullius* or to the public domain, legal theories of acquisition have, since contact, provided the legitimating rationale for territorial and cultural imperialism and for the privatization of indigenous land

and resources. A first step in undermining this process (although it is no more than that) may be to set to rest the fractured fairy tale of a neutral, apolitical legal system.

Notes

I am grateful to Alan W. Clarke for extended discussions on the issues raised in this essay and to Jack Kloppenburg and M. Annette Jaimes Guerrero for sharing research materials with me.

1   This was nicely demonstrated by the quietly reflective and rhetorically effective query that the Mennonite community employed to raise the popular conscience: "500 Years Ago the Americans Discovered Columbus on Their Shores. How Do You Think They Felt about It?"

2   The work of the American Indian Anti-defamation Council, and of activist scholars such as Ward Churchill in *Fantasies of the Master Race,* ed. M. Annette Jaimes (Monroe, ME: Common Courage Press, 1992) and *Indians Are Us?* (Monroe ME: Common Courage Press, 1994), have been instrumental in this regard.

3   This was related by Robert Antone in "Education as a Vehicle for Values and Sovereignty," an address given at the Third International Native American Studies conference at Lake Superior State University, October 1991.

4   The more probable route would be a copyright, not a patent. See 17 U.S.C. 106 (Exclusive Rights in Copyrighted Works). This would involve reducing the ceremony to some tangible expression, then claiming authorship of it. The broad construal of the salient legal terms, especially *writings (Goldstein v. California,* 412 U.S. 546 [1973]), suggests this is feasible. However, given constitutionally protected religious freedom, any suit for copyright infringement would likely be dismissed out of hand. See also 17 U.S.C. 110 (Exemptions of Certain Performances and Displays); *Robert Stigwood Group Ltd. v. O'Reilly,* 530 F.2d 1096 (2d Cir. 1976).

5   The sale of "authentic" Indian images and "genuine handmade" trinkets reaches far into the history of Euro-American/indigenous relations.

6   Various radical theorists and social critics have alluded to cultural imperialism, although few characterize it at length. My discussion differs somewhat from that of Iris Young (in "Five Faces of Oppression," *Rethinking Power,* ed. Thomas Wartenberg [Albany NY: SUNY Press, 1992]). I agree with her that it is one of several forms of oppression, but I emphasize its impact on the cultures rather than the individuals subjected to it. I move freely in this paper between references to indigenous cultures generally and Native North

American cultures more specifically, since the practice of cultural imperialism under consideration is similarly imposed upon them. However, closer analyses of how specific historical, political, cultural, and socioeconomic circumstances condition and modify such practice are needed.

7   The crassness of this commodification is stunning, as a perusal of the Berkeley, California-based Gaia Bookstore and Catalog Company readily reveals. Their 1991 catalog, for example, offers a series of oracular Medicine Cards and Sacred Path Cards (with titles such as "Medicine Bowl," "Give-Away Ceremony," and "Dreamtime") that promise "the Discovery of Self through Native Teachings." Such spirituality, noted Osage scholar George Tinker observes, is "centered on the self, a sort of Western individualism run amok" (in David Johnston, "Spiritual Seekers Borrow Indian Ways," *New York Times,* 27 December 1993, section A), whereas Indian spirituality focuses on the larger community, the tribe, and never on the individual.

8   Two illustrative examples are John Redtail Freesoul's *Breath of the Invisible: The Way of the Pipe* (Wheaton IL: Theosophical Pub. House, 1986) and Ed McGaa's *Mother Earth Spirituality* (San Francisco: Harper Books, 1990).

9   Among born-again medicine people are Sun Bear, Wallace Black Elk, Grace Spotted Eagle, Brook Medicine Eagle, Osheana Fast Wolf, Cyfus McDonald, Dyhani Ywahoo, Rolling Thunder, and "Beautiful Painted Arrow." See Churchill's *Indians Are Us?* for a powerful critique of these and other spiritual hucksters. Consider, for example, a recent flyer advertising the 1994 Rochester workshops of Brook Medicine Eagle, who is pictured in feathers, bone, leather, and braids. The text describes her as an "American native Earthkeeper" whose book *Buffalo Woman Comes Singing* (New York: Ballantine, 1991) offers "ancient truths concerning how to live . . . in harmony with All Our Relations." She is currently offering a $150 workshop on "shamanic empowerment" to "awaken the higher level of functioning possible for two-leggeds."

10 For more extensive discussion, see Leslie Silko, "An Old-Time Indian Attack Conducted in Two Parts: Part One: Imitation 'Indian' Poems; Part Two: Gary Snyder's *Turtle Island,*" in *The Remembered Earth: An Anthology of Contemporary Native American Literature,* ed. Geary Hobson (Albuquerque: University of New Mexico Press, 1979); Wendy Rose, "Just What's All this Fuss about White Shamanism Anyway?" in *Coyote Was Here,* ed. Bo Scholer (Aarhus, Denmark: University of Aarhus Press, 1984); and Churchill's *Fantasies of the Master Race.*

11 Johnston, "Spiritual Seekers Borrow Indian Ways," 1.

12 Churchill, *Fantasies of the Master Race,* 215. Spiritual leaders include Leslie Silko, Vine Deloria, Wendy Rose, Oren Lyons, Geary Hobson, Joy Harjo,

Gerald Vizenor, Ward Churchill, Russell Means, AIM, the Circle of Elders of the Indigenous Nations of North America, and many others.

13 Christopher Lind, "The Idea of Capitalism or the Capitalism of Ideas? A Moral Critique of the Copyright Act," *Intellectual Property Journal* 7 (December 1991). Lind misunderstands the nature of this protest and of the "claim being made by aboriginal artists and writers of colour . . . that whites are 'stealing' their stories" (p. 69). He insists that "(w)hat is being stolen is not the story itself but the market for the story . . . or the possibility of being able to exploit the commercial potential" of the story. Indigenous critiques are directed against the very fact of commercialization, against the extension of the market mechanism to these cultural materials by the dominant society. The claim being made is that this continues and extends a long history of oppression, that it constitutes theft of culture, of voice, of power.

14 Hobson, *The Remembered Earth,* 101.

15 Laura Keeshig-Tobias, "Stop Stealing Native Stories," *Toronto Globe and Mail,* 26 January 1990, section A.

16 Wendy Rose, "The Great Pretenders," in *The State of Native America,* ed. M. Annette Jaimes (Boston MA: South End Press, 1992), 415–416.

17 Hobson, *The Remembered Earth,* 101. Cultural imperialism is often at its apex in the academy. As a result of the stubborn influence of positivism, knowledge claims within the dominant (academic) culture continue to be regarded as value-free. An instructive example of this is Wilcomb Washburn's "Distinguishing History from Moral Philosophy and Public Advocacy" (in *The American Indian and the Problem of History,* ed. Calvin Martin [New York: Oxford University Press, 1987]). A past president of the American Society for Ethnohistory, Washburn is particularly upset about "the process of using history to promote nonhistorical causes." He reacts with consternation to the recent call for historians to "form alliances with non-scholarly groups organized for action to solve specified societal problems," which he associates with "leftist academics" and "Indian activists" (95). Washburn offers himself as an example of a historian committed to what one is tempted to call a Great White Truth, a Truth properly cleansed of all values: "[A]ll my efforts are guided by, and subject to, the limitations of historical truth. . . . There is no place in the scholarly profession of history for such distorting lenses. History to me means a commitment to truth . . . however contradictory it may be to our . . . acquired convictions about how the world should be" (97). He assumes that his work, like his conception of truth, is unburdened by such distorting lenses and remains both value-free and politically neutral. Yet note that this work includes his "recent experiences in writing Indian history, which involve combat with radical theorists on the ideological

front"; his letters to the *Dartmouth Review* in support of the use of the Indian as a symbol; his efforts abroad to "justify United States policy . . . to spike assertions of genocide . . . to disprove the assertion that . . . multinational corporations control the United States Government and seek to exploit the resources of all native peoples against their will" (94). All this, we are to suppose, is "value-free." And he goes on to claim that some will recognize his "lifelong and quixotic pursuit of the reality of the Indian as 'noble' " (97).

18 Gerald Vizenor, "Socioacupuncture: Mythic Reversals and the Strip-tease in Four Scenes," in Martin, *The American Indian and the Problem of History,* 183.

19 Martin, *The American Indian and the Problem of History,* 183.

20 Gary Snyder, as cited in Churchill, *Fantasies of the Master Race,* 192.

21 Simon Ortiz in an interview in *Winged Words: American Indian Writers Speak,* Laura Coltelli (Lincoln NE: University of Nebraska Press, 1990), 111–112.

22 Keeshig-Tobias, "Stop Stealing Native Stories," 7.

23 Pam Colorado, as cited in Churchill, *Fantasies of the Master Race,* 101.

24 Keeshig-Tobias, "Stop Stealing Native Stories," 7; Johnston, "Spiritual Seekers Borrow Indian Ways," 15. See also, for example, Ed McGaa's comments in Johnston, "Spiritual Seekers Borrow Indian Ways," 15. Wendy Rose ("The Great Pretenders") also addresses herself to rebutting this point, noting that white shamanism has touched upon something very real and that its critics are not set on hoarding or on purposively withholding spiritual knowledge: "An entire population is crying out for help, for alternatives to the spiritual barrenness they experience. . . . They know . . . that . . . part of the answers to the questions producing their agony may be found within the codes of knowledge belonging to the native peoples of this land. Despite what they have done . . . it would be far less than Indian of us were we not to endeavor to help them. Such are our Ways, and have always been our Ways" (418).

25 Cited in Churchill, *Fantasies of the Master Race,* 223–224.

26 I refer to this facet of cultural imperialism elsewhere as a "no-fault" assumption—the belief that the literary, artistic, scholarly, and commercial products of AIS are neither epistemologically nor ethically suspect or at fault, that they are legitimate and morally unproblematic vehicles of spiritual knowledge and power. (See Laurie Anne Whitt, "Indigenous Peoples and the Cultural Politics of Knowledge," in *Issues in American Indian Cultural Identity,* ed. Michael Green [New York: Peter Lang Press, 1995]). There I also address the commodification of indigenous spirituality and develop some of the epistemological issues raised by it at greater length. In particular, I focus on some central features of the dominant knowledge system that facilitate the "no-fault" assumption, features that permit and facilitate the marketing of Native America more generally.)

27 Hobson, *The Remembered Earth,* 101.

28 Churchill, *Fantasies of the Master Race,* 210.

29 Churchill, *Fantasies of the Master Race,* 210.

30 Renato Rosaldo, *Culture and Truth* (Boston: Beacon Press, 1993), 70.

31 Rosaldo, *Culture and Truth,* 70.

32 Gary Snyder, as cited in Churchill, *Fantasies of the Master Race,* 192.

33 Alberto Manguel, "Equal Rights to Stories," *Toronto Globe and Mail,* 3 February 1990, section D.

34 Leslie Silko, as cited in Michael Castro, *Interpreting the Indian* (Albuquerque: University of New Mexico Press, 1983), 161.

35 Churchill, *Indians Are Us?* 216.

36 David Lyons, "The Balance of Injustice and the War for Independence," *Monthly Review* 45 (1945): 20.

37 Gerry Simpson, "*Maybo,* International Law, *Terra Nullius* and the Stories of Settlement: An Unresolved Jurisprudence," *Melbourne University Law Review* 19 (1993): 199.

38 *Northern Pac. Ry. Co. v. Hirzel,* 161 P. 854, 859 (Idaho 1916).

39 The Dann sisters were honored for "their courage and perseverance in asserting the right of Indigenous peoples to their land" (Valerie Taliman, "Dann Sisters Win International Award for Commitment to Native Rights," *News from Indian Country* 7:20 [1993]: 1.

40 Taliman, "Dann Sisters Win International Award," 5. More detailed consideration of this case can be found in Glenn Morris, "The Battle for Newe Segobia: The Western Shoshone Land Rights Struggle," in *Critical Issues in Native North America,* vol. 2, ed. Ward Churchill (Copenhagan: International Working Group for Indigenous Affairs [IWGIA], 1990).

41 Speaking of the Antiquities Act of 1906, Walter Echo-Hawk notes that "the underlying assumption . . . is that all 'cultural resources' located on federal land 'belong' to the United States, and can be excavated only for the benefit of public museums. There are no provisions for Native ownership or disposition." (Walter Echo-Hawk, "Museum Rights vs. Indian Rights: Guidelines for Assessing Competing Legal Interests in Native Cultural Resources," *Review of Law and Social Change* 14 [1986]: 449. See this article for a discussion of the American Indian Religious Freedom Act and its implications for ownership of native resources.) The Antiquities Act has never been formally repealed, although it has been superseded by the Archaeological Resources Protection Act of 1979.

42 The term "cultural property" is generally considered to include "objects of artistic, archaeological, ethnological, or historical interest" (John Merryman, "Two Ways of Thinking about Cultural Property," *The American*

Journal of International Law 80:4 [1986]: 831). An "archaeological resource" refers to any material remains of past human life and activities that have been determined to be of "archaeological interest." See 16 U.S.C., section 470bb(1).

43 16. U.S.C. section 470(dd). However, this act, unlike the earlier Antiquities Act, does require that Indian tribes be notified of any excavation permit that might cause harm to the cultural sites. See 16 U.S.C., section 470cc(c).

44 Indeed, according to a recent article on a Colorado development known as "Indian Camp Ranch," prospective homeowners "can now purchase land where more than 200 Anasazi sites have been identified. . . . Those who buy property . . . will also be allowed to excavate sites on their land. . . . Artifacts recovered will become the property of a museum to be built in the area. Homeowners will be allowed to display recovered artifacts in their residences, provided they are turned over to the museum upon their death" (*Archaeology,* [March/April 1995], 14). According to the state archaeologist of Colorado, such land-use plans are legal.

45 C. Dean Higginbotham, "Native Americans versus Archaeologists: The Legal Issues," *American Indian Law Review* 10 (1982): 99–100.

46 Echo-Hawk, "Museum Rights vs. Indian Rights," 448.

47 Anthony Seeger, "Singing Other Peoples' Songs," *Cultural Survival Quarterly* 15:3 (Summer 1991): 39.

48 Moreover, since the 1976 Copyright Act extends copyright protection for the lifetime of the author plus fifty years, only "recent" compositions qualify for copyright protection. See 17 U.S.C., section 302(a).

49 *Amsterdam v. Triangle Publications, Inc.,* 189 F.2d. 104, 294 (3d Cir. 1951).

50 *Bleistein v. Donaldson Lithographing Co.,* 188 U.S. 239 (1903).

51 M. B. Nimmer, as cited in Maureen Baker, "La(w)—A Note to Follow So: Have We Forgotten the Federal Rules of Evidence in Music Plagiarism Cases?" *Southern California Law Review* 65 (1992): 1590.

52 *Hirsch v. Paramount Pictures,* 17 F.Supp. 816, 817 (S.D. Cal. 1937).

53 Seeger, "Singing Other Peoples' Songs," 38.

54 See *Bleistein v. Donaldson Lithographing Co.,* 188 U.S. 239 (1903).

55 17 U.S.C., section 107 (amended 1992).

56 U.S. Constitution, Article 27 (2).

57 Darrell Posey, "Effecting International Change," *Cultural Survival Quarterly* 15:3 (Summer 1991): 31.

58 Posey, "Effecting International Change," 31.

59 Posey, "Effecting International Change," 31.

60 Jack Kloppenburg, "Conservationists or Corsairs?" *Seedling* (June/July 1992), 14.

61 Roger Wallis and Krister Malm, *Big Sounds from Small People* (New York: Pendragon Press, 1984), 190–191.

62 Wallis and Malm, *Big Sounds,* 188, 199.

63 Jason Clay, "Editorial: Genes, Genius, and Genocide," *Cultural Survival Quarterly* 14:4 (1990): 1.

64 Clay, "Genes, Genius, and Genocide," 1.

65 Norman Myers, *A Wealth of Wild Species* (Boulder CO: Westview Press, 1983), 24; Garrison Wilkes, "Current Status of Crop Germplasm," *Critical Reviews in Plant Sciences* 1:2 (1983): 156.

66 Jack Kloppenburg and Daniel Kleinman, "Seed Wars: Common Heritage, Private Property, and Political Strategy," *Socialist Review* 95 (September/October 1987): 8.

67 Kloppenburg, "No Hunting!" *Z Magazine* (September 1990), 106.

68 Clay, "Editorial: Genes, Genius, and Genocide," 1; John Jacobs et al., "Characterization of the Anticoagulant Activities from a Brazilian Arrow Poison," *Journal of Thrombosis and Haemostasis* 63:1 (1991): 34.

69 Andrew Gray "The Impact of Biodiversity Conservation on Indigenous Peoples," *Biodiversity: Social and Ecological Perspectives,* ed. Vandana Shiva (Atlantic Highlands NJ: Zed Books, 1991), 67.

70 Janet McGowan, "Who Is the Inventor?" *Cultural Survival Quarterly* 15:1 (Summer 1991): 20.

71 Elaine Elisabetsky, "Folklore, Tradition, or Know-How?" *Cultural Survival Quarterly* 15:1 (Summer 1991): 10.

72 A. B. Cunningham, "Indigenous Knowledge and Biodiversity," *Cultural Survival Quarterly* 15:1 (Summer 1991): 4.

73 Brian Boom, "Ethics in Ethnopharmacology," in *Ethnobiology: Implications and Applications,* ed. Darrell A. Posey et al. (Belém, Brazil: Proceedings of the First International Congress of Ethnobiology, 1990), 150–151.

74 Boom, "Ethics in Ethnopharmacology," 149. Defined from the perspective of the dominant science, ethnopharmacology is the "scientific study of the medicinal uses of plants and animals by human groups other than the dominant Western society" (Boom, "Ethics in Ethnopharmacology," 148).

75 Boom, "Ethics," 149.

76 GRAIN (Genetic Resources Action International), "GATT, the Convention and IPRS, *Econet,* in the conference "Biodiversity" (28 June 1994).

77 Kloppenburg, *First the Seed: The Political Economy of Plant Biotechnology, 1492–2000* (Cambridge, England: Cambridge University Press, 1988), 11.

78 Kloppenburg and Kleinman, "Seed Wars," 24.

79 This was acknowledged by Illinois congressman John Porter, who, in 1990, introduced a resolution to discontinue the ongoing GATT negotiations

regarding the extension of intellectual property rights to genetic and biological resources. The difficulty with the U.S. proposal on trade-related aspects of intellectual property rights, Porter charged, is that

> it fails to consider the value of biological and genetic material and processes in developing nations, as well as the invaluable and historic contributions of local people in the use of that material.
>
> Since these people typically do not have access to representation to ensure that their interests are protected in the GATT process, we have an obligation to recognize their rights. (John Porter, "A Resolution Affecting the GATT Negotiations on Intellectual Property Rights for Genetic and Biological Resources," *Congressional Record,* 101st Cong., 2d sess., vol. 136, no. 94 [20 July 1990], E 2425).

80 Victoria Tauli-Corpus, "We Are Part of Biodiversity, Respect Our Rights," *Third World Resurgence* 36 (1993): 25.

81 Or, for that matter, little at all. U.S. patents protect "anything under the sun made by man." New life forms have been patented (*Diamond v. Chakrabarty,* 447 U.S. 303 [1980]). And the right to patent and commercially exploit human cells, even over the protests of that individual, has been recognized (*Moore v. Regents of the University of California,* 793 P.2d 479 [Cal.1990], cert. denied 111 S.Ct. 1388 [1991]).

82 Leslie Roberts, "A Genetic Survey of Vanishing Peoples," *Science* 252 (1991): 1614.

83 Roberts, "A Genetic Survey," 1614.

84 A valuable overview of these and related developments can be found in the following RAFI (Rural Advancement Foundation International) *Communiqués*: "Patents, Indigenous Peoples, and Human Genetic Diversity," May 1993; "The Patenting of Human Genetic Material," January/February 1994; and "Gene Boutiques' Stake Claim to Human Genome," May/June 1994.

85 Roberts, "A Genetic Survey of Vanishing Peoples," 1614, 1617.

86 Roberts, "A Genetic Survey," 1614, 1615. Perhaps he refers to it thus for reasons of expediency, since, "for reasons of expediency, the human genome being mapped and sequenced (by HUGO) is essentially a Caucasian one."

87 Henry Greely, "Summary of Planning Workshop 3(B): Ethical and Human Rights Implications" (Bethesda MD: Human Genome Diversity Project Organizing Committee, 1993), 22–23.

88 Paul Weiss, as cited in Greely, "Summary of Planning Workshop 3(B)," 6.

89 Beth Burrows, "Life, Liberty and the Pursuit of Patents" *The Boycott Quarterly* 2:1 (1994): 33.

90 Burrows, "Life, Liberty," 33. HGDP was unanimously denounced at the December 1993 meeting of the World Council of Indigenous Peoples: "The assumption that indigenous people will disappear and their cells will continue helping science for decades is very abhorrent to us. . . . We're not opposed to progress. For centuries indigenous people have contributed to science and medicine, contributions that are not recognized. What upsets us is the behavior of colonization (Rodrigo Contreras, as cited in Patricia Kahn, "Genetic Diversity Project Tries Again," *Science* 266 [November 1994]: 721).

91 John Liddle, as cited in Burrows, "Life, Liberty and the Pursuit of Patents," 33–34.

92 Tauli-Corpus, "We Are Part of Biodiversity," 26.

93 Tauli-Corpus, "We Are Part of Biodiversity," 25–26.

94 Tauli-Corpus, "We Are Part of Biodiversity," 26. For a copy of the "Declaration of Indigenous Peoples of the Western Hemisphere Regarding the Human Genome Diversity Project," signed on 19 February 1995 by numerous indigenous organizations, see *Indigenous Woman* 2:2: 32–33.

95 Christopher Anderson, "While CDC Drops Indian Tissue Claim," *Science* 262 (1993): 831.

96 There are other reported cases as well. According to Miges Baumann, of Swissaid, two more patent applications by the U.S. government of indigenous cell lines (from Papua New Guinea and the Solomon Islands) exist. See Burrows, "Life, Liberty and the Pursuit of Patents," 33.

97 Anderson, "While CDC Drops Indian Tissue Claim," 831.

98 Kloppenburg and Kleinman, "Seed Wars," 25.

99 Vandana Shiva, as cited in Beth Burrows, "How Do You Spell Patent?" P-I-R-A-C-Y," *The Boycott Quarterly* 1:3 (1994): 6, 5.

100 Intellectual property policies are justified in the Constitution on utilitarian grounds as a means "to promote the progress of science and useful arts" (U.S. Constitution, art. 1, sec. 8, cl. 8). Yet the lack of evidential support for the claim that patents and copyrights have indeed effectively promoted these ends has been noted (see Gerald Dworkin, "Commentary: Legal and Ethical Issues," *Science, Technology, & Human Values* 12:1 [1987]). In its place, one is generally offered appeals to "faith" that they are doing so; for example, "Faith in the private sector's ability to produce beneficial innovations is strong at the moment" (Pamela Samuelson, "Innovation and Competition; Conflicts over Intellectual Property Rights in New Technologies," *Science, Technology & Human Values* 12:1 [1987]).

101 For a characterization of oppressive conceptual frameworks and discussion of the logic of domination, see Karen Warren," A Philosophical Perspective on the Ethics and Resolution of Cultural Properties Issues," *The Ethics of*

Collecting Cultural Property, ed. Phyllis Messenger (Albuquerque: University of New Mexico Press, 1989).

102 See Kloppenburg, *First the Seed,* and Kloppenburg and Kleinman, "Seed Wars."

103 Lind, "The Idea of Capitalism or the Capitalism of Ideas?" 70.

104 Lind, "The Idea of Capitalism," 70.

105 Kloppenburg, "No Hunting!" 106.

106 Tauli-Corpus, "We Are Part of Biodiversity," 26.

107 Morton Horwitz, *The Transformation of American Law, 1780–1860* (Cambridge MA: Harvard University Press, 1977).

108 See Joseph William Singer, "Legal Realism," *California Law Review* 76 (1988).

On Revision and Revisionism: American
Indian Representations in New Mexico

THEODORE S. JOJOLA

Just a show! The Southwest is the great playground of the white American. The desert isn't good for anything else. But it does make a fine national playground. And the Indian, with his long hair and his bits of pottery and blankets and clumsy home-made trinkets, he's a wonderful live toy to play with. More fun than keeping rabbits, and just as harmless. Wonderful, really, hopping round with a snake in his mouth. Lots of fun! Oh the wild west is lots of fun: the Land of Enchantment (D. H. Lawrence, *Just Back from the Snake Dance,* Sept. 1924 [in Weigle: 1989]).

With the advent of leisure and the touring class, New Mexico became a focus of itinerant travels. *See America First* and the *Southwest Wonder Land* were credos that resounded in a 1925 introductory chapter of *Mesa, Cañon and Pueblo.* Written by adventurer Charles Fletcher Lummis, it aptly summarized an epoch of early tourism and image-building in New Mexico. Paramount in this imagery were the numerous American Indian communities that inhabited the region.[1]

What was rather curious about this period was the two distinctive and often parallel aspects of this "Indian" image-making. One was promulgated by social scientists in the fields of anthropology, ethnography, and history. The other was developed by entrepreneurs of the tourism and film industry. Among social scientists, New Mexico became a "living laboratory." Among entrepreneurs, however, New Mexico became a "living backdrop." In both instances, the investigations were dominated by outsiders who were looking for their own affirmation of a primitive and exotic humanscape.

The common denominators were the Apache, Navajo, and Pueblo peoples, but each outside group formulated its own images of what American Indians were. In 1880, for example, historian and anthropologist Adolf Bandelier wrote of the Indians at Santo Domingo Pueblo: "The women are small, and commonly ugly; the men taller, and not very handsome."[2] Similarly, in 1912, movie director D. W. Griffith, smitten with the Southwest, was reported as remarking that "the Isleta pueblo offered some of the finest scenic opportunities ever put into a picture . . . , the best setting he had ever seen for the enactment of Biblical or western plays, especially Indian plays."[3]

Both observations were intended to be all-encompassing. In the face of the exotic and primitive, the outsider draws on his or her own preconceptions and experiences to selectively appropriate elements of the "Indian." The consequent image may be a subjective interpretation, the purpose of which is to corroborate the outsider's view. This process is called revisionism and, more often than not, it entails remaking Native people apart from their social and community realities.

The dominant Indian stereotype, of course, is the face-painted and war bonnet– and buckskin–clad "chief." This image was popularized by the paintings commissioned by the Atchison, Topeka & Sante Fe Railway in the 1900s and, with the transfer of a popular stereotype into the Southwestern context, a mystification of the local cultures was achieved.[4] The Southwest Indian myth was invented as part of an "amusement" landscape. New Mexico suddenly became populated with rattlesnakes, howling coyotes, Indian chiefs, and outlaws and the scenery became reminiscent of a large outdoor stage bounded by railroad tracks.[5]

The impact of such revisionism among the Native peoples in New Mexico was appreciable. Many Natives catered exclusively to the "Indian chief" image and, for years, social scientists voiced their concerns over the disappearance of Native traditions and culture. By the time the United States Congress interceded with the creation of the Indian Arts & Crafts Board in 1935, many Native artisans were engaged in making inferior, cheap souvenirs or operating stamp-dye machines for the fabricators of mass-marketed "Indian made" replicas.[6]

But at the same time that the social scientists were promulgating laws to protect craftspeople from commercial exploitation, they also used their scholarship to develop exacting standards of "authenticity." The movement for authenticity was tied into a mission to "preserve" archaic methods and techniques. The ensuing policies, however, were formulated behind closed doors without input from the craftspeople themselves. As a consequence, standards of tribal artistic aesthetics were established which often had little to do with the standards of the tribal community and institutions such as the Southwestern Association on Indian Affairs were established to promote these.[7]

In contrast to the rigidity of these artificial standards, New Mexico, which has a complex pluralistic history of human settlement, is characterized by subtle cultural transformations and the constant adaptation of new artistic traditions among distinct communities. Many of these transformations have emerged from the interaction of diverse Anglo, Hispanic, and American Indian communities. The ability of people and their communities to adapt external traditions has been ignored by the imposition of policy designed to regulate "genuine" Indian-made items. Recent experiments among Native artists to employ genres other than turquoise, silver, wool, watercolor, and clay have usually been shunned as "inauthentic."[8]

The Southwest Indian mystique has become so pervasive that the average tourist expects the word "authentic" to imply that the artist has used a pick and shovel to procure the raw materials that went into the item. At the same time, the promotion of the Southwest Indian mystique has other troublesome aspects. Among these are the inconsistent standards used to determine the authenticity of Indian items. However rigorous, the guarantee is based solely upon ascribed qualities that depend on who is making the judgment, in what context, and for what purpose.[9] By deconstructing this mystique, it can be seen that both the social scientist and the entrepreneur contribute equally to such revisionism.

Within their own communities Native people continue to prosper. Part of this can be attributed to the maintenance of the land base or reservation. By and large, however, it has been the preservation of a communal context within this land base that has maintained the cultural integrity of Native people in the Southwest. The propensity of the New Mexico tribal communities to share the genuine expression of their cultures is what has elevated a demographic minority, 134,355 American Indians in New Mexico constituting 8.9 percent of the total New Mexico population, into the economic majority. Cultural tourism is the largest factor in New Mexico's business economy.[10]

The irony in this situation is that tribal governments play an invisible role in this industry's control. Non-Native communities such as Sedona, Arizona, and Sante Fe, New Mexico, procure the bulk of their commerce on the merchandising of authentic Indian arts, while very little of this marketing hype is present in the tribal communities. Instead, the tribal communities are witness to pockets of poverty, and their labor forces are primarily employed by the government sector. In fact, arts and crafts are seen as supplemental income activities. Items traditionally produced by Native artisans as utilitarian wares are now rarely retained in their own communities for such purposes.

Part of this situation, however, is intentional. The more culturally "conservative" the tribal community, the more apt it is to prohibit the commercial marketing of Indian items by tribal members on the reservation. Although this has less to do with the wares themselves, it often entails the use of designs and images. Unlike the medium, some designs and images do maintain religious and symbolic significance in the community.[11]

Similarly tribal people have largely rejected being the living laboratories and the backdrops for non-Indians.[12] American Indian communities have been hospitable to non-Indians during public ceremonies, but only on the condition that visitors leave only "footprints." Tribal members are prohibited from divulging information about tribal customs and religion to outsiders, especially anthropologists. In some communities, photography is prohibited. In others, some sites are restricted from public access and view.[13]

The result of such practices has been the tempering of social norms in the community. Social scientists have attributed this phenomenon to an ability of Native people to exist in both a tribal and a non-tribal world. This dualism has resulted in the reservation becoming a sort of refuge from the outside for its residents. Hence, in the absence of overt marketing and commercialism, the reservation and its bounded communities have minimized or isolated themselves from outside enterprises. In a larger sense, the place becomes "spiritual," and such spiritualism is an integral part of the migration amenity of living there.[14]

Many of the practices designed to regulate outside commercialism of tribal culture have been largely informal. What appears to be the most challenging aspect of Native American issues in New Mexico today is how the tribes will cope with the regulation of their own tourist enterprises, should they so choose. This is a relatively new phenomenon, and it comes as the result of an attempt by tribal governments to diversify their economies. For instance, both the Pueblos of Zuni and Pojoaque have begun planning their own tribal museums.[15]

The central question that remains to be answered is whether Native communities will defer to the same revisionist images that have been ascribed by the outside. As "insiders," how much cultural information will they be willing to divulge and under what circumstances? How will they revise their own image, while coping with the same issues that confront conservators today? Will they allow themselves to continue to be "living museums" or will they choose to stage pageants and reenactments designed to shroud their real community presence and deflect tourism away from their lives?

The year 1993 was designated as the Year of the Indigenous Peoples; a chance to allow Native people to confront their own images. As it turned out, the occasion was appropriated to promote the works of revisionist authors. In fact, books regarding the Southwest and its Native people have been especially hard hit. Examples range from photo essays to historical treatises.[16] The objection to these volumes is that the authors appropriated the cultural knowledge of Native people to reaffirm their own views—those of outsiders. In this way the Native voices were quashed.

What is construed by the public as the "new" Native perspective is far from new. Because revisionists affirm the exotic, the "Indian" becomes inhuman. In the process of decontextualizing, the Indian becomes curious and quaint. Like the stereotype, such imagery is never about Native America; it has everything to do with outside values.

To the non-Native mind's eye, knowledge is valuable only when it is written. In contrast, Native knowledge always has been oral. Spoken history is undervalued and consigned to be free for the taking. In a manner of speaking, this difficulty has been the downfall of indigenous people. While this oral history has been denigrated, mainstream society has allowed the outsider to legitimize it in a written manner.

Tribal peoples have been generous when it comes to the oral traditions. By being subjected to the documentation process of the oral historians they have ostensibly transferred the copyright to the authors and publishers. So far, the bulk of that scholarship has not been reciprocal. That is to say, tribal knowledge has tended to flow out of the community and has not been retained for the community's use.

One of the rare instances where this has been reversed was in 1982. At the request of the Zuni Tribal Government in New Mexico and with funding from the National Endowment for the Humanities, the Zuni History Project was initiated to bring back non-Native academics who had used Zuni knowledge in their scholarship. The invitation was laced with a warning that individuals who did not cooperate would be banished from conducting any future research. Their reports to the community were retained by the tribe and became the basis for expert testimony concerning Zuni land claims.

Other projects, outside of the Southwest but still notable, have been instituted at other tribal sites. The California Indian Library Collections Project in 1988 attempted to match the archival holdings of the University of California at Berkeley's Lowie Museum of Anthropology to the surrounding Native communities. These collections, which were assembled particularly to repatriate materials to the California tribes, included sound recordings, photographs, books, journal articles, and unpublished field notes. Similarly, Project Jukebox originated in 1986 at the University of Alaska at Fairbanks Oral History Program, a division of the Alaska and Polar Regions Department of the Elmer E. Rasmuson Library. It has worked with Alaska Native Corporations to create interactive computerized databases of their collections. What makes this endeavor unique is that it specifically adds the interpretation and identity of individual Native voices to the archival record, an element that often is forgotten in the anonymity of the oral history process.

In spite of such innovation, most Native communities still must contend with the unabashed appropriation of their creative and intellectual knowledge base. At the crux of the matter, a legal concept of "intellectual property" steadfastly is emerging. Unlike the repatriation of cultural objects or artifacts, that issue is centered around the legality of copyrighting cultural knowledge for profit.

But intellectual property is a legal concept that advances the right of the individual. It does not solve the problem of "collective" rights. In this sense, the concept of cultural property as it is evolving in the courts may be more equitable when it comes to the claim of extended families, clanships, or tribes over their cultural knowledge.

By addressing these and other important questions, Native people will be able to both demystify the Indian mystique and contribute in the revision of the prevailing stereotypes, particularly those of the Southwest Native.

Notes

1 C. F. Lummis, *Mesa Cañon and Pueblo* (New York: Century, 1925).

2 C. H. Lange and C. L. Riley, *The Southwestern Journals of Adolf Bandelier: 1880– 1882* (Albuquerque: University of New Mexico Press, 1966), 97.

3 New Mexico State Film Commission. *Mary Pickford "The Biograph Girl" and D. W. Griffith and Mack Sennett in Albuquerque, New Mexico, 1912: Produced from the Contemporary Newspaper Accounts* (Sante Fe NM: State Records Center and Archives, Report #2, July 27, 1970), 8.

4 S. Rodriquez, "Art, Tourism, and Race Relations in Taos: Toward a Sociology of the Art Colony," *Journal of Anthropological Research* 45:1 (1989): 77.

5 M. Weigle, "From Desert to Disney World: The Sante Fe Railway and the Fred Harvey Company Display the Indian Southwest," *Journal of Anthropological Research* 45:1 (1989): 130.

6 R. F. Schrader, *The Indian Arts & Crafts Board: An Aspect of New Deal Indian Policy* (Albuquerque: University of New Mexico Press, 1983), 53.

7 As seen by a new Congressional Act entitled *Expanding the Powers of the Indian Arts and Crafts Board*, which contains precise regulations pertaining to the certification of American Indian artists, such policies are still in evidence today (P.L. 101–644, 1990). See R. Zibart, "Mixing Politics and Art," *Indian Market* (Sante Fe NM: Southwestern Association on Indian Affairs, 1990), 66–70, for a brief history of the Southwestern Association on Indian Affairs.

8 An interesting example of this involved Pueblo Indian artist Tony Jojola, whose medium is glass. Apprenticed at the Pilchuck glass foundry he was originally refused a show of his glassware at the All Indian Pueblo Cultural Center. The curators cited "unauthenticity" on the basis of the medium. Today, his glassware has been acquired for the Cultural Center's museum, but only after he attained prominence in the Southwest art market (personal correspondence).

9 D. Evans-Pritchard, "The Portal Case: Authenticity, Tourism, Traditions, and the Law," *Journal of American Folklore* 100 (1987): 292, 293.

10 1990 Census of Population and Housing, U.S. Department of Commerce, Bureau of the Census. In 1990, tourism was estimated to be a $2.3 billion industry in New Mexico employing 53,000 people in the state. See J. Ditmer, "New Mexico Changing: Invading Tourists Can Sometimes Destroy Area's Historic and Cultural Values," *Denver Post*, March 16, 1991.

11 Recently the tribal council at the Pueblo of Acoma, at the prompting of religious leaders, prohibited its tribal members from producing carvings or any other arts depicting katchinas. This prohibition has alienated some

members of the community who are contesting that this action inhibits their "freedom of artistic expression" (personal correspondence).

12 In 1987, the petroglyphs surrounding the community of the Pueblo of Acoma became backdrops to the swimsuit-clad contestants of the Miss USA Pageant. Shortly thereafter, the area was hit by a series of severe storms. The elders interpreted this as an omen arising from the commercial desecration of the petroglyphs (personal correspondence).

13 These prohibitions are resurrected annually, usually under the guise of "tourist etiquette." See, for example, an extensive editorial of this issue by Joseph Suina who, himself, is a member of the Pueblo of Cochiti. See J. Suina, "There's Nothing Sinister in Pueblos' Secretive Ways," *Albuquerque Tribune*, June 28, 1991, section A9.

14 L. A. G. Moss, *Amenity Migrations*, Albuquerque Center for Research and Development, University of New Mexico, Working Paper P91–4, 3.

15 Such proposals, though, are not without controversy. A joint agreement by the U.S. National Park Service and the Zuni tribe to establish national monuments inside the reservation was rejected by a tribal citizen referendum in 1990. The vote was forced by religious leaders and the U.S. Congress subsequently passed other legislation giving Zuni leaders four more years to negotiate another agreement. G. Rosales, "National Park Service 'Stepping on Toes,'" *Albuquerque Journal*, September 30, 1990.

16 See for example "Commentaries on *When Jesus Came the Corn Mothers Went Away: Marriage, Sex and Power in New Mexico, 1500–1864* by Ramón Gutiérrez," *American Indian Culture and Research Journal* 17:3 (1993): 141–177.

American Indian Studies Is for Everyone

DUANE CHAMPAGNE

Raven, Coyote, and other trickster figures are both creators and destroyers; they shape and mold the world, but they also put constraints upon it by creating death, sickness, pain, as well as culture and institutions. It appears that academia has had a similar effect on American Indian studies. On the creative side, academia has served to preserve much about American Indian culture, history, and knowledge, and has presented Indian culture in new media forms. On the other hand, many tribal people and Indian scholars are not comfortable with what has been written, sometimes thinking that the scholarship is not correct, or that sacred knowledge is inappropriately revealed, or the tone of discussion inappropriate. In recent years, more Indian scholars have emerged within academia and introduced more sympathetic interpretations of Indian life, history, and culture. Some discussion has emerged between Indian and non-Indian scholars about various issues, although few public debates are carried out during the review of papers and books submitted for publication. Sometimes these debates are heated.[1] Debate, nevertheless, is an essential part of the academic process. An open and free forum for discussion among Indian and non-Indian scholars benefits everyone who seeks to produce accurate, substantial, and significant studies of Indian peoples.

Who should study indians?

In my view, there is room for both Indian and non-Indian scholars within American Indian studies, which includes relevant aspects of anthropology, art, religion, sociology, and other disciplines. To say that only Indians can study Indians goes too far toward excluding American Indian culture and history from the rest of human history and culture. In the final analysis, Indian nations are human groups, part of the broad history of all humanity, and therefore can be compared with other groups in technology, cultural world views, history, and adaptation to global markets and expanding state systems, etc. One does not have to be a member of a culture to understand what culture means or to interpret a culture in a meaningful way.

I say this in an ideal sense, since a frequent criticism that Indian scholars have of non-Indian scholars is that their analyses do not take into account specific characteristics of Indian cultures. Many non-Indian scholars prefer to interpret Indian life from within broad theoretical frameworks, or United States or Western historical terms, and generally place strong emphasis on expanding European economic or political activities. Even sympathetic treatments of Indians as victims of colonial pillage and military destruction often do not address the culturally specific ways in which Indian nations have survived the past five-hundred years of colonial domination. I would not say that non-Indian scholars are incapable of developing powerful cultural interpretations, but that a bias in Western scholarly culture toward economic and political interpretations directs many scholars away from cultural interpretations. Rigorous study, fieldwork, and a sensitive orientation will reward scholars, Indian and non-Indian, with greater understanding of Indian groups. I do not believe that Indian scholars have a monopoly on Indian studies. As in all human groups, culture, institutions, and social and political processes are usually understandable to most anybody who is willing to learn and who at least may observe, if not participate, in the process.

Some Indian scholars may have the advantage of direct access. Having grown up in an American Indian culture can provide considerable insight and understanding that may take a non-tribal field-worker years to acquire. Furthermore, the knowledge that an Indian scholar might have about his or her own culture often leads to the investigation of issues that non-Indian or non-tribal scholars might not consider. The mere presence of Indian blood within a scholar, however, does not ensure better or more sensitive historical or cultural understandings of Indian peoples. This can come only with training, motivation, sensitivity, knowledge, and study. An Indian scholar, with considerable background knowledge, access to informants, and participation in an Indian culture, can contribute significantly with in-depth analysis of American Indian culture and history. Such in-depth studies will enable Indian scholars to examine and extend the theories and concepts of mainline academic disciplines, as well as lay the foundation for developing their own theories. A discussion of how academic theories and concepts work, or do not work, within the study of Indian history and culture will fuel debate and lead to more general theories and concepts.

Non-Indian scholars are usually driven by theoretical or disciplinary issues that abstract segments of Indian history or culture for analysis, and often do not reflect the study of a culture as a holistic entity. Certainly, the study of Indian peoples, like other human groups, contributes to greater understanding of human culture in general, and Indians should be glad to contribute to this knowledge and welcome the contributions of non-Indian scholars. Non-Indian scholars, as well as Indian scholars, should have access to study within consenting Indian communities. As guests, scholars must respect community rules and desires to protect certain information from public view. Many communities, for example the Hopi, forbid publication of the location of sacred places or the details of certain sacred ceremonies. Scholars, Indian and non-Indian alike, must respect such wishes.

The unhappiness expressed by many Indian communities against scholars, such as anthropologists in the 1960s and 1970s, in part was due to the indifferent way in which data were collected and published, and that resulted in little benefit to the host Indian community. Indian communities are now more demanding about allowing research and are looking for greater returns from scholars. This return can be given by written reports or presentations to the tribal government, or by lending academic skills to tribal projects. The question of whether non-Indian scholars should study Indians should be answered in the affirmative. The debate, however, over scholarly presence in Indian communities should focus on the ethics and guidelines of how scholars should conduct their studies and report their results. Certainly exploitative and intrusive research should be condemned, and universities and academic disciplines need to revise and enforce their ethical codes for research conducted in Indian communities.

Research, however, need not be conducted only at the request of tribal communities. The practical and daily interests of an Indian community will rarely coincide with the research and theoretical interests of academic disciplines. That does not mean that all research should be stopped or that only research with a tangible political or economic benefit to the tribe should proceed. In that case few research projects might go forward, and considerable knowledge may be lost. Nevertheless, researchers do not have the right to conduct research within nonconsenting communities. After presentation of the proposed research to community authorities, many Indian communities will allow research that holds little direct benefit for them. Some tribes, however, may withhold permission, and the scholarly community must respect this decision.

What Is the value of American Indian Studies?

At the University of California, Los Angeles, we take the position that Indian students should take undergraduate degrees in the mainstream disciplines such as business, education, etc. We believe that it is better for Indian students to receive training and scholarly preparation in the mainstream majors rather than work on an Indian studies degree. Indian students should not go to university to learn about the central values and institutions of their cultures. Their communities are better places to gain close knowledge about their specific tribal history and culture. At the same time, we are concerned that Indian students learn about the place of Indians in United States law and history and about United States policy toward Indians, and learn to analyze and understand Indian culture and institutions. Unfortunately, most academic disciplines are not well equipped to provide this kind of knowledge or intellectual training. Consequently, we think it important to supplement the main disciplines with at least a minor in Indian studies, so Indian and non-Indian students have access to alternative interpretations of United States history, law, policy, and Indian history and culture that are not available in other academic disciplines. Indian studies programs present information and interpretations that otherwise would be overlooked. These alternative views can challenge and augment the work of the mainstream disciplines by engaging debate and providing alternative interpretations for students and scholars. Thus, courses in Indian studies provide Indian and non-Indian students with knowledge and information that will facilitate their understanding of many issues that confront Indian communities within contemporary society.

At UCLA, we favor a major in Indian studies only with sufficient student demand. Otherwise we plan to stay with a minor that will complement the work students perform in the mainstream departments. This strategy is to some extent dictated by the absence of enough faculty to support a department, and by the general absence of interest from faculty and administrators in an Indian studies department.

We offer a master's degree program in American Indian Studies, but do not have plans for a Ph.D. program. Lack of faculty is a major factor in not developing a Ph.D. program in Indian studies. Nevertheless, many of our graduates, about 60 percent, in the master's program have gone on to Ph.D. granting departments or professional schools. Many students realize they cannot obtain significant graduate level work in Indian-related topics in most contemporary graduate departments. Consequently, many attend our two-year Indian studies master's program before going on to graduate departments where mainstream coursework is required, and where there is little emphasis or help for students interested in American Indian Studies. In many ways, we think our program benefits many students, prepares them for graduate school, and gives them strong backgrounds in Indian studies that they could not obtain elsewhere.

Regulating information about American Indians

Should there be a national board of Indians to advise funding agencies, scriptwriters, and television and movie producers? Indian community members are often unhappy with the portrayal of Indians in the media. Media advisers are often not members of the Indian community, and while they are usually respected scholars or journalists, they generally do not represent an Indian perspective. Consequently, Indians are often chagrined at even the most well-intentioned attempts to portray Indian people.

There are several reasons for choosing non-Indian advisers. Often the producers are not well informed and have no clear idea of whom to choose. They consult academic sources and generally are advised to select non-Indian advisers. Since most academics do not work within Indian settings, the choices are based on scholarly reputations and scholars often are recommended by other scholars. Further, most of the money and management of large-scale media productions come from non-Indian sources. Although well-intentioned, non-Indian producers maintain administrative and artistic control over the projects. Even when Indian advisers are selected and when excellent advice is given by either Indian or non-Indian advisers, media producers are not sufficiently grounded in Indian history or culture to enable them effectively to evaluate good or bad advice. Consequently, producers tend to accept advice that fits into their plans and reject other advice. This situation often leads to the decontextualization and the dismantling of the holistic character of Indian culture and institutions, and consequently to a fragmented presentation of Indian history and culture. Since the producers are cultural members of United States society, they are operating largely within their own cultural world-view following contemporary trends in media presentation.

The shape Indian material takes in United States culture depends more on the nature of the medium than on the substance of Indian culture.

Most media productions are not produced for Indian audiences, but are produced for larger, non-Indian audiences, so that they are packaged in ways that are compatible with non-Indian world-views and understandings. There is a small group of independent Indian media producers, many of whom present Indian perspectives, but their work requires non-Indian audiences to make significant leaps in cultural appreciation and understanding. Consequently, it is doubtful that Indian producers can serve the purposes of Indian cultural expression and representation while satisfying a large commercial following in mass non-Indian markets. Since the cultural orientations and purposes of Indian and non-Indian media move in different and relatively unrelated cultural directions, it is doubtful whether a national Indian advisory board could serve the purposes of the non-Indian mass media. While such a board might bring more authenticity to the media, the media must want to present an authentic picture to the non-Indian audience, and that can only hapen if media producers perceive that authentic Indian perspectives and history are marketable and in demand by mass non-Indian audiences. While issues of Indian authenticity are debated in the media, there is a chance that such authenticity will become a primary demand by mass non-Indian audiences. I think such a situation is unlikely, though, for while there is a strong interest in Indians, there seems relatively little interest in meeting Indians on their own terms, and taking the time and energy to understand the cultural perspectives and values by which Indians live.

Issues of scholarly review
Should a national board exist for issues of academic tenure, grants, academic publishing, or academic promotion? Treatment of Indian studies scholarship in mainstream academic arenas suffers from

similar cultural disconnectedness as that found in contemporary mass media. Academic work is largely an exercise that is outside the concerns of most Indian communities and cultures. Nevertheless, some scholars are committed to making their work useful to Indian communities and, as a discipline, American Indian Studies bridges the gap between scholarship and the Indian community. The efforts of American Indian Studies, however, are not highly valued within the academic arena, and perhaps one even can say they are discouraged. This may change, but it will take time. American Indian practitioners are at risk because their academic colleagues operate from different values and cultural perspectives. Within the confines of their separate disciplines, academics have internally consistent grounds for devaluing the scholarship produced in the field of Indian studies. This presents difficulties to American Indian Studies scholars who submit work to mainstream journals and to book publishers and apply for grants and career promotions. Since Indian scholars are few, they pose little threat to mainstream scholarship, and their views are generally considered marginal.

Forming a national committee to look over academic promotions and publication review is tempting and, perhaps makes a symbolic point, underscoring the situation of Indian studies scholars. But few universities or publishers would allow such a board to oversee their review processes. Consequently, I don't think such a board would be practical. A better, more practical change would be a revolution of multicultural understanding within the academic community, with more than just lip service paid to strong, innovative scholarship within the Indian studies field. Credit should be given where credit is due. Nevertheless, I do not think such an appreciative understanding of Indian, or other non-mainstream cultures, is forthcoming. Most likely, United States academia will continue along a relatively monocultural path, leaving on the fringe those who study other cultures. You see, in the end, Raven could well have created the academic juggernaut, for it gives and takes, it creates and destroys, and it never quite moves in a direction one would like.

Note

1 See, for instance, Donald Grinde and Bruce Johansen, *Exemplar of Liberty* (Los Angeles, UCLA American Indian Studies Center, 1991); Elizabeth Tooker, "The United States Constitution and the Iroquois League," *Ethnohistory* 35 (Fall, 1988): 305–306; Bruce E. Johansen and Donald A. Grinde Jr., "The Debate Regarding Native American Precedents for Democracy: A Recent Historiography," *American Indian Culture and Research Journal* 14:1 (1990): 61–88; James Clifton, *The Invented Indian* (New Brunswick NJ: Transaction Publishers, 1990).

Why Indian People Should Be the Ones
to Write about Indian Education

KAREN GAYTON SWISHER

Several years ago I wrote an essay titled "Authentic Research: An Interview on the Way to the Ponderosa," published in *Anthropology & Education Quarterly*. It was a reflection of my dissertation experience and expressed what I learned about the importance of "minority researchers conducting research about the groups of which they are members."[1] I also have done several presentations on research in Indian education and expressed my position that Indians ought to be conducting the research and writing about it. Articles by Brown, LaFromboise and Plake, and Robbins and Tippeconnic express similar concerns. In addition, the recent White House Conference on Indian Education affirmed this belief and recommended through resolution that the United States Department of Education support a range of research by American Indian/Alaska Native scholars who are committed to addressing the needs of American Indian and Alaska Native communities. This essay is a reiteration of my convictions that Indian people should be given more authority in writing about Indian education.

Voices, stories, and perspectives

The words *voices, stories,* and *perspectives* are prevalent in recent reports of research and typify the intent of educational researchers to present more accurate interpretations of the qualitative research experience. Among the current methods being used to attempt to capture authenticity are: Listening to the voices of the people and making sure they are heard through the writing; telling the stories of the people as metaphors and examples of schooling experiences; and presenting the perspectives of others in an attempt to encourage readers to see through a different lens. However, much research still is presented from an outsider's perspective.

A recent National Dialogue Project on American Indian Education is an example of authentic research conducted about Indians by Indians. Sponsored by the American Indian Science and Engineering Society and the College Boards' Educational Equality Project (EQ/AISES), the research determined what educational changes American Indians want for American Indian youth. Indian people were not only the informants, but the principal investigators as well. In seven regional dialogues facilitated by Indian regional dialogue directors, Indian parents, students, tribal leaders, and educators discussed issues of educational change. The issues centered on beliefs that American Indians "have many educational needs that differ from those of mainstream society . . . and the assimilation objectives of American education are detrimental to the social, economic, and political well-being of their communities."[2] The report of the regional dialogues, *Our Voices, Our Vision: American Indians Speak Out for Educational Excellence,* was developed by AISES and written by the Indian staff and graduate students of the American Indian Studies Center at UCLA, and published in 1989. In addressing the area of research and publishing, the report had this to say:

> Just as the exploitation of American Indian land and resources is of value to corporate America, research and publishing is valuable to non-Indian scholars. As a result of racism, greed, and distorted perceptions of native realities, Indian culture as an economic commodity has been exploited by the dominant society with considerable damage to Indian people. Tribal people need to safeguard the borders of their cultural domains against research and publishing incursions. (p. 6)

The report went on to say that research on Indian history and culture must consider Indian perspectives. Methodology using tribal histories and other information about historical and cultural processes not found in primary and secondary source materials will avoid perpetuation of stereotypes. The writers make it clear that "American Indian scholars need to become involved in producing research rather than serving as subjects and consumers of research. Measures such as these will ultimately introduce more accurate depictions of Indian experience and lifestyles into the classroom" (p. 7). This report and others such as the *Indian Nations At Risk: An Educational Strategy for Action* and *Indian Education in America* by Vine Deloria Jr. are outstanding examples of the relevant work Indian people are doing collectively in dialogues or through public hearings or as individual scholars.

The distinguishing feature of the EQ/AISES report is the self-determination perspective. From the conception of the dialogue format to formulation of data and publication, Indian people were in charge of and guided the project; and the voices and concerns of the people were clearly evident.

Although the National Dialogue Project on American Indian Education was indeed national in scope, the final report was not distributed nationwide. In my estimation, the report of this project is as significant as the report of the Indian Nations At Risk Task Force; it apparently suffered from lack of funds for distribution.

Self-determination, potential, and confidence

Indian people believe that they have the answers for improving Indian education and feel they must speak for themselves. There is an attitude of "we can and must do it ourselves," but we need help from our friends. If non-Indian educators have been involved in Indian education because they believe in Indian people and want them to be empowered, they must now demonstrate that belief by stepping aside. They must begin to question their motives beyond wanting to do something to improve education for Indian people. In writing about Indian education, they must now defer to Indian authors, or at least co-author in a secondary position. Far too often non-Indian people have been writing the books on Indian education, so to speak. For example, just three non-Indian authors have written more than 30 articles and books about Indian education since 1985. Their authority is cited more often than the experts from whom their experience and information was gathered, and they have become the experts in Indian education recognized by their mainstream peers. This is not so much a criticism of their efforts as it is an admonition for Indian authors to publish more.

In this essay I am expressing my opinion and the opinions of my closest colleagues: In the spirit of self-determination, Indian people should be the ones to write about Indian education. And if they don't? So what? There is much work to be done and much to be written about. However, in scanning the literature, it appears that most of the books and articles focus broadly on two topics: the history of Indian education and effective teaching practices.

The history of Indian education over four centuries has been aptly written by such notable historians as Margaret Connell Szasz. Other writers such as David Wallace Adams and David H. DeJong also have researched the historical literature and presented their perspectives on the history of America's indigenous peoples. Their work has provided a valuable launching pad from which Indian scholars can develop their particular cultural perspectives and interpretations through teaching and research.

A plethora of edited books, special issues of journals, articles, and chapters in various multicultural or minority textbooks focus on effective curriculum and pedagogy regarding the education of American Indians and Alaska Natives. Much of what has been written is historically accurate and not harmful or offensive; it is sensitively, and in some cases beautifully, done. What is missing is the passion from within and the authority to ask new and different questions based on histories and experiences as indigenous people. It is more than different ways of knowing; it is knowing that what we think is grounded in principles of sovereignty and self-determination, and that it has credibility. The backgrounds, histories, traditions, cultural ways, languages, and government-to-government relationships are unique with American Indians and Alaska Natives. But the voices that communicate intergenerational meaning are missing from this literature. How can an outsider really understand life on reservations, the struggle for recognition, sovereignty, economic development, preservation of language and culture? Perhaps they can gain a high degree of empathy and act as "brokers" of sorts, but it takes American Indians and Alaska Natives themselves to understand the depth of meaning incorporated in Indian education to ask appropriate questions and find appropriate answers. A non-Indian colleague summarized the issue in this statement: The view from the outside remains the same; it's the inside view that varies.

A good example of the precept of asking appropriate questions is found in the writings about self-esteem. Using measures and procedures that were developed and normed with the mainstream, mostly Euro-American population, psychologists and sociologists have demonstrated that Indian students have problems with self-esteem and self-concept. The result has been to make cosmetic and/or structural changes.

I remember a session at one annual meeting of the American Educational Research Association several years ago where a paper was presented on effects of schooling on the self-concept of American Indian students. While the intent of the paper was benevolent, the research methodology was questioned by Dr. Beatrice Medicine, a distinguished Indian researcher, because of its Euro-American normed measures. This example is succinctly grounded in the following question: *What would the self-image of the American Indian be if it were researched by Indians?*[3]

Why haven't Indians been writing about Indian education?
They have. People like Luther Standing Bear, Ella Deloria, and Charles Eastman were writing about Indian education more than fifty years ago. They wrote about how Indian nations viewed the education of their children as a community, and about extended family

responsibility. For example, with the crafting of a cradleboard, Indian parents were considering the mental development of their unborn child. In an upright position, their baby would be in communication with his or her surroundings. Children were taught survival skills (economics), knowledge of cultural heritage (ethics), spiritual awareness (religion). The work of these authors decades ago has meaning to us as we approach the next century; it is scholarly and authentic, and it should be revisited as a basis for researching and writing about contemporary Indian education. Recent work on boarding schools by Indian researchers and writers such as Brenda Child, Jeffrey Hamley, K. Tsianina Lomawaima, Devon Abbott Mihesuah, and Paulete Fairbanks Molin, provide stellar examples of the passion I referred to earlier, balanced with their craft as scholarly researchers. Kirke Kickingbird, an attorney, and G. Mike Charleston, an educator, in 1991 co-authored a paper which thoroughly examined the political relationship between tribes/nations and the United States government as it relates to education, for the Indian Nations At Risk Task Force. In a paper published in 1994, three years after his untimely death, Charleston, who served as project director for the Indian Nations At Risk Task Force, brilliantly summarized what he had heard from Native people and observed in schools attended by Native children during INARTF hearings and visits. Fortunately the work of these and other Indian authors is available not only in education but other related fields as well.

In 1972, the Indian Education Act, initiated by President John F. Kennedy, finally was passed. Federal money was concentrated on increasing the numbers of American Indians with bachelors, masters, and doctoral degrees in education. The act was successful beyond expectations. A contemporary cadre of Indian professionals and practitioners can write about Indian education with great depth and meaning. Of all professions, more Indian people have entered the field of education than any other discipline. There are recognized Indian leaders in the field of Indian education, as well as the general field of education. Pennsylvania State University, Arizona State University, Harvard, Stanford, Dartmouth, Cornell, the Universities of North Dakota and Minnesota, among others, have benefited from Indian Education Act grants to educate Indian teachers and administrators. Many of these graduates now are making a difference in Indian education. They are leaders and they are beginning to write.

To discuss why some have not written or been published is the topic of a good qualitative research project. I cannot speculate beyond my own experience and that of my colleagues, but what I do know is that the demands placed on Indian professionals appear to be much greater than for our non-Indian colleagues. It is difficult to take a selfish stance and say no in the university experience when it means an Indian presence or perspective will not be included. My Indian colleagues and I feel a strong sense of commitment and the urgency to *do* something for our people overpowers the desire and time it takes to write. There are tangible rewards in doing something for one's community whether it is training and technical assistance or other planning and development activities. Those of us in academe know that our service records are enviable, but we often fall short in writing about our scholarly activities. Admonitions are well taken; we need to write about what we know.

In this essay I did not analyze the literature about Indian education by non-Indians comparatively, or along themes of power and authority as motives for writing about Indian education. I did think about the literature with which I am most familiar, and where a recurring theme of blaming the victim appears evident, even when authors take care not to do so. Problems still are too often situated with the individual, the family, the environment, and not in the context of school and society. The research journals focus on problems, and popular journals focus on how to remediate the problems. The successes of the many tribal schools and twenty-seven tribal colleges do not have a prominent place in the mainstream literature. What is being written about Indian education must focus on what is missing from the writings heretofore, i.e., an understanding of the issues of sovereignty and self-determination that distinguish American Indians and Alaska Natives as indigenous people of this country from other Americans.

The future

The words of Robbins and Tippeconnic written in 1985 are still accurate a decade later: "The majority of technical educational research in Indian education has been, and is still, done by non-Indian researchers. The point is not to disallow the non-Indian from performing research in Indian education. Rather, it is to encourage Indian professionals to begin to function as researchers in education. Criticism of non-Indian researchers in Indian education will continue until such time that Indian researchers are sufficient in number to significantly alter the direction of this research."[4] While the numbers of Indian professionals in Indian education are still proportionately low, the potential exists for significantly altering the direction of research and writing in Indian education. We must learn to be less complacent and more aggressive when it comes to defining our field. Magnanimous non-Indian mentors must nurture from afar and in secondary positions. There should be much collaboration and cooperation among Indian scholars and the more senior among us must nurture junior scholars and graduate students. The networks are now in place for collaboration among Indian professionals at more than one-hundred mainstream colleges and universities, twenty-seven tribal colleges, and hundreds of K-12 reservation and urban schools. A time characterized by the statement, *People come among us and tell us that they know what is best for us,* literal or implied, is long gone.[5] Indian professionals have a role and responsibility in defining what is best for us in Indian education.

Notes

1 K. Swisher, "Authentic Research: Interview on the Way to the Ponderosa," *Anthropology & Education Quarterly* 17:3 (1986): 185–188.

2 College Board and American Indian Science Engineering Society. *Our Voices, Our Vision: American Indians Speak Out for Educational Excellence* (New York: College Entrance Examination Board, 1989), 1.

3 J. E. Trimble, "The Sojourner in the American Indian Community: Methodological Issues and Concerns," *Journal of Social Issues* 33:4 (1977): 169.

4 R. Robbins and J. Tippeconnic III, *Research in American Indian Education* (Tempe: Center for Indian Education, 1985), 11.

5 E. Barlow, "Multicultural Education: Its Effective Management," *Contemporary Native American Address,* ed. J. R. Maestes (Provo UT: Brigham Young University Press, 1976).

References

Adams, D. W. *Education for Extinction: American Indians and the Boarding School Experience, 1875–1928.* Lawrence: University Press of Kansas, 1995.

Brown, A. D. "Research Role of American Indian Social Scientists." *Journal of Educational Equity and Leadership* 1:1 (1980): 47–59.

Charleston, G. M. "Toward True Native Education: A Treaty of 1992, Final Report of the Indian Nations At Risk Task Force, Draft 3." *Journal of American Indian Education* 33:2 (1994): 7–56.

Child, B. "Homesickness, Illness, and Death: Native-American Girls in Government Boarding Schools." In *Wings of Gauze: Women of Color and the Experience of Health and Illness,* edited by B. Bair and S. E. Cayleff. Detroit: Wayne State University Press, 1993.

DeJong, D. J. *Promises of the Past: A History of Indian Education.* Golden CO: North American Press, 1993.

Kickingbird, K., and G. M. Charleston. "Responsibilities and Roles of Governments and Native People in the Education of American Indians and Alaska Natives." ERIC ED 34357. Washington DC: Indian Nations Task Force, United States Department of Education, 1991.

Deloria, V. Jr. *Indian Education in America.* Boulder CO: American Indian Science and Engineering Society, 1991.

Hamley, J. "An Introduction to the Federal Indian Boarding School Movement." *North Dakota History,* 61:2 (1994): 2–9.

Lomawaima, K. T. *They Called It Prairie Light, The Story of Chilocco Indian School.* Lincoln: University of Nebraska Press, 1994.

LaFromboise, T. D., and B. S. Plake. "Toward Meeting the Needs of American Indians." *Harvard Educational Review,* 53:1 (1983): 45–51.

Mihesuah, D. A. *Cultivating the Rosebuds: The Education of Women at the Cherokee Female Seminary, 1851–1909.* Urbana: University of Illinois Press, 1993.

Molin, P. M. "Training the Hand, the Head, and the Heart: Indian Education at Hampton Institute." *Minnesota History,* 51 (Fall 1988): 82–98.

Szasz, M. C. *Education and the American Indian: The Road to Self-Determination Since 1928.* Albuquerque NM: University of New Mexico Press, 1974. *Indian Education in the American Colonies, 1607–1783.* Albuquerque NM: University of New Mexico Press, 1988.

The Contributors

Paula Gunn Allen (Laguna Pueblo/Sioux) is professor of English at the University of California, Los Angeles. She is the author of *The Woman Who Owned the Shadows* (Spinster's Ink, 1983) and *The Sacred Hoop: Recovering the Feminine in American Indian Traditions* (Beacon, 1986), and editor of *Spider Woman's Granddaughters: Traditional Tales and Contemporary Writing by Native American Women* (Beacon, 1989).

Duane Champagne (Chippewa) is an associate professor in the Department of Sociology at the University of California, Los Angeles. He is the editor of the *American Indian Culture and Research Journal* and director of the American Indian Studies Program. He is the author of *American Indian Societies: Strategies and Conditions of Political and Cultural Survival* (Cambridge University Press, 1990) and *Social Order and Political Change: Constitutional Governments among the Cherokee, the Choctaw, the Chickasaw, and the Creek* (Stanford University Press, 1992).

Elizabeth Cook-Lynn (Crow Creek Sioux) is an emeritus professor of English and Indian Studies at Eastern Washington University in Cheney, Washington. She is the editor of the *Wicazo Sa Review* and the author of *From the River's Edge* (Arcade-Little, Brown, 1991) and *Why I Can't Read Wallace Stegner and Other Essays: A Tribal Voice* (Wisconsin, 1996).

Vine Deloria Jr. (Standing Rock Sioux) is a professor of history, law, religious studies, and political science at the University of Colorado in Boulder. He is the author of numerous books and articles, including *Custer Died for Your Sins* (Avon, 1969), *God Is Red: A Native View of Religion* (Grosset and Dunlap, 1973), *Behind the Trail of Broken Treaties: An Indian Declaration of Independence* (University of Texas Press, 1974), and *Red Earth, White Lies: Native Americans and the Myth of Scientific Fact* (Scribner, 1995).

Theodore S. Jojola (Isleta Pueblo) is director of Native American studies and associate professor of planning in the School of Architecture and Planning at the University of New Mexico.

Donald L. Fixico (Shawnee, Sac & Fox, Seminole, and Muscogee Creek) is a professor and director of graduate studies in the Department of History at Western Michigan University at Kalamazoo. He is the author of *Termination and Relocation: Federal Indian Policy, 1945–1960* (New Mexico, 1986), and editor of *Native Views of Indian-White Historical Relations* (Newberry Library, 1989) and *An Anthology of Western Great Lakes Indian History* (Wisconsin, 1987).

Devon A. Mihesuah (Oklahoma Choctaw) is associate professor of history at Northern Arizona University in Flagstaff. She is the author of *Cultivating the Rosebuds: The Education of Women at the Cherokee Female Seminary* (University of Illinois Press, 1993), *American Indians: Stereotypes and Realities* (Clarity, 1996), and numerous articles on American Indian women and repatriation. She is editor of the *American Indian Quarterly*. Currently she is finishing her books, *American Indian Racial and Ethnic Identity* and *The Roads of My Relations and Other Halfblood Stories*.

Susan A. Miller (Seminole) is an instructor in the Department of History and the Native American Studies Program at the University of Nebraska–Lincoln.

Karen Gayton Swisher (Standing Rock Sioux) is chair of the Teacher Education Department and director of the Elementary Teacher

Education Program at Haskell Indian Nations University. She served as editor of the *Journal of American Indian Education* from 1990 to 1996. Her research includes learning styles, leadership/policy issues, and community-based models.

Laurie Anne Whitt (Choctaw) is an associate professor of philosophy at Michigan Technological University.

Angela Cavender Wilson, Tawapaha Tanka Win—Her Big Hat Woman —(Wahpatonwan Dakota) is a doctoral candidate in American history at Cornell University.

Index

academic freedom, 23

acculturation, levels of, 39

Acomas, 179 n. 11

Adams, David Wallace, 193

African Americans, 42, 43

Alcatraz takeover, 88

Alexie, Sherman, 126

Algonquians/Algonkins, 102

Allen, Paula Gunn, 53 n.28, 124

Almanac of the Dead (Silko), 133

American Historical Association, 105

American Indian and Alaskan Natives Professors Directory, 19 n.16

American Indian Anti-defamation Council, 162 n.2

American Indian Culture and Research Journal, 70

American Indian Ethnohistoric Conference, 87

American Indian history: aspects to include in, 37–54, 91–93, 103; defining, 85–89; development of, 99 n.22; ethics in writing, 84, 90–93; importance of, 90; Indian perceptions of, 25–26, 191–97; Indians as writers of, 14; non-Indian

perceptions of, 14–26, 86, 88–89, 91, 100–107; readership of, 13

American Indian Lives series, 120

American Indian Movement, 41

American Indian Quarterly, ix, x

American Indians: amount of literature about, 86–87, 96 n.4; appearances of, 41–43; as authoritative voices, 115; demographics of, 79; diversity among, 37–38, 94; educational needs of, 191; factionalism among, 39, 45; identity confusion among, 38; as intellectual voices, 111; images of, 115–19, 172, 186–87; life stories of, 119–24; as "living laboratories," 175–76; movies about, 93; progressives, 39; research on, x, 8–9, 10–11, 106–7; spousal abuse among, 45; traditionalists, 38, 39, 40, 50; values of, 45; world-views of, 50, 94; on writing about Others, 12, 55–64. *See also* faculty, Indian; full-bloods; mixed-bloods; *and entries for specific tribes*

American Indian scholars: advantages of, 182–83; their views, 188

American Indian Science and Engineering Society, 191

American Indian Studies, 14–16, 59, 63, 184–86

American Indian–white relations, records of, 88, 98 n.17

American Indian women: evaluation of, by males, 48–49; feelings and emotions, 46; as feminists, 40; heterogeneity among, 37–38, 41–44; intermarriage of, 43–44; mixed-blood, 43–44, 60; oppression of, 38–40; physical appearances of, 38, 41–43; power of, 44–45; struggles of, 40, 46; as writers, 17, 49 n.1, 53 n.28

American Society for Ethnohistory, 87

Andrews, Lynn, 20 n.18

Anishinabes (Chippewas), 102, 125–26

anthropologists: incompleteness of works by, 25; Indian objections to, 183–84; knowledge garned by, 9; readers of works by, 13; views of, 5, 21 n.23

Antiquities Act of 1906, 166 n.41

Apaches, 71, 78, 173

Archaeological Resources Protection Act of 1979, 149, 166 n.41

Ardener, Edwin, 2

Armstrong, Jeanette, 157

arts and crafts, and artificial standards, 174

Atchison, Topeka & Santa Fe Railway, 173

awards, academic, 6; committees, 7–8, 100, 101, 107

Bahr, Diana Meyers, 3

Bandelier, Adolf, 173

Barnes, R. H., 79

Battle of Wood Lake, 27

Behar, Ruth, 8

Bell, Betty, 124

Bennett, Robert, 80

Bentley, Christopher H., 4

Berkhofer, Robert F., Jr., 102, 104, 105

Big Foot Memorial Ride, 116

biography, American Indian, 119–24

Bird, Gloria, 126

Black Elk Speaks (Neihardt), 119

Black Hills, 101

Blue, Brantley, 69

Boas, Franz, 118

Bodmer, Sir Walter, 157

Boyd, Maurice, 3

Boyer, Ruth McDonald, 47

The Broken Chain (movie), 93

Brown, Dee, 125

Bruce, Louis, 80

Bruchac, Joe, 56, 124

Bull Child, Percy, 131

Bureau of Indian Affairs (BIA), 80, 88

California Indian Library Collections Project, 178

Calloway, Colin G., 1

Carpentier, Alejo, 133

Castaneda Don Juan, 80

Cavandish, Margaret, 121

Cavender, Elsie Two Bear, 28, 30

Ceci, Lynn, 71–72

Central Australian Aboriginal Congress, 157

Ceremony (Silko), 4, 132; clan story in, 60; difficulties in teaching, 60; sacred information revealed in, 61–62

Certificate of Degree of Indian Blood (CDIB), 19 n.16

Charleston, G. Mike, 195

Cherokee Female Seminary, 12

Cherokees, 11, 12, 40, 43, 102, 106

Child, Brenda, 49 n.1, 195

Chippewas (Anishinabes), 125–26

Choctaw Genesis 1500–1700 (Galloway), 2, 18 n.4

Choctaws, 18 n.4, 42, 48

Christianity, Indians' conversion to, 28, 39, 40, 43, 44, 107

Churchill, Ward, 144–45

Clifton, James A., 5, 68–71, 108

Cogewea (Mourning Dove), 59–60

College Boards Educational Equality Project, 191

colonialism: results of, 84; struggles against, 38, 45, 46–47

Colorado, Pam, 143–44

Columbus, Christopher, 84, 86, 88

Comanches, 4–5

Commission on Sustainable Development (CSD), 156, 161

Commission to Reestablish the Trickster, 142

Cook-Lynn, Elizabeth, 53 n.28

copyright laws, failure of, 152–53

Costner, Kevin, 113, 114

Costo, Rupert, 2

Coyote stories, 58

Crow Creek SD, 27, 30

Crow Dog, Leonard, 120

Cruikshank, Julie, 47

cultural brokers, 42, 51 n.17

cultural imperialism, 139–62; "no fault" assumption of, 165 n.26

culturalism, 39

cultural property: definition of, 166 n.42; as U.S. property, 149

culture, 97 n.12; need for Indian perceptions of, 191–97; tribal restrictions on studying, 176

Cupeños, 3

Custer Died for Your Sins (Deloria), 135

Dakotas, 27–35

Dances with Wolves (movie), 66, 93, 113

Dann sisters, 148–49

Dawson, Moses, 76

Debo, Angie, 115

Dejong, David H., 193

Delawares, 100, 102

Deloria, Ella, 118, 194

Deloria, Vine, Jr., 9–10, 129, 135, 192

de Mille, Richard, 67, 80

desecration, of Indian burial grounds, 13

Donald, Leland, 78

Duck Valley, 105

Dyea, Melissa, 51 n.16

Eagle, Clyde, 116

Eastman, Charles, 29, 194

education, Indian, 195; authors of works on, 193

En'owkin Center, 157

Erdoes, Richard, 120

Erdrich, Louise, 53 n.28, 125–26, 132, 133

Erminie Wheeler-Voegelin Award, 2, 7

essentialism, 14

ethnic fraud, 19n

ethnographic biography, 121–24

ethnohistorians, responsibilities of, 5

ethnohistory, 73

Ethnohistory, 2

Euro-Americans, standards used by, 48

faculty, Indian, 16–17, 196

The Federalist, 73

Feest, Christian, 71, 81

feminists, Indian women's views of, 40–41

feminist theory, as applied to Indian women, 49

Feraca, Stephen F., 67, 80

Five Civilized Tribes, 43

Florez, Angel, 133

Fogelson, Raymond, 98 n.15

folklore, 151–52; incompleteness of work in, 25

Fonda, Jane, 120

Fools Crow (Welch), 60

Forbes, Jack, 95 n.3

Fort Snelling, 27

Foster, Morris, ix, 7

Francis Parkman Prize, 108 n.5

full-bloods, 39, 40

Galloway, Patricia, 2

García Márquez, Gabriel, 133

Gardener, John, 131, 132

General Allotment Act of 1887, 148

genetic resources, 153

Geronimo, 71

Ghost Dance, 105

Gilbert, Madonna, 51 n.15

Gill, Sam, 67, 75–78

Glancy, Diane, 124

Gobel, Paul, 117–18

Godey's Ladies Book, 43

Golana Institute for Prehistory and Anthropology, 154

Goodale, Elaine, 116

Gramsci, Antonio, 128

Great White Truth, 164 n.17

Griffith, D.W., 173

Grinde, Donald, 72, 74

Guggenheim Award, 9

Gutiérrez, Ramón A., 1, 6, 8, 104–6

Hagan, William T., 7, 99 n.24

Hale, Janet Campbell, 53 n.28

Hall, Ed, 126

Hamley, Jeffrey, 195

Harjo, Joy, 53 n.28

Harrison, William Henry, 76

Haudenosaunee Nations, 102

Hawkeye (movie), 93

Henige, David, 28, 78

Hiawatha Indian Insane Asylum, 117

Higginbotham, C. Dean, 149

Hillerman, Tony, 117

Hinsley, Curtis M., Jr., 53 n.31

historians, methods of, 22 n.24, 87–89

history. *See* American Indian history

Hobson, Geary, 142, 144

Hogan, Linda, 53 n.28

Hopis, 8, 117, 183

Horowitz, Morton, 161

House Made of Dawn (Momaday), 60, 132, 135

Human Genome Diversity Project (HGDP), 156–58

Hurons (Wyandots), 103, 108 n.15

"identity politics," 114

"imperialist nostalgia," 145

Indian Arts and Crafts Board, 174

Indian Camp Ranch, 167 n.44

Indian Education Act (1972), 195

Indian Historian, 70

The Indian in the Cupboard (movie), 119

Indian Nations At Risk Task Force, 192

indigenous cultural resources, profits made from, 139–71

informant-based work, 122–23

Institute for American Indian Arts, 126

intellectual property, 170 n. 100, 178

The Invented Indian (ed. Clifton), 65–83

Inyangmani Hoksida, 27
Iowas, 102
Iroquoian language, 102
Isleta Pueblo, 173

Jacobs, Wilbur, 97 n.10
Jaimes, Annette, 40
Jessel, Penny, 65
Joe, Jenny R., 49 n.1
Johansen, Bruce, 72, 74
Jojola, Ted, 104
Jojola, Tony, 179 n.8

Keeshig-Tobias, Lenore, 142, 143
Kehoe, Alice, 67, 79
Kenny, Maurice, 124
Kessell, John, 105
Kickapoos, 102
Kickingbird, Kirke, 195
King, Thomas, 124
Kiowa Voices (Boyd), 3
Kloppenburg, Jack, 155
knowledge: empirical, 14; ownership
    of, 5–6

LaFleche, Susan, 45
Lagunas, 61
Lakotas, 101; women, 40
Lakota Woman (movie), 93
Lamb, Deb, 41
languages, Native, 102
Larson, Sidner J., 119
Last of the Mohicans (movie), 93
Lewis and Clark, 45
Liddle, John, 157
Limerick, Patricia Nelson, 1, 104–5,
    108
Lind, Christopher, 160
literature: as source material, 47;
    teaching, 55–64

Living Legends Oral History Collection,
    53 n.27
Locke, John, 73
Locke, Kevin, 118
Lomawaima, K. Tsianina, 49 n.1, 195
Louis, Adrian, 126
Lugones, Maria, 42
Lumbees, 69
Lummis, Charles Fletcher, 172

MacArthur Foundation Award, 8, 9
magical narrative, 132
Malcolm, Janet, 122
Martin, Calvin, 50, 96
Mason, Carol, 71–72
May, Karl, 71
Maza Okiye Win, 27, 31, 32
Mazomani, Chief, 27
McFee, Macolm, 42, 50 n.9
McGowan, 154
McLuhan, T. C., 78
McMurtry, Larry, 113
Mead, Margaret, 134
Means, Russell, 114, 115
Medicine, Beatrice, 49 n.1
Medicine Eagle, Brook, 163 n.9
Menominees, 69
Merrell, James H., 106
Mesa, Cañon and Pueblo, 172
Mesquakies, and sacred information,
    56–57
Miamis, 106
The Middle Ground (White), 100–103
Mihesuah, Devon, 49 n.1, 195
Mihesuah, Henry, 4
Mingos, 77, 103
mixed-bloods, 39–40; women, 43–44,
    60. *See also* writers, mixed-blood
mixed-blood story, as postcolonial
    story, 124–31

Mni-Sota Makoce, 27–28

Mohanty, Chandra Talpade, 40

Molin, Paulete Fairbanks, 195

Momaday, N. Scott, 47, 112, 126, 131, 132, 135

Montesquieu, 73

Moore, Mary, 120

Morgan, George, 77

Mother Earth (Gill), 76

Mother Earth, Native concept of, 75–78

Mount Holyoke Seminary, 116

music, indigenous, and copyright, 150–53

Nash, Gary, 95 n.2

Nash, Gerald, xi n.1

National Congress of American Indians, 141

National Dialogue Project on American Indian Education, 191, 192

National Endowment for the Humanities (NEH), 8, 72

Native American Studies. *See* American Indian Studies.

Native American Women (Bataille), 54 n.32

Native spirituality. *See* spirituality

Navajos, 8, 11, 58, 117, 173

Neihardt, John G., 119

New Age movement, 93; literature of, 20 n.18; and sweat lodge ceremonies, 140, 144

New Agers: as born-again medicine people, 141–42, 163 n.9; as self-appointed spokespeople for Indians, 79

Newes, 101

Newe Segobia, 101, 148

"New Indian History," 1, 2, 101

"New Indians," 11–12, 20

New Mexico, 172, 173

New Ulm MI, 31

"New Western History," 1

Noley, Grayson, 14

non-Indian scholars, 10, 86–87; concerns about Indian scholars, 70; definitions of "Indian," 66, 69; and Indian history, 81–82, 100–107

Northeast Indian Quarterly, 70

Northern Arizona University: Institute for Native Americans, 21 n.21; Institutional Review Board, 8

Northern Cheyennes, 144

O'Brien-Kehoe, Jean, 49 n.1

Omahas, 79

"150% Man," 42, 50 n.9

On Moral Fiction (Gardener), 131

oral histories, x, 24–26, 27–35, 92, 177; details provided by, 33–34; as "fantasy," 2; textualization of, 4; using, 3, 47, 190–91

oral tradition, 3, 24–25, 27–35, 132, 177

Organization of American Historians, 101, 105

Ortiz, Alfonso, 135

Ortiz, Roxanne Dunbar, 104, 105

Ortiz, Simon, 143

Otoe-Missourias, 102

Owens, Louis, 124

ownership, concept of, 161

Paine, Thomas, 134

Pamunkeys, 71

Parker, Quanah, 7

Parsons, Elsie Clews, 61

Peltier, Leonard, 102

Pierson, Kathleen, 115, 116

Plains tribes, gender roles in, 45
Plath, Sylvia, 122
Pocahontas, 45, 71
Pocahontas (movie), 112–13, 114
Pojoaque, 176
Porter, John, 168 n.79
Posey, Darrell, 152
Potawatomies, 69
Powers, Marla N., 47
Project Jukebox, 178
Pueblos, 173, 176; and Gutiérrez's
    histories, 104–6, 109; and sacred
    information, 56

Quincentennial, 82, 139
Quintana, Alvina, 48

race, 42, 97 n.12; relations, 88, 98 n.
    17
racism, 39, 40
Recovering the Word (ed. Swann and
    Krupat), 57–58
Red Power movement, 88
Riddles, Leonard (Blackmoon), 18 n.8
Riding In, James, 12
Right Livelihood Foundation, 149
Robbins, R., 190, 197
Roberts, Anna, 28
Rosaldo, Roberto, 145
Rose, LaVera, 40
Rose, Wendy, 20 n.18, 53 n.28, 124
Rural Advancement Foundation
    International (RAFI), 158, 169 n.84

Sacajawea, 45
sacred information, 55; consequences
    of scholars using, 57–58; levels of
    meaning, 58; as "tainted," 13
San Carlos Apaches, 11
Santa Fe NM, 175

Santo Domingo Pueblo, 173
scholars and scholarship. See academic
    freedom; American Indian scholars;
    non-Indian scholars; western
    scholarly bias; and entries for specific
    fields
Sedona AZ, 175
Seeger, Anthony, 151
Seneca-Cayugas, 100, 102, 103
Senecas, 106
Shawnees, 100, 102
Shiva, Vandana, 159
Shoemaker, Nancy, 1
Shoshones, 45
Silko, Leslie Marmon, 4, 53 n.28,
    60–62, 126, 132, 133, 136
Sinard, Jean-Jacques, 81
Siouian language group, 102
Six Nations, 72, 73
slavery, among Indians, 78
Smith, David, 103
Smith, John, 71
Smohalla, 76
Snyder, Gary, 145–46
Society of American Historians, 101
Southwestern Association on Indian
    Affairs, 174
spirituality: expropriation of, 10; as
    an industry, 141–46; marketing of,
    139–62
Squanto (movie), 93
Standing Bear, Luther, 194
Stanford University Press, 7
Stonequist, Everett, 42, 52 n.19
sweat lodge ceremonies, New Age, 144
Szasz, Margaret Connell, 193

Tapahonso, Lucy, 53 n.28
Tauli-Corpus, Victoria, 156
Tecumseh, 76–77

Terkel, Studs, 92
Theisz, R. D., 126
Thelen, David, 99 n.25
Thornton, Russell, 129
Thunderbird, Margo, 146
Tinker, George, 163 n.7
Tippeconic, J., 190, 197
Toelken, Barre, 57–58
Tooker, Elizabeth, 67, 72–74
Tracks (Erdrich), 132
Traditional Elders Circle, 144
Trafzer, Clifford, 4
Treaty of Ruby Valley, 148
tribalism, 41
tribal names, 102–3
tribal realism, 132
tribal stories, "borrowing" of, 113–14
trickster, 113, 181
"True Woman" ideal, 43
Turner, Frederick Jackson, 85, 89, 95, 98 n.20
Two Bear, Joseph, 28

U.N. Commission on Sustainable Development (CSD), 156, 161
United States–Dakota Conflict of 1862, 27–28, 30
Universal Declaration of Human Rights, 151
University of Alaska at Fairbanks Oral History Program, 178
University of Nebraska Press, 7, 119–20
University of Oklahoma, 8
Unktomi, 30, 35, 117
"upstreaming," 5, 107–9
Uru-eu-wau-waus, 154
U.S. Centers for Disease Control and Prevention (CDC), 158

"Vampire Project," 156–58

van Gestel, Alan, 80
Vigil, Ralph, 105
Vizenor, Gerald, 19 n., 124, 125, 142

wannabes, 59, 141
Washburn, Wilcomb, 95 n.1, 164 n.17
Weiss, Paul, 157
Western scholarly bias, 182
When Jesus Came, the Corn Mothers Went Away (Gutiérrez), 6, 7, 104–6
White, Richard, 5, 6, 8, 99 n.26, 100–103
white shamanism, 165 n.24
Winnebagos, 6, 100, 102
womanism, 41
women of color, heterogeneity among, 37. *See also* American Indian women
Wong, Hertha Dawn, 11–12
World Council of Indigenous Peoples, 157, 170 n.90
World Intellectual Property Rights Organization (WIPO), 151–52
Wounded Knee (1973), 41, 88
Wounded Knee Creek, 105, 116
writers, mixed-blood: failures of, 127–31; as outside tribal cultures, 129–30; as self-centered, 137; themes of, 124–31; undocumented, 12
writers, Indian women as, 17, 49 n.1, 53 n.28
written records, unreliability of, 2–3
Wyandots, 6, 100, 102, 103, 109 n.15

Year of the Indigenous Peoples, 177
Young, Iris, 162–63
Young Bear, Ray, 56, 63, 131
Young Bear, Severt, 126

Zunis, 176, 177–78

Acknowledgments

Portions of the introduction, by Devon A. Mihesuah, previously appeared as "Voices, Interpretations, and the New Indian History: Comments on the *American Indian Quarterly*'s Special Issue on Writing about American Indians," *American Indian Quarterly* 20:1 (Winter 1996).

These essays were previously published in the *American Indian Quarterly* 20:1 (Winter 1990): "American Indian History or Non-Indian Perceptions of American Indian History?" and "Grandmother to Granddaughter: Generations of Oral History in a Dakota Family," by Angela Cavender Wilson; "Commonalty of Difference: American Indian Women and History," by Devon A. Mihesuah (in a slightly different form); "Ethics and Responsibilities in Writing American Indian History," by Donald L. Fixico; "Licensed Trafficking and Ethnogenetic Engineering," Susan A. Miller; "American Indian Intellectualism and the New Indian Story," by Elizabeth Cook-Lynn; "On Revision and Revisionism: American Indian Representations in New Mexico," by Theodore S. Jojola; "American Indian Studies Is for Everyone," by Duane Champagne; and "Why Indian People Should Be the Ones to Write about Indian Education," by Karen Gayton Swisher.

"Special Problems in Teaching Leslie Marmon Silko's *Ceremony*," by Paula Gunn Allen, was previously published in the *American Indian Quarterly* 14:4 (Fall 1990).

"Comfortable Fictions and the Struggle for Turf: An Essay Review of *The Invented Indian: Cultural Fictions and Government Policies*," by Vine Deloria Jr., was previously published in the *American Indian Quarterly* 16:3 (Summer 1992).

"Cultural Imperialism and the Marketing of Native America," by Laurie Anne Whitt, reprinted from the *American Indian Culture and Research Journal* 19:3 (1995) by permission of the American Indian Studies Center, UCLA. © Regents of the University of California.